# AWAKEN YOUR GENIUS

# AWAKEN YOUR GENIUS

Escape Conformity,
Ignite Creativity, and
Become Extraordinary

## Ozan Varol

**PUBLIC**AFFAIRS
*New York*

PublicAffairs
Hachette Book Group
1290 Avenue of the Americas, New York, NY 10104
www.publicaffairsbooks.com
@Public_Affairs

Printed in the United States of America

First Edition: April 2023

Published by PublicAffairs, an imprint of Perseus Books, LLC, a subsidiary of Hachette Book Group, Inc. The PublicAffairs name and logo is a trademark of the Hachette Book Group.

The Hachette Speakers Bureau provides a wide range of authors for speaking events. To find out more, go to www.hachettespeakersbureau.com or call (866) 376-6591.

PublicAffairs books may be purchased in bulk for business, educational, or pro-motional use. For information, please contact your local bookseller or Hachette Book Group Special Markets Department at special.markets@hbgusa.com.

The publisher is not responsible for websites (or their content) that are not owned by the publisher.

Print book interior design by Jeff Williams.

Library of Congress Cataloging-in-Publication Data

Names: Varol, Ozan O., 1981– author.
Title: Awaken your genius : escape conformity, ignite creativity, and become extraordinary / Ozan Varol.
Description: First edition. | New York : PublicAffairs, 2023. | Includes bibliographical references.
Identifiers: LCCN 2022042348 | ISBN 9781541700369 (hardcover) | ISBN 9781541700390 (ebook)
Subjects: LCSH: Thought and thinking. | Creative ability. | Autonomy.
Classification: LCC BF441 .V27 2023 | DDC 153.4/2—dc23/eng/20221212
LC record available at https://lccn.loc.gov/2022042348

ISBNs: 9781541700369 (hardcover), 9781541700390 (ebook), 9781541703568 (international edition)

LSC-C

Printing 2, 2023

*Dedicated to all the teachers who helped awaken my genius—particularly:*

*Şakir Kan*
*Baise Kan*
*Neriman Minisker*
*Robert Rice*
*William Chisholm*
*Jonathan Rau*
*Anne Kozlu*
*Steven Squyres*
*William Birdthistle*
*Jane Latimer*

# Contents

*A genius is the one most like himself.*

—THELONIOUS MONK

*What lies behind us and what lies before us are
tiny matters compared to what lies within us.*

—HENRY STANLEY HASKINS

*Originality consists of returning to the origin.*

—ATTRIBUTED TO ANTONI GAUDÍ

# Introduction

# It's Time to Wake Up

*There's a worm addicted to eating grape leaves.*
*Suddenly he wakes up . . . and he's no longer a*
*worm. He is the entire vineyard, and the orchard*
*too, the fruit, the trunks, a growing wisdom and*
*joy that doesn't need to devour.*

—RUMI, "THE WORM'S WAKING"

Dreams feel real when you're dreaming.

You find yourself in the middle of the action, unaware of how you got to where you are. You don't wonder how you regressed to your childhood or how you managed to grow wings and fly. It's only when you wake up that you realize you were dreaming.

Our lives work much the same way. It's hard to remember how we got to where we are, why we do what we do, and why we believe what we believe.

Think about it: How did you end up with the route you take to work every day? The way you brush your teeth? The side of the bed you sleep on? The way you take your coffee?

How did you adopt the beliefs you hold dear and the opinions that are so tightly woven into your identity? When was the precise moment in your life that you declared yourself to be a liberal, a conservative, or a fill-in-the-blank?

Which of these beliefs were truly your own choice? And which ones were implanted by your community, your schools, and your family?

It's hard to say.

We have little idea how we ended up here. We just know we're here, so we keep going. We sleepwalk through life. We get stuck in our rehearsed way of operating in the world. We choose things out of habit, not desire. We reaffirm the same beliefs, think the same thoughts, and make the same choices that lead to the same outcomes.

In a very real sense, our past becomes our future. What we chose earlier dictates what we do today. We drag ourselves into the same predictable tomorrow by reliving yesterday.

We say that some people march to the beat of a different drummer. But implicit in this cliché is that *the rest of us march to the same beat*. This is true to a disturbing extent. We're told from an early age not to cause a ruckus, to do what it takes to fit in without looking like we're trying.

We become defined by beliefs that aren't our own. We find ourselves on well-worn paths that were never ours to walk. We follow directions from other people who don't know us and who have no idea where we want to go. We color between the lines of sketches drawn by someone else.

As a result, we become a supporting actor in our own life.

We're conditioned to look for external patches to internal holes—to trust strangers more than we trust ourselves. This conditioning works well for the self-help industry: The "three principles of this" or the "five secrets to that" are just a credit-card swipe away. Corporations and governments, empowered by increasingly sophisticated algorithms, know us better than we know ourselves—leaving us vulnerable to control and manipulation.

Deep down we know we're destined for more—that we weren't put on Earth to do what we often do—but we feel imprisoned by our unnatural indoctrination and programming. We become addicted to the reality we want to escape.

The price we pay for living in this world is betraying who we are—and disconnecting from the genius within.

Inside you is a vast reservoir of untapped wisdom. You are made up of every experience you've had, every story you've heard, every person you've been, every book you've read, every mistake you've made, every piece of your beautifully messy human existence. Everything that makes you *you*—a huge treasure waiting to be explored.

All that wisdom is concealed under the masks you wear, the roles you play, and the decades of social conditioning that have taught you to think like your teachers, to think like your parents, to think like your tribe, to think like influencers and thought leaders—to think like anyone but yourself.

As a result, we become strangers to ourselves. Many of us go from birth to death without knowing what we really think and who we really are.

Here's the thing: No one can compete with you at being you. You're the first and the last time that you'll ever happen. If your thinking is an extension of you—if what you're building is a product of your own genius—you'll be in a league of your own. But if you suppress yourself, if you don't claim the wisdom within, no one else can. That wisdom will be lost, both to you and to the world.

Think of humans as individual puzzle pieces that combine to build a beautiful collective. Each piece is important. Each piece is idiosyncratic. The puzzle cannot be completed with a billion corner pieces all of the same shape and color. What makes each piece different is also what makes it valuable to the collective. If you copy or conform to the other pieces, the world loses its full shape and color.

The puzzle pieces among us who embody their true shape and color are extraordinary. They stand out from the crowd—because they don't copy the crowd. They're not at the mercy of outside forces—because they sculpt those forces. They can't be misdirected by others—because they self-author their life.

They also embody the magic of Teflon. They operate unconstrained by the opinions of others—and their own past opinions and identities. They think and act with genuine independence, offering up insights direct from their own depths.

These extraordinary thinkers are geniuses. By genius I don't mean great talent or intelligence. A genius, in the words of Thelonious Monk, "is the one most like himself." Genius, in its Latin origin, refers to the attendant spirit present at birth in every person. Each of us is like Aladdin, and our genie—or our genius—is bottled up inside of us waiting to be awakened.

Once they awaken their genius, extraordinary thinkers share it with the world around them. They channel the energy that brought them into existence and turn it into the art only they can create. They don't just resist or disrupt the status quo—they reimagine the status quo and change the foundations of what's possible. In the words of Apple's "Think Different" campaign, they're misfits, rebels, troublemakers—round pegs in square holes.

But the goal isn't just to think differently. Someone who walks left simply because others are walking right is a conformist of a different kind. They're still living in reaction to others, not on their own terms. The same is true for people who reject scientific facts and instead embrace conspiracy theories about flat Earths and lizard governments. They think these theories are the product of their own thinking when in fact they've been captured by a tribal narrative. Rebels without a cause, they've let their thinking become even more conformist. Strong convictions are a sign of the conventional-minded, not of the independent-minded.

We've been conditioned to fear independent thinkers. Once you get people to think for themselves, there's no telling where they'll go. Independent thinkers are a constant danger to the status quo and the people who benefit from it. Kings tremble, and their rule tumbles, when independent thought stirs.

Thinking *for* yourself doesn't mean thinking *by* yourself. It also doesn't mean you're better than other people or that you should fall in love with your own thoughts the way Narcissus fell in love with his own reflection in a pond. The myth of the lone genius is just that—a myth. As I'll explain later, a diverse community of thinkers who *don't* think alike can be a mirror for you and help you see depths you'd otherwise miss. An orchestra of the *un*-like-minded, with every member playing their own best internal melodies, produces a whole symphony that is more than the sum of its parts.

In this era of mass manipulation, when so many otherwise intelligent people have been seduced by lazy thinking, what must it feel like to act instead of react? To be confident that your beliefs are your own? To stop operating on autopilot? To carve your own path as a leader and creator? To act from your imagination instead of your programming? To show up as the extraordinary puzzle piece that you are instead of contorting yourself into the shapes you're told to be? To make your own dent in the universe?

This book is for aspiring universe denters. It's a practical book for impractical people. It will give you the tools you need to wake up and find yourself—and to discover the melodies that only you can play in the symphony of life.

The book is organized into five parts.

The first part, *The Death*, is about **eliminating who you are not, so you can begin to discover who you are.** Here you'll enroll in a school of unlearning. I'll reveal how we lose ourselves when we tie ourselves to an identity, a belief, a tribe, a job, another person, or our old self. You'll discover how to declutter your mind so you can find the genius within and focus on what matters. You'll learn how to uninstall your unnatural programming, discard what no longer serves you, and abandon what *is* so you can figure out what *could* be.

The second part, *The Birth*, is about **finding your way back to the real you**. You'll learn how to discover your first principles, your fingerprints, and your shape and color—the qualities that make up your genius. I'll reveal how you can diversify yourself and embrace your multitudes—instead of falling into the trap of defining yourself as a single, static, unevolving person. You'll learn how to create your own doors in life, instead of contorting yourself to fit through the doors that happen to be open.

The third part, *The Inner Journey*, is about **igniting your creativity**. In this part, I'll explain how to think for yourself, create original ideas, and make something out of nothing by tapping into your inner wisdom and mining yourself for insights. You'll learn why creativity is less about forcing ideas to come and more about unblocking obstacles that prevent their natural flow. I'll reveal practical ways to discover the big fish swimming in the depths of your own oceans. By the end of this part, you'll be equipped with practical strategies for creating art that matters—whether it's a book, a business, or a breakthrough idea.

The fourth part, *The Outer Journey*, is about **exploring the outer world and finding the balance between what's inside and what's outside**. I'll reveal my approach to filtering information and detecting bullshit. I'll explain why we become intellectually imprisoned so easily and how to escape the tyranny of the new, the convenient, and the popular. You'll discover how to look where others don't look, to see what others don't see, and to find the extraordinary in the ordinary. You'll learn why success stories fool us, how well-meaning advice often misleads us, and what you can do to stop comparing yourself to others.

The fifth part, *The Transformation*, is about **your future**. I'll reveal why life is a jungle gym, not a ladder, how planning can blind you to better possibilities, and how to start walking before you see a clear path. You'll learn why your safety net might be a straitjacket, how letting go can be an act of love, and why a life lived carefully is a half-dead life.

When you wake up from the slumber of your past, the illusion of the Matrix will drop away and, like Neo, you'll begin to see all the 1s and 0s. Waking up will be jarring. The new self that emerges may seem foreign to you because it's been suppressed for so long. Side effects include headaches, existential crises, and really confused friends.

There will always be a reason to keep coloring inside the lines drawn for you by others—or the ones you've drawn for yourself. It will be agonizing to leave behind what feels comfortable to pursue what's uncomfortable—and to step into the unknown, where all things that never existed are created.

But as Zora Neale Hurston wrote, "There is no agony like bearing an untold story inside you."[1] This book is here to help you uncover that story, tap into your inner wisdom, and give birth to your genius, your true self—the person you were meant to be.

You don't need a red pill or ruby red slippers to start this journey.

You're already home.

Turn the page and start to walk back to yourself.

To help you put the principles in the book into action, I've created several free resources on my website, which is an important extension of this book.

Visit ozanvarol.com/genius to find:

- A summary of key points from each chapter
- Worksheets, challenges, and other exercises to help you implement the strategies discussed in the book
- A place to sign up for my weekly newsletter, where I share one big idea that you can read in three minutes or less (readers call it "the one email I look forward to each week")

# A Note to You from This Book

*I've been waiting so long*
*for you*
*to pick me up.*

*I reach out to you across time and space.*

*I see all your chapters.*
*Magic in your madness.*
*Light within your eyes.*
*Unfulfilled desire in your veins.*
*Unspoken words on your underlip.*
*A ray within your DNA.*

*I'm here to be your mirror,*
*reflecting the best and the worst of you.*

*I'm here to be your shovel,*
*helping you unearth what's already within.*

*I'm here to give you paper cuts,*
*telling you things you don't want to hear.*

*But I won't change my words just so you'll*
        *love me.*
*I won't offer you a sugared soda or a bland tea.*
*I'll serve you my truth—nothing but my big, beautiful,*
        *messy truth.*

*Remember: I am not your truth.*
*Your truth is within.*

*I won't tell you how to live.*
*(That would stop you from living.)*
*I'm not a lecture or a sermon.*
*There's no test at the end.*
*You can skip parts of me.*
*Take what works and leave the rest.*
*Disagree with me and tell me what I missed.*
*Ask your own questions and find your own answers.*

*I believe in words*
*(I am a book after all!)*
*But what I most believe lies beyond them.*

*My words will unlock your words.*
*My wisdom will unlock your wisdom.*
*My story will unlock your story.*

*I'll sit with you in the dark,*
*as you return to your light.*

*I can't wait*
*to delight*
*in the*
*extraordinary you.*

# PART I

# *The Death*

Part I has three chapters:

1. **Uneducate:** On repairing the damage caused by the education system
2. **Discard:** On letting go of who you are *not* so you can discover who you *are*
3. **Detox:** On decluttering your mind so you can see the wisdom within and focus on what matters

Along the way, I'll reveal:

- One of the worst pieces of advice (that's frequently repeated)
- Why persistence can backfire
- A counterintuitive way to generate original ideas
- Your most scarce resource (hint: it's not your time or money)
- What the snake can teach you about living on your own terms
- The dark underbelly of meditation
- The three tactics I use to keep an open mind and avoid confirmation bias
- Why you'll never feel "on top of everything" (and what to do about it)
- The biggest lie we've been told about productivity
- The one emotion we're starving for—and how it can help you see yourself more clearly

# 1

# Uneducate

*Re-examine all you have been told in school or church or in any book, dismiss whatever insults your own soul.*

—WALT WHITMAN,
PREFACE TO *LEAVES OF GRASS*

## "There's no trouble with this child"

Gillian Lynne was considered a problem child.[1] She did terribly in school. She couldn't sit still, let alone focus. She was so hyperactive that people would call her Wriggle Bottom.

This was the 1930s in Britain, and the acronym ADHD didn't even exist. Concerned that her child had a disorder, Lynne's mother took her to see a doctor.

That doctor's visit would radically change the course of Lynne's life.

What's important is what the doctor did *not* do. He did not label Lynne as "difficult." He did not tell her to calm down. He did not automatically medicate her.

Instead, he decided to follow a hunch. He turned on the radio and asked Lynne's mother to leave the room with him.

The minute the adults left, Lynne's body began to move. As the music filled the air, she couldn't contain herself and started dancing

3

all around the room, even leaping up on the doctor's desk. "What I hadn't noticed," Lynne writes in her autobiography, "was that his door was one of those beautiful old glass ones with etched designs, through which the doctor and my mother were watching."[2]

As he watched Lynne dance, the doctor smiled and turned to her mother.

"There's no trouble with this child," he said. "She is a natural dancer—you must take her immediately to dance class."

(Can we pause the story here for just a second? How *amazing* was this doctor?)

That prescription—*Take her to dance class*—changed Lynne's life. When she arrived at dance school, Lynne found a whole room of people just like her—"people who had to move to think," as she put it.

What followed was a lifetime of dance. Lynne danced in the Royal Ballet and choreographed *Cats* and *Phantom of the Opera*, two of the longest-running shows in Broadway history. Looking back at that moment in the doctor's office, Lynne says, "I really owe my whole career . . . and I suppose my life to this man."

Most schools treat students the way airlines treat economy-class passengers. The same bag of pretzels is served at every cramped seat. Regardless of their unique perceptions and curiosities, every student is served the same curriculum, the same lessons, and the same formulas.

Efficient? Yes. Effective? No.

It's hard to make people interested in a subject they don't care about. When he was a student, the astronomer Carl Sagan hated calculus.[3] He believed that calculus was invented by ill-meaning educators for "intimidation purposes." His attitude changed only after he picked up the book *Interplanetary Flight* by Arthur C. Clarke. In the book, Clarke used calculus to calculate interplanetary trajectories. Instead of being told "calculus is good for you," Sagan could now see for himself why calculus was helpful to know.

He could use it to solve problems that he thought were worth solving.

In their early years, children are moved by genuine curiosity. They stare at the world, wrapped in awe, and take nothing for granted. They approach life, not with the assumption that they know (or should know) the answers, but with the desire to experiment and absorb.

They may ask questions like: *If the world is spinning, how are we able to stand still? Why does the ground feel cold if the Earth's core is so hot? How do the clouds float without falling?* These terrific questions annoy adults who believe they aren't even worth asking. (Take a moment and try to answer them.)

"Children enter school as question marks and leave as periods," writes Neil Postman.[4] Too often, schools cure students of curiosity, dispelling any desire they have to pursue what they're interested in. Instead of asking their own questions and figuring out their own answers, students are compelled to memorize someone else's answers to someone else's questions.

When students enjoy what they learn, doing schoolwork doesn't feel like work. It feels more like play. Enjoyment of school also boosts academic performance. In a study of over 12,000 students in the United Kingdom, those who reported enjoying school at age six performed much better on standardized tests at age 16, regardless of IQ or socioeconomic background.[5]

When I was five years old, my parents enrolled me in kindergarten. Instead of picking a kindergarten for their child, as most parents do, they told me that I would get to pick where I went to school. Unbeknownst to me, they had already vetted nearby kindergartens and found three suitable and affordable ones that they presented to me as a choice.

We visited each kindergarten, and I got to ask the questions that were important to me ("What kind of toys do you have?"). This was a formative moment—one that has stayed with me to this day. For the first time in my life, I felt empowered to make my own choices within the guardrails my parents had set. I could think for myself rather than depend on anyone else to do my thinking for me.

Telling children to "attend this" or "do that" isn't good enough—in the same way that the instruction "learn calculus" wasn't good enough for Sagan. But if you allow people to follow their own interests—and commit to a destination they care about—they come alive.

Spend less time on the "what," as in *Here's what we're doing*, and more time on the "why," as in *Here's why we're doing it*. Show your child how geometry and fractions will help them fix their bike. Explain to your employees how the new marketing strategy they need to execute will help land a worthy moonshot. Rally your customers by embedding a purpose into the heart of what you do.

If you do this, the student will become a learner. The employee will become a team member. And the customer will become a passionate advocate.

Because the trouble isn't with them.

They just need to go to dance class.

And once they are moved, they will move the world.

## "What did you learn in school today?"

*Osmosis is the process by which molecules pass through a semipermeable membrane in order to balance concentrations.*

I was pacing back and forth, memorizing material for my high school biology exam. Pacing put me in a trance of sorts, allowing the semipermeable membrane that is my brain to absorb the molecules of information that I was supposed to learn.

But I wasn't learning anything. I was regurgitating a string of meaningless words that defined osmosis, and I had no idea what those words actually meant. I didn't know what made a membrane semipermeable (as opposed to completely permeable) and how in the world molecules knew to balance concentrations. (Did they have little brains that told them what to do?)

My other classes were no different. In the chemistry lab, there was one right outcome that our "experiment" was supposed to produce. If we didn't get that outcome—if the experiment produced something unexpected—there was no room for curiosity. It meant we had performed the experiment incorrectly and had to repeat it until we got it "right" while our classmates trekked off to the movies.

The word educate is related to the Latin word *eductus*. And *eductus* means to "educe" or to "draw out" of a "person something potential or latent."[6] In other words, education is supposed to help students develop and ripen what's already within them.

Most education systems do the opposite.

There's no drawing out. There's only stuffing in—of knowledge and facts. The teacher fills the empty tanks of young minds with the "content" of the course. The student absorbs knowledge by osmosis and regurgitates it on the exam. Education is all about the passive accumulation of yesterday's answers to yesterday's questions. Students aren't taught how to overhaul old facts, generate tomorrow's knowledge, and answer questions that haven't even been asked.

To memorize isn't to understand.

You can't learn yoga by memorizing yoga poses. You can't learn to ride a bike by reading a book about it. And you can't learn science by memorizing the definition of osmosis. There's a difference, as Richard Feynman says, "between knowing the name of something and knowing something."[7]

This teaching-by-telling approach puts the focus on the person in front of the class. Many schools thrive on students outsourcing their thinking to someone else and depending on the teacher for the right answer. Well-meaning teachers are crushed under the constraints of required outcomes that push them to standardize and teach to the test. Independent thought is sacrificed for simple and scalable compliance, and compliance is rewarded with a good grade and a piece of paper called a diploma.

What's worse, all the "learning" takes place in an environment that resembles a dictatorship. Strict hierarchy is maintained. Any unauthorized movement is subject to discipline. Essential bodily functions require a hall pass. Rules are imposed arbitrarily: Even though chewing gum doesn't impede learning, the behavior is still punished.

Although educators pay lip service to valuing creativity, many end up discouraging it in practice. Research shows that teachers rate highly creative students as less desirable in the classroom.[8] This finding has been replicated in numerous studies: Creative students are unconventional students, and unconventional students are often disfavored by their teachers.[9]

As a result, schools end up unteaching creativity. Kids unlearn how to make art, they unlearn how to speak up, and they unlearn how to take initiative and ask critical questions. They are rewarded for thinking like the teacher, thinking like the school board, or thinking like the textbook author—not for thinking for themselves or questioning what they learn.

I excelled in this system. I graduated first in my law-school class, earning the highest grade point average in the law school's history. That doesn't mean I was smarter than other students or that I would be the best lawyer my law school ever produced. (In fact, I left the practice of law after just two years.) My GPA indicated one thing and one thing only: I was good at taking exams and figuring out what my professors were looking for. After I took each final exam, I would promptly forget just about everything I had learned for it, and what little I remembered quickly became outdated.

Most exam booklets should have the words LET'S PRETEND inscribed in big block letters on the cover, just so everyone is aware of what's about to take place.[10]

*Let's pretend that the questions on this exam are important.*

*Let's pretend that there's a single, absolutely right answer to every question.*

*Let's pretend that the answer has been determined by someone far smarter than you.*

*Let's pretend that the answer is fixed for all time.*

A typical question in this game of "Let's pretend" might be "Who discovered America?" A question like this closes off all inquiry by demanding a one-dimensional, Eurocentric answer like "Christopher Columbus."

Yet a far more interesting question is, "How do you discover who discovered America?"[11] That question leads to even more questions: "What does 'discover' mean?" "Weren't there millions of people already living in America when the Europeans arrived?" "Were the native people always here?" "If not, how did they arrive? By foot? By boat? From where?" "Where would you look to find out?"

These questions—which defy simple answers—are the types of questions that students will encounter in real life. Students leave school perfectly equipped to thrive in a world that doesn't exist outside the classroom. They feel lost because, in life, there are no clearly defined problems with a single, clearly defined solution.

Later on in life the authority figure might change—say, from a teacher to a manager—but the underlying approach remains the same. The manager demands compliance, and the worker conforms. The business then gets bogged down by dogma and resistance to change.

So let's stop asking, "What did you learn in school today?" That question perpetuates the outdated conception of education as an endeavor whose only purpose is to teach students the right answers.

Instead, let's ask, "What made you curious today?" or "What questions are you interested in exploring?" or "How would you figure out the answers?" or any other question designed to get students to think for themselves and to put a question mark at the end of conventional wisdom.

If a child asks you, "How did the dinosaurs die?," resist the impulse to launch into a lesson about an asteroid hitting the earth. Instead ask, "What do you think could have killed them? How would you figure it out?" When they give you an answer, ask them for more answers. Let them see that there's often more than one way of framing the question and more than one possible answer to it.

If an employee comes to you and says, "What should I do about this problem?," don't immediately deliver a quick and efficient fix. Let them suggest solutions on their own. When you spoon-feed right answers to others, you're acting like a personal trainer who "helps" clients by lifting their weights for them.

In the end, the ability to reimagine conventional wisdom is far more important than the ability to regurgitate it.

## Where have all the artists gone?

"How many artists are there in the room?"

This is the question that Gordon MacKenzie, a longtime artist at Hallmark Cards, would ask while visiting schools.[12]

The response was always the same.

In the first grade, all the kids would leap from their seats and raise their hands.

In the third grade, roughly 10 out of 30 kids would raise their hands.

By the sixth grade, only one or two would reluctantly raise their hands—while others in the class looked around to see who would admit to such deviance.

"Every child is an artist," Pablo Picasso purportedly said. "The problem is how to remain an artist once he grows up."[13] As student loans and mortgages begin to mount, we get stuck in old patterns and lose sight of the artist within.

Our vocabulary reflects this shift. We don't even call it "art" anymore. We call it "content." A part of me dies inside when someone calls themselves a "content creator."

Content is something you stuff inside a bag. It's something you produce on an assembly line. No one wants to get up in the morning and read content over coffee. And no truly self-respecting creator wants to generate content either.

Because content is normal. Content is fungible. Content creators can be replaced. Artists can't.

Art isn't just something that poorly compensated artists do inside a studio. Art isn't just related to objects. As long as you're reimagining the status quo—as long as you're disturbing the peace, in James Baldwin's memorable phrase—anything you do in your life can be art.

The new strategy you design at work is art.

The way you raise your children is art.

The way you decorate your home is art.

The way you talk, the way you smile, the way you live your life—it's all art.

If you call your creations "content," or if you refuse to think of yourself as an artist, the results will reflect that mindset. What you create will be ordinary. You'll reinforce the status quo. You'll bore people to tears. And you'll be wildly out of touch with a rapidly evolving world that requires all of us to be artists.

The seven-year-old daughter of the artist Howard Ikemoto once asked him, "What do you do at work?"[14] He replied: "I work at a college, where my job is to teach people how to draw." She replied, bewildered, "You mean they forget?"

Yes, they do. Ever look at yourself in the mirror and wonder what happened? You probably don't feel nearly as old as you look. It's because there's an ageless center within you that has remained young, even as your body has physically aged. And there's an artist with a permanent studio in that ageless center—that inner first-grader leaping from their seat to tell the world they are an artist. The more we can reconnect with that inner artist and recapture our youthful wonder, the better off we will be.

So take out your metaphorical crayons and finger-paint.

Your blank canvas is waiting for you.

What will you create?

# 2

# Discard

*Every act of creation is first an act of destruction.*
—ATTRIBUTED TO PABLO PICASSO

## The skin you live in

The snake is the ancient symbol of transition.[1]

Unlike human skin, the skin on a snake doesn't grow as the animal grows.[2] During its lifetime, the snake's insides outgrow its outsides, and the animal reaches a point where it must discard the older skin in favor of the new.

This process is *uncomfortable*. The snake rubs and scratches until it's able to literally crawl out of its old skin. When the snake succeeds in completing the process, a new vibrant skin emerges in place of the old. But when the snake fails to shed its skin, it can grow blind and die.

Over the course of my life, I've worn and shed many skins: Rocket scientist. Lawyer. Law professor. Author and speaker.

Each transformation was preceded by an uncomfortable feeling that something wasn't quite right. I'd make some adjustments here and there, but there came a point where my old skin couldn't sustain my inner growth. What once made sense no longer did.

Take, for example, my transition from rocket science to law. I majored in astrophysics in college and worked on the operations team for the Mars Exploration Rovers mission. I loved working on the mission and navigating the practical challenges of putting a rover on the Martian surface. But I didn't love the substance of the theoretical math and physics classes I had to take. Over time my enthusiasm for astrophysics began to wane and I became more interested in the physics of society. Although it meant walking away from the four years I had poured into rocket science, I honored my curiosity as it flowed in a different direction and decided to go to law school.

To discard was to temporarily lose my balance. But not discarding would have meant losing myself.

We often mistake ourselves for our skin, but our skin isn't us. Our skin is just what we happen to be wearing right now. It's what suited us yesterday. Yet we often find ourselves unable to leave what we've outgrown. We stick to a job that's great on paper but soul-sucking in practice. We remain in a dysfunctional relationship, refusing to recognize that it's not working out. We sacrifice the possibility of what *could be* for the self-constructed prison of what *is*.

When you're not changing who you are, you're choosing who you are. The decision to remain the same is a choice—and it's not the natural one. Our physical skin changes every month or two.[3] But the skins made up of our beliefs, relationships, and careers are far more sticky.

Discarding runs counter to conventional wisdom. We've all heard that well-intentioned advice: *Don't ever give up*. We prize grit and perseverance and attach a huge stigma to quitting. Quitting is undignified. Quitting means you failed. "Winners never quit, and quitters never win," as the popular saying goes.

Yes, many people quit when they should persist. You shouldn't give up on your goal simply because things got hard or because you fell down a few times.

Yet many people persist when they should quit. Grit is important—but not if it blinds you to other possibilities. Determination is meaningless if you're repeatedly doing what's not working or clinging to something long after it has outlived its purpose. The 37-year-old you has little in common with the 27-year-old you. If you have any doubts about that, check out the social-media posts you wrote 10 years ago. Once you're done cringing over what your past self decided to share with the world, consider why you should stick to the decisions that person made. What you did yesterday doesn't have to control what you do today.

Even positive things can eventually become a burden. In a Buddhist parable, a man builds a raft to cross a raging river and safely reaches the other side. He picks up the raft and starts walking into a forest. The raft begins to snag in the trees, impeding the man's forward progress. Yet he refuses to let go of the raft. *This is my raft!* he objects. *I built it! It saved my life!* But to survive in the forest he must let go of the raft that saved his life on the river.

Make no mistake: Peeling back your old skin is painful and jarring. There's a certainty to it. You've worn it for years, if not decades. It makes you feel safe and comfortable. Over time it has become your identity, so cultivating a new skin requires changing who you are.

Adding is easy, but subtracting is hard—really hard. When we've invested time and resources in building something, the sunk-cost fallacy kicks in and prompts us to stay the course. (*I've spent two years on this project, so I can't quit now!*) We behave like a snake that stubbornly clings to its old, dead skin even as the new skin urgently tries to emerge.

We crave what we don't have, but we fear losing what we do.

If you've been successful on a path you've outgrown, you're up against another formidable foe: your ego. The part of you that gets off on titles, pay raises, and accolades will not go down without a serious fight. It will kick, it will scream, it will do everything in its power to convince you that you're making the biggest mistake of your life. Your ego will ask, *If I stop doing this thing that I've been doing for years—if I abandon the title of lawyer or senior director—what will I lose? More importantly,* who *will I be?*

But there's another, more important question you should be asking:

*What will I gain if I let this go?*

Many of the positive impacts in my life have come from subtractions, not from additions. I'm more proud of what I have stopped doing than of what I have done.

When you don't act—when you cling to the skin you've outgrown—you risk leaving a canvas unpainted, a book unwritten, a song unsung, and a life unlived. If you keep that dead-end job that sucks your soul, you won't find the career that allows you to shine and light up the world. If you keep reading a terrible book because you've already read the first few chapters, you won't find that quake book that shakes you to your core. If you remain in a dysfunctional relationship because, despite all its failures, you're still convinced you can "fix" the other person, you won't find a relationship that feeds your soul.

Keep in mind the cost of failing to act, the pain of stagnancy, and the death of your potential. As the saying goes, many a false step is made by standing still.

What's more, discarding is often impermanent for humans. You can do what a snake can't do: If you miss your old skin, you can put it back on. You can start over. For example, if founding a start-up doesn't work out for you, you can go back to the corporate world. You'll still have all the skills that made you successful to begin with, and now you'll also have the benefit of a founder's perspective. Returning to where you once were isn't the same as never leaving. You'll know you've found your place—even if that place is back where you began.

If life feels heavy, you might be choosing to carry a raft that no longer serves you. If it feels hard to fit into old patterns, old relationships, or old thoughts—if you're tired of participating in business as usual—it might be time for you to do some shedding. Even if the new skin doesn't perfectly fit you, discarding the old skin will give you a much-needed sense of agency over your life. Proving to yourself that you're in charge and that you can create your future is a priceless gift.

To keep growing and stay healthy, plants must be pruned. Humans work the same way. Once you prune what's no longer serving you—once you stand naked before the wind with layers of old skin shed—you'll begin to see yourself.

As you eliminate who you are *not*, you will discover who you *are*.

## You are not your identity

*I have already lost touch with a couple of people I used to be.*

—JOAN DIDION, *SLOUCHING TOWARDS BETHLEHEM*

We inherit an initial identity from our parents: *American. Scottish-German. Catholic. Jewish.*

Later on, the expectations, ideals, and roles implanted in us by others become part of our identity: *Jock. Nerd. Troublemaker.*

Our choice of career adds another layer: *Marketer. Accountant. Lawyer.*

Our self-perceived traits add still more layers: *"I'm a perfectionist." "I don't display my emotions." "I'm awkward in social settings."*

Brick by brick, we build an identity for ourselves that defines what we can do, what we can believe, and what we can achieve in our lives. We then expend an extraordinary amount of energy defending and maintaining these identities.

"What hurts a lot of people, particularly famous people," Kobe Bryant once said, "is they start valuing themselves for 'what' they are, the way the world sees them: writer, speaker, basketball player. And you start believing that what you are is who you are."[4]

Our identity is a construct. It's a story we tell ourselves, a narrative we craft to make sense of our selves and our place in the world. We then become a prisoner to this narrative, constricting our thinking and adjusting our behavior to fit our identity. Our language often reflects this inflexible posture. *I'm a Democrat. I'm a Republican. I'm vegan. I'm Paleo.*

We confuse identity with self, but identity obscures the self. Identity tricks you into believing that it is you when identity prevents you from becoming you. You are not your diet. You are not your political party. You are not your résumé or your LinkedIn profile. You are not the house you own or the car you drive. To describe yourself with a single, fixed identity is to insult your vastness and conceal and suppress the multitudes within you.

We end up serving our identity rather than changing our identity to serve us. Our narratives become self-fulfilling prophecies. If you tell yourself you're awkward in social settings, you'll avoid social settings, which will weaken your socialization muscles and make you even more awkward. If you tell yourself you don't display your emotions, you'll choose to live a guarded life and build even higher walls. If you call yourself a perfectionist, you'll change your reality to live up to that label by constantly aiming for some unachievable mirage of perfect.

Identity also makes it easier for the powers that be to slice and dice us into categories and subcategories. If you have a fixed identity, it's easier for an algorithm to show you the gadget you're guaranteed to buy, for a politician to craft messaging to get you riled up, and for a media company to narrowcast ideas that will appeal to you. To refuse to be typecast in this way shifts the power of choice back to you.

The fewer labels that follow "I am . . . ," the more freedom you have to step into who you are. This is what Buddhists call unbeing—dropping the veil of identity so that your true self can emerge. "To become no one and anyone, to shake off shackles that remind you who you are, who others think you are," as Rebecca Solnit writes.[5] If you can confuse the algorithm or the market researcher—if there's no checkbox that captures your multitudes—you'll know you're on the right path.

To give birth to yourself—to the person you were meant to be—you must forget who you are.

The rest of this chapter will share suggestions on how to untether yourself from your identity so you can be free.

## You are not your beliefs

*You're going to find that many of the truths we cling to depend greatly on our own point of view.*
—OBI-WAN KENOBI,
IN *STAR WARS: EPISODE VI—RETURN OF THE JEDI*

There's an old saying in academia: *Academic politics are so vicious because the stakes are so small.*

I experienced the truth of this saying firsthand. In my early years as a professor, I upset several prominent scholars by writing a series of articles that bucked conventional wisdom in my field.

During one particularly memorable conference dinner, a senior scholar was so offended by my work that he hurled a series of insults in my direction across the dinner table while bits of spaghetti alfredo flew out of his mouth. (I will exercise the good taste not to share what he said, though it's tempting.)

It was hard not to take attacks like these personally. My heart rate would increase, my blood pressure would skyrocket, and I would get defensive, clinging to my arguments as if they were a life raft protecting me from impending doom.

My academic beliefs got wrapped up in my identity—and became my biggest weakness. This was *my* article, *my* argument, *my* idea. This was *me*.

Once we form an opinion—our own very clever idea—we tend to fall in love with it. Doctors fall in love with their diagnoses, politicians religiously toe the party line, and scientists ignore competing hypotheses. What we think becomes who we are. Our beliefs, expressed consistently over time, rigidify. It becomes impossible to determine where our beliefs end and where we begin.

Facts don't drive our beliefs. Our beliefs drive the facts we choose to accept—and the facts we choose to ignore. We assume that facts and logic are on our side and that our opponents have blinded themselves to the truth—even though we're in the same position more often than we realize.

When our beliefs and our identity merge, we embrace a belief system simply to preserve our identity. Any attempt to change our minds—whether by ourselves or, worse, someone else—strikes us as a threat. When someone says, "I don't like your idea," we hear, "I don't like you." Criticism turns into verbal violence, and simple disagreements become existential death matches.

My experience at the academic conference reminded me of a parable. A group of blind men come across an elephant for the very first time in their lives.[6] Each man inspects this strange animal by touching a different part of its body. One man touches the trunk and says that the animal is like a thick snake. Another feels its side and describes it as a wall. Another touches its tail and says it's like a rope. In one version of the parable, the disagreements reach a fever pitch. The men accuse each other of lying and come to blows. "It's a snake, you idiot!" "No, moron, it's a wall!"

The moral of the story is simple: Perception shapes reality. We don't see things as *they* are. We see things as *we* are.

Although our experience might be accurate, it's limited and subjective. It's not the whole truth. We're not seeing the elephant in the room. We're feeling only one piece of it.

The senior scholar and I were acting like the blind men in the parable. We were too blinded by our beliefs to see each other's perspective.

Now when I disagree with someone, I try to take a different approach. Instead of immediately assuming they're wrong and I'm right, I ask, *What would have to be true for their perspective to be accurate? What are they seeing that I'm not seeing? What part of the elephant am I missing?*

When you engage with others, the goal isn't to judge them or berate them—not even in your own mind. The goal isn't to persuade them or to win the argument either. Research shows that the more we try to convince others, the more we convince ourselves—and the more rigid our beliefs become.[7] Instead, the goal should be to understand and get curious about the other person's view of the elephant—to try to figure out what they are seeing and why. "Tell me more" instead of "You're wrong and here's why."

Here's an unusual way to implement this curiosity-over-victory mindset. When you're about to disagree with someone, don't say anything until after you've restated what the other person has said *to that person's satisfaction.*[8] And that person, in turn, can't respond to you until they restate what you said to your satisfaction. This rule disrupts the typical social dynamic where you're so focused on crafting your own clever retort that you stop paying attention to the other person. Try it out in your next work meeting or contentious conversation. And remember Haruki Murakami's advice: "To argue, and win, is to break down the reality of the person you are arguing against. It is painful to lose your reality, so be kind, even if you are right."

Every time you spot a new perspective, you change how you see the world. The world itself hasn't changed. But your perception of it has. If I'm stuck over here only able to touch the elephant's ear, the only way for me to understand the tusk is through another human being.

This doesn't require you to change your own mind. It simply requires you to see someone else's point of view. "It is the mark of an educated mind," Aristotle once said, "to be able to entertain a thought without accepting it."[9]

The trick is to separate your identity from your beliefs to see them clearly, evaluate them honestly, and discard them if necessary. Once you take off the blinders composed of your beliefs, you can see the world—and yourself—more clearly.

Here are three ways you can put this mindset into practice:

### 1. Don't blend ideas into your identity.

Write your opinions in temporary ink so they can be revised. Instead of saying, "This is what I believe," say, "This is how I currently understand this issue." This wording makes it clear that our ideas and opinions—just like ourselves—are works in progress, continually changing and improving. "'What I believe' is a process rather than a finality," as Emma Goldman put it.[10]

### 2. Ease the blow on your ego.

The hardest part about thinking differently is admitting that what you once believed is now wrong. That's an admission that most egos are unwilling to make.

So tell your ego it wasn't wrong. To ease the blow, tell yourself that you were right given what you knew—given your partial view of the elephant. But now that new information has come to light about other parts of the elephant you couldn't see before, your beliefs should change. This way, you're not canceling your past self. You're simply updating it.

*3. Ask yourself a simple question.*

Take one of your firmly held beliefs. Ask yourself, *What fact would change my opinion on this subject?*

If the answer is, *No fact would change my opinion,* you don't have an opinion.

You *are* the opinion.

## The beauty in complexity

*Out beyond ideas of*
*wrongdoing and rightdoing,*
*There is a field.*
*I'll meet you there.*

—RUMI, "A GREAT WAGON"

"I love you, I love you, I love you," Megan told her mother on the phone. "I'll talk to you in ten days."

Megan then went off to a silent meditation retreat. This symbolized the turning of a new leaf after a breakup. Ten days of inward focus would help restore her. The retreat center she had chosen promoted meditation as a "universal remedy for universal ills" that provides "total liberation" from "all suffering."

During the retreat, Megan would have to give up her cell phone and maintain a mandatory "noble silence." Every day, she'd meditate for nearly 11 hours, sitting cross-legged on a rug and focusing on her breath.

On the seventh day of the retreat, things took a dark turn for Megan.

During meditation, she began to feel heavy, and an "immense fear" gripped her. She began to lose hold of reality—and of herself. She kept thinking: *Is it the end of the world? Am I dying? Is Jesus punishing me?*

When Megan's mom and her younger sister went to pick her up from the meditation center, Megan resisted. "You're not really here," she told her sister. "I'm creating you. You're just a projection."

After she returned home, Megan's troubles did not relent. A few months after the retreat, she took her own life.

When I first read Megan's tragic story in an article by David Kortava, I was tempted to treat it as an extreme outlier.[11] I've been meditating regularly for nearly a decade and have been an evangelist for its benefits.

Conventional wisdom paints meditation as a universal remedy. Ariana Huffington captured the prevailing sentiment in an interview: "The list of all the conditions that [meditation] impact[s] for the better—depression, anxiety, heart disease, memory, aging, creativity—sounds like a label on snake oil from the 19th century! Except this cure-all is real, and there are no toxic side effects."

But reality, as is often the case, is more nuanced. For many people, meditation restores well-being. For others, it does the opposite.

One study conducted a systematic review of 83 research studies on meditation that included over 6,700 participants. Sixty-five percent of the studies reported at least one type of adverse effect resulting from meditation. "We found that the occurrence of [adverse effects] during or after meditation practices is not uncommon," the researchers concluded, "and may occur in individuals with no previous history of mental health problems."[12]

I shared this research with readers on my email list to meditate on the dangers of thinking in rigid categories of black-white, good-bad, right-wrong, yes-no. It was one of my most popular posts, and most readers appreciated the central point: There's no such thing as a universal remedy. Even a "good" thing isn't good for all people under all circumstances.

Interestingly, I also received more hate mail for that article than anything else I've written in recent memory. Here's a sample:

"You're scaring people away from meditation. What is wrong with you?"

"This article is beyond irresponsible. I'm unsubscribing."

"You're a fraud. Do better."

Ironic, isn't it? Some of the most ardent practitioners of meditation were quick to respond with anger to an article that merely introduced nuance and ambiguity.

Very un-zen.

I think their reaction was all too human. We have a hard time tolerating ambiguity. We find it much easier to sort things into simple, rigid categories and to keep them there. Meditation is good. Meditation is useless. College is essential. College is pointless. Elon Musk is a hero. Elon Musk is a villain.

Instead of seeing all the gray between these extremes, we reject any evidence that introduces doubt. From this perspective, it's better to suppress peer-reviewed information about the potential adverse effects of meditation than to distort a neat, one-dimensional picture of meditation as a universal good.

We do this with people too. We divide the world into heroes and villains, oppressors and oppressed. This is the standard Hollywood template: The good guys defeat the bad guys, and everyone lives happily ever after. You can't expect anything bad from the good, nor anything good from the bad. There's no room for nuance or fine judgment. And the template works—because it appeals to human nature.

Janus was a Roman god with two faces. His superpower was his ability to look in different directions simultaneously. Independent thinkers act like Janus and can consider multiple perspectives at the same time. The goal isn't to reconcile the contradictions or resolve the oppositions. It's to embrace them. It's to live with them. It's to realize that light can be a wave *and* a particle. It's to understand that a meditation practice that works wonders for one person can cause problems for another.

Our preference for binary thinking is partially a product of our education system. Schools are factories of certitudes. They don't bother us with ambiguity or let nuances get in the way. We learn, for example, that democracy triumphed over tyranny in World War II. But we forget that the Soviet Union was also among the victors.

There is no "I guess" to be found in a textbook. None of the knowledge in a textbook is tentative or a work in progress. The world is a series of one-dimensional, right or wrong answers discovered by people far smarter than you. Your job is to memorize them and move on.

Certitudes then replace all thinking. They become a substitute for understanding. They bend reality to match the narrative. They create stark divisions that alienate people with a different perspective.

In leaping to certainty, we skip the holy ground of uncertainty— of not being sure, of keeping an open mind. Those are the conditions required for spotting nuances and planting the seeds of new ideas. We don't have to weigh all perspectives equally or ensure that every conceivable point of view is represented. It's more about keeping an open mind and realizing that one set of truths doesn't negate another.

I like to keep my opinions loosely held. I entertain thoughts without accepting them. From time to time I even flirt with hypocrisy: I believe one thing, but I do the other. If I find myself being hypocritical, I take that as a sign that my mind might be changing—and that's a good thing for a mind to do from time to time. The more loosely attached I am to my beliefs—which is precisely what meditation teaches—the more likely I am to change my mind.

"The test of a first-rate intelligence," F. Scott Fitzgerald once wrote, "is the ability to hold two opposed ideas in mind at the same time and still retain the ability to function."[13] Reality begins to emerge only when we set aside our tendency to think in clean categories and realize that almost all things exist on a continuum. Along that continuum, answers change depending on time and context. An answer that's closer to right today could be closer to wrong tomorrow.

Instead of committing ourselves to a single opinion, we can entertain multiple views and reduce our attachment to any one of them. Instead of singing a single melody, we can add a countermelody. Instead of marching to a consistent beat, we can dance our dance, delighting in surprising rhythms.

If you can let contradictory thoughts dance with each other without your head exploding, they'll produce a symphony brimming with additional music—in the form of new ideas—far superior to the original.

When you adopt this mindset, you gain the magic of perspective and see through the smoke and mirrors created by one-dimensional stories.

In the end, there's so much beauty in complexity. A world of multitudes is far more interesting—and accurate—than a world of certitudes.

## You are not your tribe

Henri Tajfel had a personal interest in studying genocide.[14]

He was a Polish Jew who served in the French Army during World War II. He was captured by the Germans but survived the Holocaust because the Germans didn't realize that he was Jewish. Although Tajfel escaped death, many of his friends and family didn't.

He dedicated his professional career to answering a seemingly simple question: *What motivates discrimination and prejudice?*

Tajfel and his colleagues ran a series of experiments.[15] They assigned volunteers to different teams based on their answers to random questions. The subjects were asked, for example, which one of two abstract paintings they liked better. Based on their answers, they were assigned to a group made up of others who expressed the same preference.

These were relatively meaningless, artificially created groups. There was no shared history between the members and no inherent reason for conflict to develop.

Yet the participants quickly developed group loyalty. They were more likely to distribute monetary rewards to the members of their own group at the expense of the others—even when they received no rewards themselves and even when alternative strategies would benefit both groups.

In other words, it took the most trivial of distinctions for the participants to divide themselves into "us" and "them." Simply telling people that they belonged to one group and not the other was sufficient to trigger loyalty toward their own group and bias against the other.

Tribes are at the core of the human experience. Thousands of years ago, loyalty to our tribe was vital to our survival. If you didn't conform, you'd be ostracized, rejected, or worse, left for dead.

Tribes endure in modern society in different ways. Modern tribes organize themselves around different identities—Democrats and Republicans, Yankees fans and Red Sox fans, nerds and bros, Crossfitters and Pelotoners, Dead Heads and Little Monsters.

Once we're in a tribe, we tend to identify with that tribe. We become part of the tribe, and the tribe becomes part of us.

There's nothing inherently wrong with tribes. They connect us to a like-minded community and create opportunities for connection. But tribalism becomes dangerous when it turns rivals into enemies, when it suppresses diverse thinking, and when it pushes individuals to do things they wouldn't do on their own.

This type of dangerous tribalism thrives in a sea of disconnected people looking for belonging. And who doesn't crave belonging these days? We are disconnected from our neighbors, disconnected from nature, disconnected from animals, disconnected from the universe, and disconnected from most things that make us human.

Tribes are the magnet that attracts the metal of our craving to belong. They assure us that we're right and morally superior. They force us into a different reality where it becomes impossible to see—let alone comprehend—another worldview. We become "the Few, the Proud, the More or Less Constantly Appalled at Everyone Else," as David Foster Wallace put it.[16]

Over time, the tribal identity becomes our identity. Once identity and tribe fuse, we let our tribe determine what's appropriate for us to read, watch, say, and think. We pick up social-media cues about what our tribe is thinking, and we toe the line. If our tribe hates Joe Rogan, we hate him too. If our tribe believes that immigrants are destroying our country, we believe it too. We forfeit our voice. We forfeit our choice. That warm, fuzzy, satisfying feeling of belonging trumps everything else—including thinking for ourselves.

We follow narratives, not evidence. We judge the message by the tribal affiliation of the speaker. We accept information endorsed by our tribe without investigating it or thinking it through for ourselves. Conversely, we reject information from competing sources regardless of its quality.

Any sign of detribalization—any deviance from the expected code of conduct—threatens tribal groupthink. It introduces uncertainty into tribal certainty. It raises the danger that others might follow suit. So if you disobey or disagree—if you push back against your own tribe or add nuance to categorical thinking—you are shamed, canceled, and shown the door.

In *Fahrenheit 451*, Ray Bradbury describes a dystopian society where the government burns books to ashes and then burns the ashes. It's easy to see this novel as a cautionary tale about a totalitarian state that bans books.

What's harder to see is another story line where the real culprit is not the government, but the people. In *Fahrenheit 451*, it's the tribes—the dog-lovers, the cat-lovers, the doctors, the lawyers, the leftists, the rightists, the Catholics, the Zen Buddhists—who pour the kerosene, light the fuse, and push their government to do the same. Although authors don't get to control how their books are interpreted, Bradbury insists that this is the primary message of the book: Junior dictators, in the form of ordinary citizens, rooting out seemingly controversial ideas can be just as dangerous as an oppressive government.[17]

A frequently prescribed remedy for tribalism is empathy. But research shows that people are biased in their expression of empathy.[18] The members of our own tribes get empathy. Others get a punch to the gut. We belittle them (*I told you so*). We ostracize them (*If you're not with us, you're against us*). We ridicule them (*What an idiot*). We see others, not as people trying to make sense of the same elephant from different angles, but as morally corrupt or unintelligent.

We reject people who don't follow our norms.

We reject people who have a different perspective.

We then reject people who don't reject the right people.

Intelligence isn't a defense against this tendency. In fact, research shows that people with higher cognitive abilities are more susceptible to stereotypes because they're better at detecting patterns.[19]

Although technology has torn down some barriers, it has erected others. We've been algorithmically sorted into echo chambers, where we're bombarded with ideas that reiterate our own. When we see our own ideas repeatedly mirrored in others, our confidence levels skyrocket and our views become even more extreme.[20] Opposing beliefs are nowhere to be seen, so we assume that they don't exist or that those who adopt them must be out of their minds. Even on the rare occasions that other perspectives appear on our feeds, it's easy to disconnect from them. Simply unsubscribe, unfollow, or unfriend—until all our acquaintances are winnowed down to those who parrot our worldview.

Shouting matches have replaced reasoned engagement. The ideology of different tribes is varied, but the argument style is disturbingly similar: *My position is based on facts and logic, but my opponents are immoral, biased, and downright ignorant. If only they'd open their minds—if only they'd read such-and-such a book or listen to so-and-so's take—they'd totally get it.*

We engage with others, not to understand them, but to convince our own group that we belong. Arguments have turned into membership cards that we wave on social media and beyond to make sure that everyone knows what team we play for. We gain acceptance for what we say and what we believe—not for who we are.

These debates aren't between right and wrong. They're one wrong pitted against another wrong. And the truth isn't in the middle. The truth isn't even in the room. It's nowhere to be seen.

Be careful if you find yourself in a place where only acceptable truths are allowed. Taboos are a sign of insecurity. Only fragile castles need to be protected by the highest of walls. The best answers are discovered not by eliminating competing answers, but by engaging with them. And engagement happens in groups built, not on taboos and dogma, but on a foundation that celebrates diverse thinking.

When we preach, when we lecture, when we blindly attempt to impose our truth on others, when we pour the kerosene and light the fuse, when we allow our tribes to determine what's acceptable and what's not, we can't see others or ourselves clearly. And we endanger the future of humanity.

To engage with competing perspectives is to betray your tribe. By asking another group how they see a particular issue, you're seeing them. By trying to understand them, you're humanizing them. By questioning the tribal narrative—its core weapon—you're reducing the tribe's power.

And that's exactly what we need to do. If our group identity doesn't replace our own—if we can develop a strong sense of self independent from our tribes—we can ask questions that no one is asking and see what others are too blind to see.

When you're not identified with any one side—when you're not on the team holding the tusk or the trunk—you can be the observer who steps back and sees the entire elephant in all its glory.

## I see you

*Sawubona* is a standard Zulu greeting.[21]

But its meaning goes far deeper than your typical hello. *Sawubona* literally means "I see you." It refers to seeing in a more meaningful sense than the simple act of sight. *Sawubona* means, "I see your personality. I see your humanity. I see your dignity."[22]

*Sawubona* says you're not an object to me. You're not a transaction. You're not a title. You're not just another person standing in line between my Starbucks macchiato and me. You're not the jersey you're wearing or who you voted for in the last election.

You exist. You matter. You can't be reduced to a label, an identity, or a tribe. You're a memory to someone. You're a living, breathing, imperfect human being who has experienced joy and suffering, triumph and despair, and love and grief.

The traditional response to *sawubona* is *ngikhona*. It means "I am here," but its meaning also goes deeper: "It tells the observer that you feel you have been seen and understood and that your personal dignity has been recognized."[23]

When we feel understood in this way, we vibrate on each other's frequency and see each other's perspective, instead of moving past it.

This is an exceedingly rare quality in a world where we refuse to make eye contact with our opponents, let alone see the world through their eyes.

*Sawubona* doesn't involve any grand gestures. It means becoming curious about someone else's view without trying to convert them to our own.

It means engaging with others even when we don't endorse all their actions.

It means resisting attempts to slice and dice us into groups and subgroups.

It means reminding ourselves that beauty thrives in diversity—including diversity of thought.

It means seeing difference as a curious delight to learn from instead of a problem to be fixed.

It means remembering our common humanity even when we disagree.

It means choosing to see in a world that has stopped seeing.

## Take a shot of awe

"Oh my God! Look at that . . . over there!" astronaut Bill Anders screamed.[24]

The Apollo 8 mission marked the first time a manned spacecraft entered into lunar orbit. As the spacecraft circled the Moon, Anders spotted an object coming up on the horizon and alerted his crewmates, Jim Lovell and Frank Borman.

The object was the Earth. The three men became the first humans to see our home from 240,000 miles away—and captured the moment in an iconic photograph called *Earthrise*. These three astronauts—Greek for star sailors—set sail for the Moon, and in so doing, they found the Earth.

From the vantage point of the Moon, we saw ourselves for the very first time. A vibrant blue-and-white marble against a backdrop of lifeless cosmic black. There were no borders between nations. No reason for people living in one pinprick corner of this tiny ball to hate the occupants of another. No cause for our worries and preoccupations to overshadow life's beauty. "To see the Earth as it truly is, small and blue and beautiful in that eternal silence where it floats," the poet Archibald MacLeish wrote, "is to see ourselves as riders on the Earth together, brothers on that bright loveliness in the eternal cold."[25]

At one point during the mission, Lovell lifted his thumb to the spacecraft window and covered the entire Earth with it. Behind his thumb lived over five billion people and everything he had ever known. The Earth was a "mere speck in our Milky Way galaxy and lost to oblivion in the universe," he wrote.[26] Lovell began to question his own existence. He had hoped to go to heaven when he died. But he realized he had gone to heaven when he was born.

Distance provided clarity. "From out there on the moon, international politics looks so petty," Apollo 14 astronaut Edgar Mitchell explained. "You want to grab a politician by the scruff of the neck and drag him a quarter of a million miles out and say, 'Look at that, you son of a bitch.'"[27]

Whether it's to the Moon, or to a foreign land here on Earth, we travel "initially, to lose ourselves; and we travel, next, to find ourselves," as Pico Iyer writes.[28] Stay too long in your home and you get jaded and lose all perspective. The breath of foreign air jolts you out of your entrenched ways and opens you up to new ways of being.

The French call this *dépaysement*, the disorientation you feel when you travel to a strange land. Your world becomes topsy-turvy. Your sense of proper and improper flips. You learn to laugh at things that would anger you at home. The majority becomes the minority. Surrounded by the echoes of a language you don't know, you return to infancy when your mother tongue was foreign to you. You become a young fool again.

These conditions are ideal for discarding your old skin. Our beliefs, perspectives, and habits are tied to our environment. Change your environment, and it becomes easier to dislodge what's no longer serving you. This is why many smokers find it easier to quit when they're traveling. Their new environment doesn't have the same smoking associations as their home.[29]

There's another reason why the *Earthrise* photo is so powerful. It triggers an emotional response to see our blue home rise above the gray lunar surface. It's the same emotion that captivates us when we lose ourselves in nature, experience the birth of our child, or ponder the vastness of the universe.

That emotion—awe—is sorely lacking in our lives. There are problems at work, stress at home, and anxiety in the news. We're starving for awe, deprived of one of the most fundamental emotions that connects us to others and makes us more humble in our thinking.

Awe doesn't just give you goose bumps. It wakes you up. It quiets the ego and loosens your attachment to your old skin. In a series of studies, participants who watched awe-inspiring videos of the night sky expressed less conviction about their beliefs on capital punishment and more willingness to engage with others who held different views on immigration.[30] Another study found that awe increases people's awareness of the gaps in their knowledge.[31]

If you're in a rut and feeling stuck in your old skin, take a shot of awe. Get lost in a foreign land. Go outside on a cloudless night and consume one of the most potent mind-altering substances— the night sky.

When you return home, your home won't have changed. But you will have. "We shall not cease from exploration," T. S. Eliot wrote, "and the end of all our exploring will be to arrive where we started and know the place for the first time."[32]

# 3

# Detox

*There are many things of which a wise man might*
*wish to be ignorant.*

—RALPH WALDO EMERSON, "DEMONOLOGY"

## Free your mind (and the rest will follow)

It was a composer's worst nightmare.[1]

Out of nowhere, he began to hear ringing and buzzing in his ears. Over the next few years, his hearing steadily declined. To hear his own music, he would pound on the piano keys with such force that he often wrecked them.

His condition continued to grow worse, and there was no hope of treatment. This was the 1800s, when deafness was poorly understood. What gave his life meaning—sound—was permanently disappearing from it.

By his mid-forties, he could no longer hear music.

Even though sounds played only in his imagination, he continued to compose. After all, music is a language, and he had spent his entire life mastering it. He knew how musical notes sounded, and how different instruments worked together. He could write an entire symphony without hearing a single note.

His deafness disabled, but it also enabled. The less he could hear, the more original he became. "Deafness did not impair and indeed may even have heightened his abilities as a composer," wrote his biographer.[2] His early work had been heavily influenced by his instructor, Joseph Haydn. When he became deaf, he couldn't hear the musical fashions of his time, so he wasn't influenced by them.

With the soundtrack of other musicians tuned out, he fully tuned in.

His originality, according to the Yale music professor Craig Wright, "rests in the sounds his disability forced him to hear internally."[3] His deafness allowed him to develop a unique compositional style that distilled music into its fundamental elements. He then took those elements and pushed them forward by repeating a chord or rhythm over and over at higher pitch and with increasing volume. That style would define him as one of the greatest composers of all time.

It would make him Beethoven.

Imagine Beethoven sitting in front of a piano. No distractions. No chatter. No music. Certainly no smartphone and no internet. Just the notes dancing in his imagination.

For most of us, this type of solitude feels deafening, so we fill the silence with other people's thoughts and opinions. "All human misfortune comes from . . . not knowing how to remain quietly in one room," Blaise Pascal wrote in the 17th century.[4]

Since then, the problem has gotten only worse. It's never been easier to access information than it is today. That ease of access brings many conveniences, but it also makes it too easy to see what other people are thinking. In Beethoven's time, you'd at least have to go to a library or a newsstand to get information. Now facts and opinions are just a click-and-scroll away.

Every notification plays someone else's tune. Every email transports us to someone else's reality. Every breaking-news flash plugs our brain into drama and conflict. In Shakespeare's timeless words, we live in a tale "full of sound and fury, signifying nothing."

Amid all that sound and fury, we can't hear ourselves. Other people's sounds deafen our ears, and their colors blind our eyes.

When you turn down the volume of other voices, you'll begin to hear a subtle melody, the whispers of a new voice. That voice will seem strange yet familiar—as if you've heard it before, but you can't quite recall where.

Eventually, you'll recognize that voice as your own. You'll meet yourself again—for the first time in a long time.[5]

In this state, you're alone, but not lonely. You're speaking with the one person who has been and will be your constant companion: your own self. Ideas you've missed will become audible in the silence.

The path to tuning in to the genius within begins by tuning out the noise without.

You'll find that there's a wise being inside you who already knows the next chapter in your story and the next melody in your symphony.

## Your most scarce resource

I woke up in the middle of the night, utterly confused.

I had been dreaming—of an equation. I was in a classroom, and on the blackboard there was a simple equation written in chalk:

$$0.8 * 0.2 = 0.16.$$

To be clear: I rarely ever dream about math. When I do, it's often a nightmare about bombing a theoretical physics final in college.

Even though this was no nightmare, the equation really bothered me. The middle school math checks out: 0.8 multiplied by 0.2 in fact equals 0.16. What bothered me was the underlying implication: The product of two numbers could be less than each number (0.16 is less than both 0.8 and 0.2).

The outcome makes sense to the astrophysicist in me. But in the dream I was staring at this equation as a mathematical beginner, completely befuddled by the result. How could that be? If you multiply two numbers together, shouldn't the result be greater than each part?

Dreams are written in disappearing ink. But this one lingered for a while, as if a message was embedded within it that I needed to learn.

And then the message hit me: When we operate at a fraction—at a 0.8 or a 0.2 instead of a full 1.0—we compromise the output.

Most of us go through life functioning at a fraction in everything we do. We check email during Zoom meetings. We shove a sandwich into our mouth with one hand while scrolling through our phone with the other. We check our email before we get out of bed and continue to check it more times than we realize (for the average American, the daily number is 74).[6] On average, Slack users check their messages every five minutes—fragmenting their attention at an absurdly high rate. The irony of Slack is that it prevents people from having any.

When we work, we think about play. When we play, we think about work. We inhabit an in-between state—we're neither fully here nor fully there. As a result, our output suffers. What we produce becomes less than what we put in. We achieve only an iota of our full capability.

Where's your phone this very second? If you're like most people, the answer is "within arm's reach." We've become inseparable from our phones. We walk with them, have dinner with them, and even take them into the bathroom to share the most private of moments. They're the first thing we grab in the morning and the last thing we check before we go to bed.

We've been tricked into believing that, if we're not always "on," we'll miss out on some crucial piece of information. But in responding to the fear of missing out, we become reckless with our most scarce resource.

Your most scarce resource isn't your time or money. It's your attention. There's a reason why we call it *paying* attention. Treat it like you would your money (because it's more important than money). Save it, invest it, and spend it where it matters most. And remember: Today's "free" services—like social media—aren't free at all. You're paying a fortune in terms of fragmented attention and lost focus.

Attention doesn't scale: We can pay attention to only one thing at a time. That's why it's worth so much. Economic forces have recognized the value of this scarce resource and turned it into a commodity. Social media is in the attention-selling business. You hand your attention to them for free, and they sell your attention for a fee. When you open their app, they make money, and when you close it, they lose money.

From one moment to the next, your reality is defined by what you pay attention to. Your attention empowers and magnifies its object in your mind. The easiest way to change your reality is to change how you use your attention.

When people meet a great leader, they often say, "She made me feel like I was the only person in the room." Imagine giving that type of complete attention to everything you do—and making that thing the *only* thing in the room.

Not just deep work, in Cal Newport's memorable phrase. But deep play. Deep rest. Deep listening. Deep reading. Deep love. Deep everything.

This mindset requires being aware of your own limitations. When I write, for example, my output begins to significantly drop after about two hours. By the fourth hour, I'm operating at a 0.2 at best. If I keep pushing, I know I'll write gobbledygook that isn't even worth editing. I'm much better off taking my hands off the keyboard and giving my attention to something else.

"Just as neurons that fire together wire together, neurons that don't fire together don't wire together," Nicholas Carr writes.[7] As you spend more time bouncing around from one distraction to another and less time focusing on a single activity, the neural networks that support those old functions begin to weaken. We pick up a book and find ourselves reading the same paragraph over and over. We can't sit through a film or have a long conversation without reaching for our phone. Our focus constantly flickers.

"A wealth of information," as Herbert Simon says, "creates a poverty of attention."[8] If your attention is fragmented and impulsively pulled in a million different directions, you won't be able to remember much. You can't make associations, connect dots, and form new insights. You can't think.

Academic research supports this commonsense conclusion: Heavy multitaskers perform worse on simple cognitive memory tasks.[9] When you're suffering from attention overload, your ability to process information and transfer it to long-term memory significantly decreases.

The solution isn't just to be mindful of what you're doing. It's to choose one activity over others. It's to refuse to shred your attention into tiny, useless pieces by switching tasks roughly every 10 minutes, as the average knowledge worker does.[10]

There must be intention to your attention and purpose to your focus. Often we operate impulsively, moving from one notification to the next, one email to the next, living our lives in a frantic blur. But if you slow down for just a moment and intentionally give your full attention to what you'll do next, you'll trigger an internal defibrillator that can jolt you back to life and bring you closer to your full capacity.

It's like the way a great leader might shake your hand and greet you. *Hello, activity. It's great to meet you. I'm choosing to engage with you. I'm going to treat you like you're the most important person in the room and ignore everyone else.*

Ask yourself on a daily basis: *How do I want to use my most scarce resource today? Where do I want to direct my attention?* Also ask, *What am I paying attention to that doesn't deserve it? While I pay attention to that, what am I not paying attention to?*

0.8 * 0.2 = 0.16. There's now a Post-it note on my desk with that equation. It serves as a constant reminder to live deep instead of operating at a fraction of my capacity.

## This is toxic

*A fly sat on a straw on a puddle of donkey urine.*
*Full of pride, it lifted up its head and said:*
*"I am the captain of this ship,*
*master of this ocean!"*

—RUMI

"What's on your digital morning rotation?" he asked.

"Digital morning what?" I replied.

"Digital morning rotation," he repeated. "The first few apps or websites you check every morning."

I'm not the sort of person who has a "digital morning rotation," I was about to blurt out indignantly. But in the split second before I opened my mouth, I realized I'd be lying.

I did, in fact, have a digital morning rotation. Every morning—before I even had my morning coffee—I checked Instagram, Facebook, my favorite news website, and my favorite sports website. If something was trending, I wanted to know. If someone liked my post, I wanted to know. If some news was breaking, I wanted to know.

I followed this routine to get grounded and connected, but it would do the opposite. It was the digital equivalent of gorging on a giant bucket of M&Ms for breakfast every morning. I'd lose all grounding, deep-fry my brain in a pool of 1s and 0s, and make myself nauseous in the process.

Information is like food. Some of it is toxic. And even healthy information can become toxic in high doses. Once ingested, information can wreak havoc on your mind, taking up precious space in an already cluttered environment. In-*form*-ation forms us from within. If you consume junk, your life becomes junk. Garbage in, garbage out.

The bottomless tanks of the internet repeatedly reload with new junk. By the time we've completed the rotation, we're already behind. It's time to start over to catch up on everything we missed. It's an endless game of whack-a-mole that leaves our mind in constant hyperventilation.

Imagine that someone collected all the information that you ingest daily—your friends' Facebook status updates, clickbait articles, meaningless Tweetstorms—put them in a book, and said: *I want you to read all this from start to finish*. You'd almost certainly say no. Yet the same information handed to us in micro-installments scattered throughout the day becomes more digestible. It's death by a thousand cuts.

What's more, the smoke lingers long after the fire is out. Even after we move on to the next thing, we still find ourselves worrying about a work email sitting in our inbox, envying photos from a friend's beach vacation, or wondering what Kim Kardashian might be doing this very moment.

There's information that's objectively junk—like your ex-partner's dating life or that clickbait article with the title "10 Adorable Child Stars Who Didn't Age Very Well."

And then there's junk information dressed up as healthy. These are the breaking-news reports that conveniently break in predictable cycles or op-eds that masquerade as unbiased reports designed to inflame our emotions.

It's easy to rationalize ingesting this type of information. We've been seduced into believing that we must "stay current" and "keep up with the times." In a time of great social and political upheaval, acquiring information feels urgent—but lacking the space to think properly creates its own emergency.

Sherlock Holmes compared the brain to an empty attic. You can decorate your brain-attic with whatever furniture you choose, but space is limited. Everything that's in your brain is there at the expense of something else.

Consider these eye-opening statistics. The average person spent 145 minutes per day on social media in 2021.[11] The average adult reads 200 to 260 words per minute.[12] The average book is roughly 90,000 words. If the average adult read books instead of using social media, they would read anywhere from 118 to 153 books a year. Every moment you spend ingesting junk information is a moment you're not spending on a book that can transform you.

If you're curious about what I allow into my brain-attic, here are the trade-offs I've made.

I look for sources with a higher signal-to-noise ratio. I generally prefer audiobooks over podcasts, books over blog posts, and evergreen articles over breaking news. The reason is simple. Books are curated and edited in a way that most podcasts and blog posts aren't. It takes a year to write a book, but only a few hours to draft a blog post. Two hours of a podcast conversation might have one gem buried in it, but two hours of an audiobook might change your life.

For several reasons, I significantly limit my news consumption. The ad-driven business model has turned news into a form of entertainment rather than a faithful reporting of global events. News has become a form of professional wrestling for intellectuals: A scripted drama unfolds in the ring, and readers cheer on their favorite wrestlers as they beat the crap out of each other with folding chairs.

What's more, the enormous demand for content can't be met by actual news, so old news is recycled and the same breaking story breaks in a dozen different ways. We tune in to the news to stay informed, but the news ends up making us *less* informed by generating artificial drama and conflict. The media repeatedly press the same buttons in our amygdala, indulge our outrage, and trigger our anxiety.

The news also warps our perception of reality. Much of what's important isn't considered newsworthy. Hypnotized by headlines, we assume the world is filled with cynicism and gloom. Many mental health problems, as Robert Heinlein wrote, "can be traced to the unnecessary and unhealthy habit of wallowing in the troubles and sins of five billion strangers."[13]

Rather than get caught up in the frenzy and speculation that characterize the 24-hour news cycle, I'd much rather read about what happened after the dust has settled—and after some level of clarity has emerged. The type of clear-headed retrospective I'm looking for appears in books and long-form articles published after the news is no longer new.

I also use "read later" and "watch later" lists. If something looks interesting, I usually don't read it or watch it right away. Instead, with a click, I save it to my "read later" or "watch later" list. I'm amazed at what happens when I go back through these lists. With the benefit of time, what looked irresistible in the moment turns out to be uninteresting junk. I regularly eliminate half of what I put on those lists. The goal, as Oliver Burkeman advises, is to treat these lists "like a river (a stream that flows past you, and from which you pluck a few choice items, here and there) instead of a bucket (which demands that you empty it)."[14]

These are the trade-offs I've made, but they may not be the right ones for you. Your brain-attic is *your* space. You get to decide what comes in and who stays. If you're not intentionally making that decision, someone else is. And that someone else is going to decide based on their best interest—not yours.

## An ode to a thought

Hello, I'm a thought.

I'm the result of a million variables all coming together to spark me into existence.

I've been waiting to come online in your mind for a long time now.

I decided to reveal myself to you this morning when you were in the shower, a time when the channel to your subconscious is open—for a brief moment.

Here I am now, appearing as a distant echo in your mind. I'm not strong yet. I'm just a flicker. A slow nudge. A delicate water bubble floating through your depths and slowly rising through your atmosphere.

I knock on the door of your mind. Knock knock! Here I am! Do you see me? I come bearing gifts. An idea you've yet to notice. An insight that will solve the problem that's been bugging you. An opportunity you've been missing.

But no one answers. Your mind is so noisy that you don't even hear me.

You step out of the shower, dry yourself off, and reach for your phone.

My bubble is burst, and I vanish forever.

## A resistible impulse

Imagine two boxes of cookies.

In one box, the cookies are individually wrapped in foil. You must unwrap each cookie before you can eat it. In the other box, the cookies aren't wrapped. There's no partition, so each cookie can go directly into your mouth.

In research studies, this minor distinction ends up producing a major difference.[15] People took much longer to finish a box of individually wrapped cookies. They also gambled less when their funds were divided across several envelopes rather than placed in a single envelope.

The partition—whether it's a foil or an envelope—prompts people to be more conscious of their behavior. Being forced to pause for a moment and contemplate what they're doing leads to more self-control. It turns an unconscious compulsion into a conscious choice.

The same approach can help with managing mind clutter. You don't need to wrap your smartphone in foil (though that would probably help). The goal is to insert a mental speed bump between you and your most impulsive behaviors—to put life in slow motion just enough to make you pause and consider what you really want to do. *Do I want to keep stuffing my face with more cookies? Do I want to keep scrolling through social media? Is pressing this button the very best thing I could do right now?*

The remedy doesn't require abstention. You don't need to give up your smartphone or quit social media. For most people, going cold turkey isn't sustainable anyway—or even desirable. In general, I'm skeptical of all-or-nothing approaches, which attack the symptom, leaving the underlying cause intact. Once the diet ends, people tend to relapse.

Instead, the goal is to be more intentional and less impulsive. When you find yourself reaching for your favorite source of distraction, pause for a moment. Observe the itch without scratching it. Ask yourself, *What need am I trying to fulfill? What is driving this desire?* We often reach for our distractions to satisfy an unmet need for excitement, escape, or intrigue.

But our distractions don't reliably fulfill these needs. Every now and then they might give us a momentary sense of excitement, but that feeling quickly fades. And what we think will spark joy or add meaning often does the opposite. We become so lost in our distractions that we don't even notice our body is horrified.

Here's a little exercise. Go ahead and put the book down and pick up your smartphone. Spend at least 10 minutes going through your favorite sources of distraction—social media, email, the stock market, whatever it might be. Once you pull yourself out of the rabbit hole, come back to the book.

Check in with yourself. How do you feel? Do you feel satisfied? Happy? Or are you feeling some unexplained discomfort? A low-level buzz of stress just below the surface? An unfulfilled hunger for excitement or intrigue?

Here's what often happens to me. Twitter makes me neurotic. Facebook makes me feel like I'm reliving the worst parts of middle school. Instagram makes me feel "less than." The news makes me feel like the whole world is going to hell in a handbasket.

It's not discipline that has made me more resistant to bingeing on these distractions. It's having learned, after repeatedly observing myself, that they often leave me feeling worse.

Even though they frequently make us feel lousy, these services keep us returning by exploiting our psychological weaknesses through variable rewards. In a lab setting, mice respond most strongly to intermittent reinforcement. If they press a lever and get rewarded with a treat every time, they eventually lose interest. But if the reward is variable—sometimes they get a treat and sometimes they get nothing—they become hooked.

Research shows that dopamine rises, not from the reward itself, but from the anticipation of the reward. And when the reward is doled out on an unpredictable schedule—when you introduce "maybe" into the equation—the resulting dopamine spike rivals the boost produced by cocaine.[16] This is one reason why slot machines are so addictive. You pull the lever repeatedly, but you're rewarded only intermittently.

You might feel sorry for the senior citizen mindlessly pulling a slot machine lever for hours. But you're doing the same thing every day on your smartphone. Every time you pull up your inbox or social-media feed, you're pulling a lever. Our phones dangle inter-mittent love outside our cage like rat treats. The goods arrive, just like slot machine rewards, on an unpredictable schedule. We turn into digital vampires, feasting on our feeds and forever seeking the dopamine jackpot.

As the saying goes, there's a reason why only drug dealers and Silicon Valley companies call their clients "users." But this partic-ular addiction is socially acceptable. Just look around an airport terminal. If everyone sucking on their digital pacifier were smoking a cigarette instead, we would announce an epidemic.

Unlike online rewards, time unfolds on a predictable schedule, so we become complacent about it. Time is always there—until it's not.

How would you like to spend your limited time here on Earth? Do you want to look back on your life and realize that you spent huge chunks of it keeping up with the Kardashians? Or do you want to focus on what matters and create art that you're proud of?

Remember Annie Dillard's timeless wisdom: "How we spend our days is, of course, how we spend our lives."

## You can't keep up

I feel guilty.

I feel guilty about the unread books sitting on my bookshelf.

I feel guilty about the unlistened podcasts waiting in my pod-cast app.

I feel guilty about the newsletters I haven't opened, and the classic movies I haven't watched.

I feel guilty about the unanswered emails in my inbox.

I feel guilty about somewhat envying people who lived in the 16th century and lacked access to the printing press—let alone the internet—and therefore had no obligation to "keep up" with the mountain of information available to their 21st-century descendants.

I feel guilty until I realize this: I can't keep up. You can't keep up. *No one* can keep up.

It's impossible to stay ahead of the melt on the ice-cream cone.

I'm not saying that you *may* not get to everything. I'm saying that you *definitely* will not. No day will ever come—not even in the distant future—when you'll feel "on top of everything" on your overcrowded plate.

This might sound unfortunate, but it should be liberating. It's only when I realize I can't keep up that I can focus on what actually matters. I become more selective about what I take in. I'm more liberal with the unsubscribe button. Life is too short to force-march yourself through a book you're not enjoying because of a delusion that some amazing insight will show up on page 183.

Everyone I know is stuck on some book. They're still acting like high school students forced to finish every book they were assigned, no matter how hard the slog. Instead of giving up, they stop reading altogether because they feel guilty about reading anything else. (If this book hasn't sparked your interest yet, you have my permission to stop reading.)

So let some of the ice cream melt—and let some bad things happen.

"Bad" comes in degrees. Not all bad things are created equal. There are the big bad things that could lead to catastrophe, and those of course are worth preventing. But then there are the little bad things that won't have any long-term consequences.

We often don't distinguish between these two categories, treating all bad events as equally bad. To avoid that pitfall, ask yourself, *Is this a little bad thing or a big bad thing? What if I let it fall through the cracks? What might happen, and how likely is it to happen?*

I'm not suggesting that you become careless. Quite the opposite. The goal is to be careful and intentional about which balls you're willing to drop so you can keep juggling the balls that matter the most.

Here's the thing: Something, somewhere is wrong all the time.

So let some emails go unanswered. Let some people complain. Let some opportunities slip by.

It's only by letting the little bad things happen that you can accomplish the great things.

## The biggest thing holding you back

"I am here today to cross the swamp, not to fight all the alligators."[17]

I came across this quote from an anonymous NASA employee in the terrific book *The Art of Possibility*. The quote resonated because we often do the opposite. We fight the alligators instead of crossing the swamp.

The swamp is a scary, uncertain place. We may never reach the other side. And if we do cross it, we're afraid of who we might become.

So we fight the alligators to hide from the discomfort of crossing the swamp. We spend our time doing what we know best— tackling our emails, attending endless meetings—instead of finishing this project or launching that product. The alligators are visible—they're right in front of us—but the shore seems distant in time and space. On any given day, a random email sent our way takes priority over the things that actually matter.

It's not like fighting alligators is completely unjustified. They're there after all. They *might* present a danger to us. As the alligators scream their 100-decibel sirens for attention, we feel compelled to fight them. Rather than being proactive, we spend most of our days—and our lives—playing defense.

All this churn *feels* productive, but it's not. We're getting things out of the way, but out of the way of what exactly? We're slaying the alligators, but the shore isn't any closer. We're winning each battle, but we're losing the war.

As Tim Ferriss writes, "Doing something unimportant well does not make it important."[18] What makes you a successful venture capitalist is the quality of the deals you close—not the number of your Twitter followers. What makes you a successful writer is the quality of your books—not how often you hit inbox zero. What makes you a great software engineer is the quality of your software—not the amount of time you spend in meetings. What makes your product successful is its remarkability—not the camera angle you use for the TV commercial promoting it. While we're busy tackling small tasks that we've convinced ourselves we *have* to do, we avoid the more complicated projects that will take us to the next level.

Extraordinary people ignore the alligators to focus on crossing the swamp. They don't spend their days dutifully checking off items from a to-do list. Their work is too big to be reduced to checkboxes.

Counterintuitively, a to-do list can be a powerful driver of procrastination. When you put all your to-dos in the same place and give them equal treatment, you give yourself another reason to clean your desk or call your insurance company instead of writing your book proposal.

You don't need to ditch your to-do list. You also don't need to replace it with a four-part matrix, a special app, or a stylish journal.

It's simple. Decide what's important and relentlessly prioritize it. Make it one of your to-dos to determine whether you've got the right to-dos. Identify the alligators in your life—the shallow concerns that aren't helping you cross the swamp. Ask yourself,

*What do I do just to make myself* feel *productive? Is this helping me cross the swamp? Or is it an alligator that's distracting me from what's important?* Then get to work on erasing those alligators from your to-do list. Stop trying to do more things and start doing the things that matter.

Instead of asking, *What's most urgent right now?*, ask, *What's the most important thing I could be doing? And why am I not doing it?* Urgent, by definition, doesn't last. But the important persists.

In the end, we have a choice.

We can keep fighting alligators and wait for a magical springboard to show up and catapult us to the other side. (Spoiler: There are no magical springboards.)

Or we can ignore the alligators, focus on the important instead of the urgent, and cross that swamp, inch by inch.

## Never stop never stopping

*Why are you so afraid of silence? Silence is the root of everything. If you spiral into its void, a hundred voices will thunder messages you long to hear.*

—RUMI

Nature, according to Aristotle, abhors a vacuum. He argued that a vacuum, once formed, will be filled by the dense material surrounding it.

I also used to abhor a vacuum. Whenever I found a vacuum in my life, I would fill it—no, stuff it—with the dense material surrounding it in an attempt to be "productive."

Productivity was tied to my identity. The fear of not doing enough was the fear of not being enough. I had to hustle, cut carbs, and continuously polish my morning routine to feel worthy. I tied my sense of accomplishment to how quickly I could clear my to-do list or how many times I could reach inbox zero. I was ever on the lookout for a new hack, a new system, or a new app that would allow me to squeeze more productivity out of my day for someone else's benefit.

I always felt the *need* for the next thing. When I was a professor, I'd write multiple academic articles simultaneously. Whenever I needed a break from one, I'd switch to another. The week after my last book, *Think Like a Rocket Scientist*, was published, I started drafting the proposal for the book you're currently reading. This mode of operating made me prolific, and being prolific gave my life meaning.

I know I'm not alone.

We worship at the altar of productivity. We idolize people who don't succumb to distractions like burnout, sickness, or sleep. Who can argue with getting more done in less time—more words per minute, more miles per gallon, more widgets per hour?

Nothing captures the prevailing hustle culture better than the chopped salad. The chopped salad is optimized to free the eyes and one hand of a knowledge worker from the odious task of eating so they can keep working. It allows its consumer, as Jia Tolentino writes, "to send emails for sixteen hours a day with a brief break to snort down a bowl of nutrients that ward off the unhealthfulness of urban professional life . . . because he needs the extra time to keep functioning within the job that allows him to afford a regular $12 salad in the first place."[19]

For me, the chopped-salad lifestyle came at a serious cost. I was so productive within my current state that I couldn't see outside of it, and I missed opportunities lurking in plain sight. As a self-constructed pandemonium raged around me, I didn't have the space or time for good thinking, and without good thinking, I couldn't make good decisions. I then spent much of my time correcting the resulting missteps.

Busyness is contrived significance. It's a form of laziness. It's a way of moving fast, but without direction. It's a numbing agent that people use to avoid looking within and panicking when they see what's inside.

If you're constantly in a fight-or-flight state, expecting a saber-toothed tiger to leap from the bushes, you'll feel resistance to tuning in for answers. Because, if you look inside, you won't notice the threat outside. If you're preoccupied with survival and constantly reacting to perceived crises, you're trapped on the bottom rung of Maslow's hierarchy of needs. You won't have the capacity to think for yourself and uncover your best insights.

If you slow down, you won't get left behind. You'll use less energy, you'll go faster, and you'll go deeper. The pedal-to-the-metal mentality is the enemy of original thought. Creativity isn't produced—it's discovered. And it happens in moments of slack, not during hard labor. Taking your foot off the pedal can be the best way to accelerate.

This sentiment is captured by a slogan commonly attributed to the Navy SEALs: "Slow is smooth, smooth is fast." These people work with sniper rifles and grenade launchers. Your PowerPoint presentation pales in comparison. If SEALs can slow down, so can you.

Ideas often don't arrive with a bang. There's no parade. The big thing never screams that it's a big thing. At first glance, the big thing actually looks quite small. If there's no void in your life—if your life is full of constant chatter—you won't be able to hear the subtle whisper when it arrives.

One of the biggest lies we've been told is that productivity is all about doing. But your best work will come from *un*doing—from slowing down and giving yourself time and space.

Mother Nature is a great teacher. She obeys an ancient formula: Sit still. Wait for things to come. Trees don't try to produce fruit year-round in an absurd attempt to be more productive. They lie dormant through the fall and the winter, shedding their leaves and conserving resources. You can't make a tree grow faster by tugging on it or watering it more than the soil can absorb.

Humans also have seasons. In some seasons, it's time to act. In others, we're better off easing up, stepping back, and allowing space for the water to be absorbed. The artist Corita Kent, during one of her dormant periods, would sit idle and watch a maple tree grow outside her window. "I feel that great new things are happening very quietly inside of me," she said. "And I know these things have a way, like the maple tree, of finally bursting out in some form."[20]

Being idle isn't the same thing as being lazy. A vacuum isn't something to be automatically filled. As the saying goes, it's the silence in between the notes that makes the music. It's only by letting go that you can receive and by becoming empty that you can be filled.

The void can't be reserved for your twice-a-year vacation in the sun. Shut down the noise, if only for a little bit, throughout your day. Give yourself permission to lounge in bed after waking up. Put yourself in airplane mode. Sit and stare at the ceiling. Wander aimlessly through a park without listening to a podcast or audiobook.

Allow interior silence to oppose contemporary chaos. Sink into the rhythm of no rhythm.

Because everything is born from the emptiness of the void.

Great new things are happening quietly inside of you.

Give them the time they need to bloom in all their glory.

Visit ozanvarol.com/genius to find worksheets, challenges, and exercises to help you implement the strategies discussed in this part.

# PART II

# *The Birth*

Part II has two chapters:

1. **Spectacularly You:** On becoming extraordinary by becoming more like yourself—and finding your first principles and your superpowers
2. **Discover Your Mission:** On finding and living your purpose

Along the way, I'll reveal:

- Why you're in a jail cell of your own making (and how to get out)
- The fascinating story of the appliance salesman who became one of the best-selling musicians of all time
- Why most people choose the wrong career (and what to do about it)
- The email that changed my life
- The problem with pursuing happiness
- Why "follow your passion" is bad advice (and what to do instead)
- A simple question you can ask to assume control over your life
- The secret to stop overthinking and start doing

# 4

# Spectacularly You

*They laugh at me because I'm different.*
*I laugh at them because they're all the same.*
—ATTRIBUTED TO KURT COBAIN

## Embrace your purple

To belong.

For much of my life, that's what I wanted most.

I was an only child living in Istanbul, a sprawling city of millions. Growing up, I spent most of my time holed up in my room in the small apartment we lived in.

I had eccentric tastes that made me feel different. From an early age, my favorite spot was inside my own head. I fell in love with computers and books. I taught myself how to code and lost myself in the fantasy worlds created by Isaac Asimov and others. Carl Sagan spoke to me through the original *Cosmos* series on Betamax tapes. I didn't speak any English, so I had no idea what he was saying. But I listened anyway.

My differences remained largely harmless until I got to fourth grade. As elementary school students, we wore the same outfits to school—a bright blue uniform with a crisp white collar—and the boys all had the same buzz cut.

Well, all boys except me.

I had a laissez-faire approach to haircuts, which drew the ire of the school principal, a bulldozer of a man better suited to work as a prison warden. He spotted my longer-than-standard hair during a school assembly and began grunting like a winded rhinoceros. He grabbed a hair clip from a girl and stuck it in my hair to shame me publicly—as retribution for nonconformity.

Shame, for Turks, is worse than death. I never skipped a haircut again.

Once my eccentricities turned into liabilities—once I began to get pushed around literally and proverbially—I turned into an octopus, changing my colors to match the colors around me. I even changed my favorite color. When people asked, instead of revealing that my favorite color was purple, I'd say it was blue. Because blue was what normal boys were supposed to like, and I really, *really* wanted to be normal.

I learned to be a good boy, to tetris myself into shape to become what the world expected of me. *This is what you're supposed to think. This is who you should be afraid of. This is who you should spend your time with. This is the approved list of games for you to play. This is the kind of future you should want. You've got three options: doctor, lawyer, or engineer.* My oh my!

When I started middle school, my sense of *un*belonging kicked into high gear. It wasn't just my hair that was different. Unlike my public elementary school, where I rubbed shoulders with students from similarly humble economic backgrounds, my private middle school catered largely to Istanbul's wealthy elite. My parents could barely afford the tuition, but they found a way to make it work. This was my best option for learning English and getting a shot at attending college abroad.

I spent much of middle school assuming that I was missing some belonging chip that came preinstalled in everyone else. I could talk for hours about sci-fi books or HTML programming, but I had never played tennis or heard of Prada. Fashion sense—or even basic color coordination—didn't come naturally to me. I had an admittedly lowbrow taste in music and preferred the catchy tunes of Ace of Base over the infinitely more popular Nirvana.

I remembered the lesson my school principal taught me in fourth grade. I started to treat my interactions with others like my haircuts, obsessively observing what was normal. I would anticipate what other people thought and wanted, and I'd change my colors accordingly.

It worked beautifully. My social circle expanded, and over time I became a master at fitting in.

Whether it's a suit, a dress, or yourself, fitting in works the same. You cut a thought here, you alter a preference there, and you adjust a behavior over here—until you fit into the mold.

But unlike clothing, an altered self barely resembles the original. To be sure, glimmers of my actual self would shine through with certain people and in certain contexts, but I frequently played the role I was expected to play—until I became unrecognizable, even to myself.

When I moved to the United States for college, I had to start all over again. I traded my skinny European jeans for cargo shorts. I joined a fraternity and mastered the art of beer pong. My accent was one of my distinctive qualities, but by the end of sophomore year, that too had faded. ("Dude, there is something happening to your accent!" my roommate Joe blurted out one night between sips of Milwaukee's Best.) I was a skinny kid with a funny name from a foreign country halfway around the world, but if I *talked* like them, I thought I could *be* them.

I was as un-Muslim as someone raised in a majority-Muslim country could be. If there was a Muslim hell, I was definitely going there. But that didn't matter on September 11. When the twin towers fell, the fact that I grew up in Turkey overshadowed everything else. Islamophobia consumed even people I had considered good friends, and I found myself the target of bigoted comments. Just when I thought I had finally fit in, I was once again exposed.

Even when they worked, my attempts to fit in brought only a superficial sense of belonging. It wasn't *me* that belonged. It was a tailored version of me.

It starts slowly. You begin to say things that contradict what you actually believe. You nod along like it makes sense. You forget your own boundaries and invite others to breach your soul. Over time you become a fugitive in your own sanctuary.

Trying to fit in makes it harder to belong. As Brené Brown describes it, "Belonging is being accepted for you. Fitting in is being accepted for being like everyone else. If I get to be me, I belong. If I have to be like you, I fit in."[1]

I remain a work in progress. I still fight the tendency to crawl back into my conformist skin and change who I am in a futile attempt to fit in. In many ways, my writing is self-help—I write in part to help myself, to reconnect with who I really am, and to show my true colors to the world.

I also take small actions every day to embrace my eccentricities. Every now and then I rock out to Ace of Base. My Spotify playlists are musical Armageddon. They are where good music goes to die. But I love them. They remind me to step into my self rather than become a stranger to it.

Shortly after my now-wife, Kathy, and I first met, she asked me, "What's your favorite color?"

I was about to blurt out "blue," but I swallowed the word and returned to myself.

"Purple," I said, "I love purple."

She looked at me and smiled one of her gorgeous, infectious smiles.

"Ever since I was a kid," she said, "I wanted to marry a boy whose favorite color is purple."

And I knew I finally belonged.

## How to be remarkable

In 1954, Johnny Cash walked into the audition room at Sun Records.

At the time he was a nobody. He was selling appliances door to door and playing gospel songs at night. He was broke, and his marriage was in ruins.

Cash decided to sing a gospel song for his audition. It was what he knew best. What's more, gospel was all the rage in 1954. Everyone else was singing it.

The audition, as depicted in the movie *Walk the Line*, didn't go as Cash planned.[2] As Cash begins to sing a dreary gospel song, the record label owner, Sam Phillips, feigns interest for all of 30 seconds before interrupting Cash.

"We've already heard that song," Phillips scoffs. "A hundred times. Just like that. Just like how you sang it." The song, he says, is the "same Jimmy Davis tune we hear on the radio all day, about your peace within, and how it's real, and how you're gonna shout it." He asks Cash to sing "something different, something real, something you felt," because that's the kind of song that truly saves people.[3]

"It ain't got nothing to do with believing in God, Mr. Cash," Phillips says. "It has to do with believing in yourself."

This rant jolts Cash out of his conformist, let-me-sing-you-some-good-old-gospel attitude. It brings out the part of him that's been buried by a crushing mortgage, a stale marriage, and too many years in the Air Force.

He collects himself, starts strumming his guitar, and begins singing "Folsom Prison Blues."

In that moment, he stops trying to be a gospel singer.

He becomes Johnny Cash.

He walks out of the audition room with a record contract. All because he rejects his natural tendency to conform and embraces everything that sets him apart from others—his somber demeanor, his distinctive voice, and the dark black clothes that would later earn him the nickname "The Man in Black."

We assume following the herd makes it safe. We hide behind what's expected and what's accepted. We'd rather be wrong collectively—we'd rather fail singing the same gospel song that everyone else is singing—than risk failing individually. So we chase trends, adopt the latest fad, and, as Cash would say, walk the line.

Think back to the emails you received from dozens of companies at the beginning of the Covid-19 pandemic. They inevitably included some variation of the same boring title ("Special Message from our CEO about Covid-19") and repeated the same clichés ("Dear valued customer") and worn-out sound bites ("in a time of unprecedented uncertainty").

In business, as in life, most people work from the same uninspiring template. We're wired to emulate others, especially in times of unprecedented uncertainty (see what I did there?). We copy and paste from our peers and competitors, assuming they know something we don't. We believe that the only audience worth reaching is the biggest one, so we round off the edges, erase our fingerprints, and start singing gospel.

The response "no one does it that way" stops a conversation before it begins. If no one does it that way, it can't be done. If no one does it that way, we don't know what might happen. If no one does it that way, we're not going to do it that way.

This "monkey see, monkey do" approach creates a race to the center. But the center is too crowded with other gospel singers competing for ever-shrinking slices of the pie. People often want to "aim for the biggest, most obvious target, and hit it smack in the bull's eye," the musician Brian Eno says. "Of course with everybody else aiming there as well that makes it very hard to hit." The alternative? "Shoot the arrow, then paint the target around it," Eno explains. "Make the niches in which you finally reside."[4]

Bruce Springsteen made his own niche. He knew his voice wasn't great. He could play the guitar, but "the world was filled with plenty of good guitar players, many of them my match or better," he writes.[5]

Instead of aiming for the same target as others, Springsteen shot his arrow and then painted the target around it. He doubled down on the quality that made him different from other musicians: his ability to write songs. Springsteen became a sensation for writing songs that capture the blue-collar spirit ("For my 19th birthday I got a union card and a wedding coat") that show the distance between the American dream and the American reality ("Waste your summer praying in vain for a savior to rise from these streets"), and that allow his audience to find pieces of themselves in his music ("I want to know if love is real"). The same man initially dismissed by audiences, agents, bandmates, and just about everyone else eventually became a rock 'n' roll sensation.

Oprah Winfrey has a similar story.[6] She was fired from her first job as an evening news reporter. The reason? She couldn't separate her emotions from her stories. Instead of trying to erase her emotions, Winfrey embraced them. That distinctive quality eventually made Winfrey the world's most compassionate interviewer and turned her into a household name.

Becoming extraordinary requires becoming more like yourself. When you do that, you become a magnet that attracts some people with the same force that repels others. You can't be liked by all and disliked by none. If you aim for that unachievable objective, you'll only reduce the force of your magnet—the very source of your strength. The only way to attract people who like purple is to show your purple.

Embracing your purple doesn't work if it's inauthentic. If it's a gimmick. If you're just trying to get attention or zigging simply because everyone else is zagging. This isn't rule breaking for the sake of rule breaking—rebelling without a cause against the establishment. Rather, it's an intentional bending of the rules, driven by a desire to live in a way that's aligned with who you are.

Here's the thing: We notice things because of contrast. Something stands out because it's different from what surrounds it.

If you blend into the background—if you show no idiosyncrasy, no fingerprints, no contrast, no anomaly—you become invisible.

You become the background.

It's only by embracing, rather than erasing, your idiosyncrasies—the things that make you spectacularly you—that you can become remarkable.

## One of these things is not like the others

I love walking into a bookstore and discovering new books.

Not the best-selling books sitting on everyone's bookshelf, but the undiscovered gems. Books that have yet to break through. Books that have fallen out of mainstream awareness. Books published by smaller publishing houses without massive marketing budgets.

Over the past few years I've noticed a disappointing trend in some bookstores that I used to frequent. The trend carries important lessons regardless of what you do for a living.

You walk in and you're greeted by a massive best-sellers section displaying all the usual books. You make your way past all the new best-sellers, and the books highlighted on the other shelves are the old best-sellers. You ask a staff member for recommendations, and he suggests three books from—you guessed it—the best-sellers section.

All the books on all the shelves are organized in alphabetical order by the author's last name—a system designed for the rapidly shrinking category of people who walk into a bookstore knowing exactly what book they want to buy.

There's no personality in this type of bookstore. No quirkiness. No charm. Nothing that's remarkable. Nothing that improves on the online retail experience. So why should potential customers go out of their way to visit you?

Bookstores can't compete with online retailers on price and availability. But they can do what online stores can't do: give people a personalized experience.

And that's what the best bookstores do. They provide real curation by real human beings that goes beyond ads, algorithms, and best-seller lists. They organize their shelves in a delightful way that helps customers discover books they're going to love. Instead of just putting books in alphabetical order, these booksellers create categories like "Time Travel," "Page Turners You Can Read in a Weekend," "Must-Read Books You've Never Heard Of," and "Young Adult Books That Adults Will Also Love."

Across industries, consider Virgin America. Back in 2007, the airline filmed a hilarious airline-safety video that ditched the conventional instructions.[7] My favorite line: "For the 0.0001 percent of you who have never operated a seat belt before, it works like this." That line created a point of connection—it's something people have been thinking about but haven't verbalized. (*Why do they still teach people how to fasten their seat belt?*) The airline also embraced its purple and adopted soothing purple lighting for its cabins instead of the headache-inducing white lights that illuminate most airplanes. These features helped Virgin America stand out in a crowded market filled with airlines offering virtually identical products. By the time other airlines followed suit, Virgin America had already established itself as the hip leader of fun in airline travel.

When it comes to fun in ice cream, Ben & Jerry's traditionally led the pack with pun-packed flavors like Cherry Garcia and Karamel Sutra. But after it was acquired in 2000 by Unilever, a huge multinational company, Ben & Jerry's lost some of its flavor. Newly appointed executives eliminated jobs and closed plants, draining company morale.[8]

Things took a turn for the better when Jostein Solheim was appointed CEO in 2010. His commitment to the company culture was soon tested with a proposal for a new ice-cream flavor. It was called Schweddy Balls, a name based on a well-known *Saturday Night Live* skit.[9]

Would he green-light the flavor? It would be a risky move. Some parents' groups would be outraged. Some stores would refuse to carry it. But there was something more important at stake: the distinctive soul of Ben & Jerry's. After a tumultuous decade, Solheim's people needed to know that their leader would embrace the company's purple. He approved the new flavor.

The response from some retailers was hostile, as expected. During a meeting with Ben & Jerry's executives, the CEO of Walmart screamed at the top of his lungs, "I'm not going to sell Schweddy Balls!" This anecdote alone was worth whatever pain the new flavor would create for the company. From then on, Ben & Jerry's had its mojo back.[10]

Yes, the new ice-cream flavor was edgy. But edges define the puzzle piece and set it apart from the rest. Your edges become the reason why people talk about you and choose you over others. If you round off the edges and erase your useful idiosyncrasies, you turn into plain vanilla ice cream. And plain vanilla ice cream isn't remarkable. The same goes for a bookstore that organizes its shelves the same way as every other bookstore, an airline that repeats the same dull safety warnings, or a gospel singer delivering the same song in the same way.

Step back and ask, *What is our edge? What can we offer our customers that will delight them (and us!)? How can we share our unique personality in a way that will set us apart from every other business offering the very same thing?*[11]

There may have been a great reason 20 years ago for organizing all your proverbial shelves in alphabetical order by the author's last name.

But if you don't reimagine how things are working today, someone else will.

## The most dangerous form of imitation

When people talk about imitation, they often refer to copying from others.

But there's a more dangerous type of imitation: self-imitation. When you first taste success, there's a strong temptation to rinse and repeat—to copy and paste what you did before.

I experienced that temptation when writing the book you're reading now. When I wrote my last book, *Think Like a Rocket Scientist*, I hadn't written anything worth imitating. I had no notion of where the book would go. I was free to explore, play, and shape my clay in the way that I wanted.

With this book, my record is no longer blank. I now have something I need to live up to—something that this book is going to be compared against. So in writing this book, I initially copied the same formula that made *Think Like a Rocket Scientist* successful—the same structure, the same format, the same everything.

But it wasn't working. The words stopped flowing. The more I stuck to the previous formula, the harder writing became. So I let it go. Instead of forcing myself to stick to what was no longer working, I became curious about what was coming up during the process—the ideas, topics, and themes presenting themselves moment to moment—and leaned into the uncertainty of it all.

Copying dilutes the qualities that made the original sing. This is why sequels and remakes rarely capture the magic of the original. Once I abandoned the formula, the words began to come. My fingers felt freer on the keyboard, and eventually they began to dance. I wrote a record number of words in a month.

"You have two options," Joni Mitchell says. "You can stay the same and protect the formula that gave you your initial success. They're going to crucify you for staying the same. If you change, they're going to crucify you for changing."[12]

I'd rather get crucified for changing. I don't want to sit at the pottery wheel aiming to re-create the last best thing.

Remarkable happens when you stop copying others—especially your own past self—and start making the art that only your current self can make.

## Master the principle behind the tactic

I vaguely remember the first time I saw a pop-up on a website. It was exciting! *Look, a tiny little box! It came out of nowhere! It's like someone knows I'm here.* I couldn't type my email address fast enough to opt in for that 10 percent off coupon that I didn't even want.

In just a matter of weeks, pop-ups began to, well, pop up on every website. That initial euphoric feeling quickly turned into annoyance. When the tactic became popular, people began to ignore it. Pop-ups became like the seat belt announcement on an airplane: repeated so many times that it blended into the background.

In cooking, if you use someone else's recipe and you know your way around a kitchen, you can basically get the same Instagram-worthy dinner. But life doesn't work that way. It's the beauty of life that the exact same ingredients and the exact same recipe can produce wildly different results for different people.

Yet it still feels safe to copy other people's recipes. If you fail—if the same tactic doesn't produce the same result for you—you can blame the cookbook.

But when you blindly follow other recipes, you grow dependent on them. You can't understand the logic behind the recipe or master the foundations of cooking. You just go through the motions—add a teaspoon of salt here and half a cup of olive oil there—without knowing what those ingredients do. As a result, you can't troubleshoot when something goes wrong or change the recipe to make it your own.

Julia Child wasn't a natural-born cook. She fumbled with recipes on her own but couldn't master the art of cooking—until she attended Le Cordon Bleu cooking school at the age of 37. As Laura Shapiro writes, "Learning to cook at the Cordon Bleu meant breaking down every dish into its smallest individual steps and doing each laborious and exhausting procedure by hand." This process allowed Child to understand "for the first time the principles governing how and why a recipe worked as it did."[13]

Having mastered the foundations of cooking, Child could teach them to the public on television. And that was part of her charm: She didn't hide behind a recipe. She revealed how each step worked and why she did what she did. She led the viewers through the mysterious process of cooking—and gave them the same foundations that had allowed her to achieve her own results. Armed with those foundations, a novice cook could take control in the kitchen.

Control is the key word here. Most of us have given up control—to recipes that other people use and to recipes we've used in the past. Process, by definition, is backward looking. It was developed in response to yesterday's problem. If you keep doing what you're doing—if you keep planting the lightning rod where lightning struck last—you will, at some point, stop being remarkable and lose what makes you great. Regaining control requires being intentional about what you do, instead of blindly copying what others are doing or mindlessly repeating what you've done in the past.

And being intentional requires knowing *why* you're doing what you're doing.

Does that weekly status meeting serve a clear purpose? Or are you holding the meeting because it's easier to keep doing what you've always done—and avoid having a difficult conversation with that one person who enjoys having the meeting?

Is your brainstorming session just a venue for people to sound smart? Or is it actually producing valuable ideas and tangible decisions?

What is that pop-up on your website for? Is it producing the results you seek? Or is it there simply because someone told you it'd be a good idea to put it there?

Instead of copying tools, tactics, and recipes, master the principle behind them.

Once you know what the principle is—once you know the *why* behind the tactic—you can create your own extraordinary *how*.

## The first principles of you

If you've ever read a business book, you probably know the story of Kodak's downfall. In 1975, a young Kodak engineer developed the first digital camera. But instead of commercializing the technology, management decided to suppress it because it would compete with Kodak's traditional film photography business.

Kodak eventually found itself being disrupted by the same technology it had first developed in-house and then shelved. Although the company later entered the digital market, its efforts were too little, too late—tantamount to rearranging deck chairs on a sinking *Titanic*.[14] Kodak went bankrupt in 2012.[15]

But there's another, far more important story from across the Pacific that hasn't been repeated and retold. And that's the story of Fujifilm.

With the rise of digital cameras, Kodak's primary film rival, Fuji, faced a similar problem. Its core photographic film market was shrinking dramatically. But unlike Kodak, Fujifilm's management was willing to let go of its historical baggage and overcome the stubborn "this is who we are and what we do" mentality.[16]

To reimagine the future, Fujifilm leaders asked, "What are our first principles—the core capabilities of our company that can be repurposed in new ways? What other industries could benefit from what we do exceptionally well?"

The answer? Cosmetics.

Yes, you read that right. In 2007, Fujifilm launched Astalift, which sells high-end skin products for—fittingly—"photogenic beauty."

Photography and skin care may seem to have nothing in common. But appearances deceive.

It turns out that the same antioxidants that protect photographic film from harmful UV rays can do the same for human skin. It also turns out that collagen—which makes up about half the materials in film—is also the most abundant protein in skin and a common ingredient in beauty products.

So the company applied its historical experience with collagen and antioxidants to manufacture a formula for skin care. Departments at Fuji that had worked on film photography for decades were repurposed to develop cosmetic products.

In 2012, when its film competitor Kodak declared bankruptcy, Fuji's diversified annual revenues exceeded $20 billion. The company continues to redeploy its assets into exploring new frontiers, including health care, pharmaceuticals, and life sciences. Many of these spin-off ventures have failed. But Fuji's few big successes have compensated in spades for the ideas that didn't take off.

Fuji never completely gave up on film. To protect its history and culture—its own version of pun-packed ice-cream flavors—it still produces film products, even though they account for only a tiny fraction of its profits. That share, however, is growing as nostalgia for analog images and physical media boosts the popularity of traditional film products.

This is the power of first-principles thinking—of distilling a system into its core ingredients and building it back up in a different way.

Other examples abound. YouTube started out as a video dating website. On February 14, 2005—before swiping was a thing—the three founders of YouTube launched a website to allow single people to create videos to introduce themselves to eligible partners.[17] "Just three guys on Valentine's Day that had nothing to do," as company cofounder Steve Chen explained. Their attempt to play Cupid didn't work. So they took the company's underlying technology and created a service that allows people to easily upload videos of all kinds.

Before becoming a massive $16 billion company, Slack used to be a game developer called Tiny Speck.[18] In the early 2010s, the company made a multiplayer online role-playing game called Glitch. The game had an internal chat tool that allowed users to communicate with each other. When Glitch failed to find a sustainable audience for its game, the founders took the internal chat tool from the game and made it a stand-alone product.

The power of first-principles thinking can be used far beyond the world of business. You can also use this thinking to find the raw materials within yourself and build the new yous. Take a moment to tease out your own basic building blocks—the Lego blocks of your talents, interests, and preferences.

Here are some questions to consider. What makes you *you*? What are some of the consistent themes across your life? What feels like play to you—but work to others? What is something that you don't even consider a skill—but other people do? If you asked your best friend or partner, what would they say is your superpower—the thing that you can do better than the average person?

We tend to distrust our superpowers—what comes relatively easily to us. We value what's hard and devalue what's easy. We've been convinced that if we're not in pain—if we're not constantly grinding, hustling, and struggling—we're not doing it right. But in life it's possible to create diamonds without immense heat and pressure.

Consider the skills behind each activity in which you excel. For example, if you're great at organizing events, that doesn't just mean you're a good event organizer. It means you can communicate well, rally others, and create memorable experiences. Those skills may suit you for a much wider array of pursuits than you realize.

One of the consistent themes in my own life has been storytelling. As a child, from the moment I learned how to type on my grandfather's Underwood typewriter, I wrote stories. I spent much of my time in elementary school writing—screenplays, stories, and articles for a magazine I started (my parents were the only readers). Later in my adult life, I used storytelling as a lawyer to tell persuasive stories on behalf of my clients. Then, as a professor, I told stories to captivate and inspire my students. Now, as an author, I use storytelling to convey ideas in a memorable way. The recipe changes, but the core ingredient remains constant.

Your first principles as a person are often the qualities you suppress the most—because they make you different from others.

Play is one of those qualities for me. I excelled at being playful as a child, and when that quality began to get in the way of conformity, I suppressed it with discipline. I'm still getting reacquainted with my playful side, and my best writing happens when my inner child comes out to play.

Your inner child often holds the key to unlocking your first principles. Originality consists of returning to the origin, as the

Catalan architect Antoni Gaudí purportedly put it. So reconnect with your own origin. What did you love doing as a child—before the world stuffed you with facts and memos, before your education stole the joy from what you enjoy, and before the word *should* dictated how you spend your time?

What made you weird or different as a child can make you extraordinary as an adult. Tap into those faint memories and use them as inspiration for what you do now.

Once you've deconstructed your key components, build yourself anew from the ground up. But don't just copy what was there before. Reimagine as you go. Recombine your first principles in new ways to seek out potential new futures. Apply yourself to a new career or a new industry, as Fujifilm and Slack did. Pivot to reach different audiences, as YouTube did.

When you discover your first principles, you'll begin to step into all of your staggering richness and complexity.

## Diversify yourself

*I am large, I contain multitudes.*

—WALT WHITMAN, "SONG OF MYSELF"

Imagine eating the same thing every day, breakfast, lunch, and dinner.

That's what millions of people in Ireland did in the early 1800s.[19] They ate almost exclusively potatoes of the Lumper variety, with the average laborer consuming around 14 pounds of potatoes every day.

This single-crop system kept the population fed—until steamships from the Americas brought with them an unwelcome visitor to Irish shores.

The visitor was a pathogen called *Phytophthora infestans*. The name is Greek in origin: It means plant destroyer. The pathogen rapidly obliterated Irish potato crops, turning those essential tubers into inedible slime.

The Great Famine that followed lasted seven years. By 1852, one million people had perished, and a decade after the famine, more than two million had left the country for good, causing the population to plummet by nearly 25 percent. Numerous factors played into the tragedy, including the ineffectiveness of the British government and the cruelty of the British landlords who evicted their farmer tenants.

Another major contributor to the famine was the lack of genetic diversity in Irish potatoes.[20] Much of the country's poorest depended on the Lumper variety, which proved to be particularly vulnerable to the plant destroyer. As a result, the pathogen decimated both the crops and the people who depended on them for survival.

A lack of diversity in any system—whether it's agriculture, business, or a human being—renders it vulnerable. Companies become obsolete after they overinvest in the same potato varietals year after year. If you've defined yourself only as a seller of physical film, then, like Kodak, you'll ignore the digital revolution. If you've defined yourself as a maker of dash-mounted GPS units, you'll make the mistake Garmin made and ignore the smartphone revolution. If you've defined yourself as a brick-and-mortar video rental store, you'll ignore the streaming revolution and go the way of Blockbuster. In each of these cases, a lack of diversity undermined evolution and paved a company's way to extinction.

Consider RIM, which developed the BlackBerry brand of smartphones. "I'm a poster child for not doing anything but what we do," said Jim Balsillie, the company's former chair and co-CEO, during an interview. The interviewer asked Balsillie whether he was thinking of diversifying RIM beyond the BlackBerry. His response? "No," followed by laughter. "We are a very poorly diversified portfolio. It either goes to the moon or it crashes to the earth,"

Balsillie said, laughing again. "But it's making it to the moon pretty good," he added with a smile.[21] Steady as she went—until it hit an asteroid called the iPhone. In just five years, from 2009 to 2014, RIM's market share of smartphones in the United States plummeted from nearly 50 percent to less than 1 percent.[22]

Xerox's legendary research lab, PARC, invented the first personal computer as we know it, including pivotal innovations like the mouse, Ethernet networking, laser printing, and the graphical user interface. Then, they did nothing with it. Xerox was, after all, a manufacturer of office copiers, not computers. Instead, Xerox gave an official tour of PARC, including the personal computer it had developed, to a man named Steve Jobs. Jobs took meticulous notes, hired away PARC's top talent, and then, inspired by what he had seen, created the Lisa, the precursor to the Mac.[23]

If these organizations hadn't tied their identities to their most successful product, their Lumper potato, they might have seized these new opportunities when they arose.

The obstinate grip of a single identity also affects people. We're taught to show only one part of ourselves—one dimension, one personality, and one profession. Hence the cliché questions, "What will you be when you grow up?" or "What do you do for a living?" The underlying implication is clear: You are defined by what you do—you're a doctor, a lawyer, or an engineer—and what you do is a single, static thing.

If your identity is bound up with your profession, what happens if you lose your job—or decide you don't want to do it anymore? What happens when that specialty you've spent a lifetime perfecting becomes obsolete?

The only escape, the only path to genuine resilience, is through diversity. Treat yourself like your financial investments and hedge your bets. Once you've figured out your first principles, mix and remix them. Pursue multiple interests. Diversify *yourself*. If you have a diversity of traits and skills that you can recombine and repurpose, you'll enjoy an extraordinary advantage to evolve with the future.

Diversifying isn't octopus-like color shifting—changing who you are to blend into your environment. It's stepping into the fullness of you—all of you. It's understanding that you are an unfinished, and unfinishable, human being. To think that you are only one thing—that there is a single, static *you*—is inconsistent with the very nature of a life, where you learn from each experience and evolve.

Diversification doesn't just ensure your resilience. It also becomes a source of new strength. "To create," as François Jacob said, "is to recombine."[24] Successful creators tend to follow their curiosity and branch out: Rappers write novels. Actors paint. Entrepreneurs make films. Nobel Prize–winning scientists are roughly three times more likely than the average scientist to pursue artistic hobbies.[25] Intuitively, they understand that each medium of expression informs others, that time spent on a secondary project adds richness and depth to their primary work, and that pursuing multiple avenues provides a liberating sense of security. We all need our own personal R&D departments where we can experiment with new dimensions.

Diversifying yourself also makes it easier to take potentially valuable risks. If you take a moonshot with one aspect of your life—and miss the moon entirely—you'll still land on solid ground.

Amelia Boone is an attorney for Apple as well as an endurance athlete. When she first started training, she couldn't do a single pull-up. Since then, she's won the World's Toughest Mudder three times. The race, which lasts for 24 nonstop hours, makes a marathon look like a casual stroll.

When Boone broke her femur, she could no longer race. But the injury didn't hit her as hard because she used the recovery time to reconnect to what she loved about being a lawyer. She still had a leg to stand on.[26]

When diversifying, the more unusual the combination, the greater the potential value. It's certainly helpful for a singer to learn to dance, but there's nothing distinct or unusual in that mix. Rarer combinations, however, lead to unexpected benefits. A doctor who can code. A contractor with a flair for public speaking. An engineer who knows the law. A football player who performs ballet, as Heisman Trophy winner Herschel Walker did.[27] When people call you a contradiction in terms—too complex to categorize—you'll know you're on the right track.

When you live a hyphenated life, it also becomes futile to compare yourself to others. There's no standard playbook for a Turkish American rocket scientist–turned-lawyer-turned-professor-turned-author. By refusing to follow a fixed path myself, I've been able to write my own story. And it's been a rollicking tale so far, with plenty of exciting plot twists along the way. From the outside, all this change might seem dizzying, but thanks to a diversified identity, life has become a rewarding, choose-your-own-adventure game for me.

The future belongs to those who transcend a single story or identity.

These people don't define themselves by what they do or what they believe. They may practice law, but they're not lawyers. They may act, but they're not actors. They may support a Democratic candidate, but they're not Democrats.

They can't be captured by a single story.

They plant the seeds for multiple crops.

They are large.

They contain multitudes.

# Discover Your Mission

*People of accomplishment rarely sat back and
let things happen to them. They went out and
happened to things.*

—AMERICAN AVIATOR ELINOR SMITH

## The screenplay of your life

The 29-year-old actor stared at his bank account statement.[1]

He had only $106 left to his name.

His acting career was going nowhere. He couldn't afford the rent on his cheap Hollywood apartment. He even tried to sell his dog because he didn't have enough money to buy dog food.

To take his mind off things, he decided to watch the world heavyweight title fight. Reigning champion Muhammad Ali was facing off against Chuck Wepner, a relatively unknown club fighter. The fight was supposed to be an easy win for Ali. But defying all odds, Wepner fought for 15 rounds before being knocked out.

Against one of the greatest boxers of all time, this supposed nobody held his own. Inspired by this triumph of the human spirit, the actor decided to write a screenplay. Since he couldn't get acting jobs in other people's movies, he would create a lead character for himself to play. He grabbed a Bic pen, lined sheets of paper, and started writing.

He finished the script in just three and a half days.

One day, on his way out the door from another failed audition, he turned around and, on a whim, mentioned his script to the producers in the room. Intrigued by the premise, the producers read the script, loved it, and offered him $25,000 to purchase the rights. But they had a condition: They wanted a big-name actor with a big box-office draw to play the lead.

The actor refused.

He had written the script so that *he* could play the lead. "I'd rather bury [the script] in the back yard and let the caterpillars play [the lead]," he told his wife. "I would have hated myself for selling out."

The producers mistook the actor's refusal for a negotiating tactic, so they kept increasing the offer. To $100,000. Then $175,000. And then $250,000. Finally, $360,000.

He refused to budge.

The producers kept insisting that they needed a big star to play the lead, but the actor wanted to live by the moral of the story he told in the script—about the importance of going after your dreams and having faith in yourself.

The producers finally relented and green-lit the film on the condition that the budget be kept low. The film was shot in only 28 days. To make ends meet, the actor cast several family members in the film, including his father, brother, and wife—and even his dog, Butkus.

The film beat all expectations. It went on to earn $225 million in global box-office receipts and won three Academy Awards in 1977, including Best Picture.

The movie was *Rocky*, and the actor was a young Sylvester Stallone.

Most people in Stallone's position would have given up the lead to another actor and just sold the script. But Stallone wanted to be an actor. With his long-term guiding principle clear, the decision was simple. He wasn't going to throw away an opportunity to star in a potential blockbuster—playing a role created specifically for him—even if it meant walking away from a lucrative deal with nothing to show for it.

If you put a seed upside down in the ground, the sprouting plant will right itself. Roots know which direction they need to point in order to grow and will turn themselves until they get there.[2] But unlike plants, most people who know they're pointed the wrong way will still keep growing in that direction—simply because that's what they've always done. As a result, they end up living a life out of alignment with who they are.

Ask yourself: *What do I want from my life? What do I really want?*

Deciding what you want can be incredibly hard, particularly if you've spent your life—as most of us have—going along with what others want for you or chasing what you've been told you *should* want.

Here are a few ways to get started.

Forget following your passion, which is far too difficult to figure out. Instead, follow your curiosity. What do *you* find interesting? Say yes to the tiny internal clues nagging you to learn more about botany, take welding classes, or pick up that sewing hobby you abandoned. The things that pique your curiosity aren't random. They will point you to where you need to go. Unlike your appetite, indulging your curiosity will increase your curiosity. The more you follow the bread crumbs, the more they tend to appear.

Ask yourself: *What would I do if no one could know about it— if I couldn't tell my friends about it or post on social media about it?* The principle behind this question is simple: It doesn't matter how good it looks or how prestigious it is. Trying to impress an invisible jury will often force you to conform and prevent you from taking bold actions that bring you into alignment with yourself. Any choice is a poor choice if it doesn't bring you alive.

"Don't ask what the world needs," as Howard Thurman says. "Ask yourself what makes you come alive, and go do that because what the world needs is people who have come alive."[3] I used to think that doing things that brought me alive was self-indulgent. But it's quite the opposite. Going after what you want isn't a burden on the world. It's a beacon. When you do that, you establish a new way of existing that others can follow. When you shine, you help others shine, to paraphrase Lizzo.[4] When you let light hit your prism, you cast a rainbow that extends far beyond yourself.

To figure out what brings you alive and what leaves you depleted, keep an energy journal. Track when you feel engaged and enthusiastic—and when you feel bored and restless. Follow the subtle signals from your body—when it relaxes and expands, when it tightens and contracts. The more specific your observations, the better ("When I was answering emails this afternoon, I noticed I was clenching my gut"). Sometimes you can't explain why you love something, but you know that it warms you and delights you. Since we spend a lifetime ignoring these internal signals, it's easy to miss them unless we're paying close attention. Learn the signals your body sends you when you come alive and start following those signals.

Be careful about chasing moments that make you feel *happy*. In the most important moments of my life, I didn't feel happy. I felt anxious about the path ahead. I didn't feel good enough. I didn't feel ready enough. I felt *heavy*—intimidated by a load that I was sure I couldn't carry.

Yet I still did the thing. Happiness came only after a wave of other emotions washed through me (and knocked me around a bunch). If you pursue only happiness, you won't ever leave your comfort zone. Because stepping outside your comfort zone is, by definition, uncomfortable.

Also ask yourself, *In my ideal life, what does a Tuesday look like?* That's a question I learned from acting teacher Jamie Carroll. It's easy to dream about the Saturday night moments: getting promoted, booking an amazing acting role, or landing a book deal. But those moments are few and fleeting. The rest of the time, it's the Tuesdays—the everyday.

You might be thinking: *I can't just do what I want!* Maybe you assume that, if you had the freedom to do what you wanted, your life would just be cigarettes, booze, and mindless video games for days on end. With free rein, sure, you might engage in these activities for a little while, but you'd eventually get bored. You'd find that these are very poor substitutes for desires that have remained unmet—a feeling of adventure, flow, and engagement—that can be fulfilled in far more constructive and long-lasting ways. It's only by giving yourself permission to do what you think you want that you discover what you truly want (and what you don't want).

Finally, consider your life's purpose. What is your "why"? Why are you here? If you were writing your own obituary describing your life, what would it say? If you were lying on your deathbed, what would you regret not doing? Your life's purpose is often connected to your first principles. Review them again and consider how you can use your first principles to express yourself.

The North Star, Polaris, is known for being fixed, but it's not. Like all other objects in the sky, it moves—so much so that in about 2,000 years it'll no longer be the North Star.[5] What you want from your life can also change as the world changes around you and as you change as a person. In fact, pursuing your curiosity will inevitably change you, by taking you off the path you've followed in the past and introducing you to new ways of being in the world. As long as you choose it intentionally, there's nothing wrong with changing your direction.

Once you're clear on what you want, say no to things that don't matter and opt out of meaningless races that don't bring you closer to it. If you don't decide your guiding principles ahead of time—out of the heat of the moment—you'll let the seemingly urgent crowd out the important.

Jim Carrey says that his father, Percy, could have been an amazing comedian. But Percy assumed that it was foolish to try to make a living with comedy, so he made a safe choice and took a job as an accountant. He was later fired from that job, and Carrey's family became homeless. Looking back on his father's life, Carrey says: "You can fail at what you don't want, so you might as well take a chance on doing what you love."[6]

In finding our life mission, we often run away from what we don't want instead of running toward what we *do* want. We make our choices based on "fear disguised as practicality," as Carrey says. It can be scary to go after what you want. Because if you go for it, you may not get it.

Carl Sagan dedicated his life to looking for evidence of extraterrestrial life. He failed. He never found it. But he got millions of people—including me—excited about the stars. He made numerous contributions to humanity that transcended his own life and helped us understand the cosmos we are lucky to live in.

As long as you enjoy the journey—and as long as you create art you're proud of—who cares if you don't reach your destination?

You've already won.

## Dreamers and doers

Discovering your life mission requires action. You must pull on the threads, push the buttons, and experiment to discover your next steps.

Most people don't experiment. Some don't act at all and remain stagnant. These are the armchair adventurers—people who overthink everything, find themselves in a rabbit hole of pros and cons, and take no action because they're afraid of making the wrong move. And then there are people who jump prematurely from idea to execution. They skip experimentation because they believe that reality will only confirm their half-baked theories.

If there's any formula I've followed in my life, it's this: Stop overthinking and start experimenting, learning, and improving.

Experimenting beats debating. Action is the best teacher. You can make all the pros-and-cons lists you want, but it's hard to know what will work and what won't work unless you try.

In my prior life as a law professor, I taught countless students who had come to law school for all the wrong reasons. Someone had told them they were "good at debate." Their uncle was a successful lawyer. They loved watching *Law and Order* when they were growing up, so they always wanted to be a prosecutor.

In each case, reality didn't match their sky-high expectations. The mismatch resulted from a failure to experiment in order to determine for themselves whether a career in law was the right fit for them. Most people don't bother to figure out what it's *really* like to be a lawyer. Or a neurosurgeon. Or a podcaster.

Thinking about law school? Stop watching *Law and Order*. Don't take questionable advice from your uncle. Instead, go sit in on a law-school class. Intern at a local law firm.

Considering neurosurgery? Talk to neurosurgeons and learn about their day-to-day reality. What is their Tuesday like? Collect multiple perspectives. Shadow a neurosurgeon for a day. Talk to neurosurgeons who enjoy what they do and—more importantly— talk to neurosurgeons who didn't enjoy the work and left the field.

Want to be a podcaster? Launch an experimental podcast, commit to recording 10 episodes, and see if you enjoy it.

To experiment is to be humble—to acknowledge that you're uncertain how your idea will pan out. Experiments also reduce your attachment to a particular idea. You haven't committed to moving to Singapore. It's just a two-week visit to see if you like it. Be sure to vary your experiments so that you can compare options to see which works best for you. Don't just visit Singapore. Also visit Istanbul, Hong Kong, or Sydney.

The goal isn't to be "correct." It's to discover. As you walk down different paths, you'll sometimes hit a dead end. Or you'll discover that a path you tried wasn't the right one for you. Yes, your summer as a law-firm intern may have been miserable. But at least you didn't waste three years of your life and incur unnecessary law-school debt. You learned that the practice of law isn't for you and opened yourself up to other possibilities.

Lion trackers call this "the path of not here." As lion tracker Boyd Varty writes, "Going down a path and not finding a track is part of finding the track. . . . No action is considered a waste, and the key is to keep moving, readjusting, welcoming feedback. The 'path of not here' is part of the 'path of here.'"[7] The worst mistake, whether on the trail or in life, is being paralyzed by the options and failing to try any of them.

Here are three questions I ask when I run experiments.

1.  *What am I testing?* You're running an experiment, so you need to know what you're testing. Will I enjoy podcasting? Do I want to live in Singapore?

2.  *What does failure look like? What does success look like?* Define your criteria for failure and success at the outset, when you're relatively clearheaded—before your emotional investments and sunk costs cloud your judgment.

3.  *When will the experiment end?* "Someday" isn't a good answer. Pick a firm date when you'll evaluate whether the experiment is working and put it on your calendar. It's much easier to start things than to end things, so it's important to have an exit plan.

The best experiments have an "I wonder what will happen" quality to them. It's that uncertainty that unlocks the door to possibility. Experiments that produce unexpected results tend to be far more valuable than experiments that confirm what you already think.

With this mindset, life turns into a forever experiment in your very own laboratory. Instead of fixating on a static self, you try on possible selves. Instead of making firm plans, you experiment with different futures—and allow your path to emerge as you discover what works for you and what doesn't.

## The problem with chasing gold medals

Jason Alexander, famous for playing George Costanza on *Seinfeld*, was nominated eight times for an Emmy award.

He never won.

Glenn Close was nominated eight times for an Oscar.

She never won.

Carl Sagan was nominated for membership in the National Academy of Sciences, one of the highest honors in science.

He was rejected. Most of the academic establishment disdained Sagan for popularizing science and voted against his membership.

Isaac Asimov didn't hit the *New York Times* best-seller list until his 262nd book.[8] That's *not* a typo. That's 43 years writing 261 consecutive non-best-sellers.

Does this mean that Close and Alexander are bad actors? That Sagan was a lousy astronomer? Or that Asimov's first 261 books all suck?

Of course not.

Yet, in our own lives, we often define our worth by referring to the number of medals we have collected along the way. We want to be chosen by the people who were chosen before us. We want the external validation, the pat on the back—the gold medal. We let someone else determine whether we're good enough. Once we get approval, life becomes a tightrope to not lose that approval.

"I have made the most wonderful discovery," Napoleon is purported to have said. "Men will risk their lives, even die, for ribbons!" We focus on collecting ribbons—social-media followers and impressive job titles—forgetting that vanity metrics rarely move the needle on what matters. We seek applause instead of improvement. We pursue goals that are unaligned with ourselves. We play meaningless games and win meaningless prizes.

The more we value vanity metrics, the more we fear failure. The more we fear failure, the more we strive for guaranteed success. And the more we strive for guaranteed success, the more we color inside the lines and the less remarkable we become.

If you base your internal compass on external metrics, it will never be stable. The compass needle will always waver because approval is fickle. Stability requires a compass that's based on your own values, not the values of others.

Alexander, Close, and Sagan couldn't control how the academy members voted. Asimov couldn't control how many people bought his books. You can't control whether your boss gives you a promotion or whether you get the job you want.

If we were assessing people based on outcomes beyond their control, we'd assume that every lottery winner must be a genius.

A simple question for you: *Is this within my control?*

Don't hand the controls of your life over to any other pilot. You have your own sense of direction and balance. Focus on what's yours to shape—and ignore the rest.

## Have you had enough?

We had had enough. More than enough.

My wife, Kathy, and I were driving back from one of our favorite restaurants in Portland. During the drive home, we were chatting about how stuffed we both were. Kathy turned to me and said: "It's strange. When it comes to eating, we know when we've had enough. But we don't do that in other aspects of life."

She was right.

We try to squeeze in another hour of work—even though we've worked enough.

We try to make more money—even though we make enough.

We want more attention and more praise—even though no amount of it will make us happy over the long haul.

Our body is wise. When we stuff ourselves, it loudly tells us to stop eating.

But our ego is foolish. It's chronically dissatisfied. It craves more money, more attention—more everything—even though we have more than enough.

You want to be a millionaire? Once your bank account reaches seven figures, you'll start aiming for eight. You want 1,000 followers? Once you get there, you'll want 10,000—and then 100,000. You want to keep up with the Joneses? Once you do, you'll want to keep up with the other, more accomplished Joneses—the ones with a nicer house and fancier car. If you don't define what "enough" looks like for you, the default answer will always be "more."

As the saying goes, growth for the sake of growth is the ideology of the cancer cell. The more-more-more monster will never be satiated. It'll never have enough money to prevent every hardship, enough stability to fend off every uncertainty, and enough power to defeat every challenge.

So ask yourself: *What does "enough" look like for me? How will I know when I get there?* The beautiful thing about "enough" is that defining it is up to you. Once "you decide you have enough, then you do," as Seth Godin writes. "And with that choice comes a remarkable sort of freedom. The freedom to be still, to become aware and to stop hiding from the living that's yet to be done."[9]

I'll leave you with a famous story that Kurt Vonnegut tells of a conversation he had with Joseph Heller, the author of the novel *Catch-22*.[10] The two were at a party hosted by a billionaire. Vonnegut turned to Heller and said: "How does it make you feel to know that our host only yesterday made more money than your novel *Catch-22* has earned in its entire history?"

"I've got something he can never have," Heller replied.

"What on earth could that be, Joe?" Vonnegut asked.

"The knowledge that I've got enough."

## Be careful what you measure

When I first became a professor, I was amazed by how much the *U.S. News & World Report* rankings influence decisions for both students and faculty.

The *Report* ranks colleges and other degree programs in the United States. The rankings rely on a formula to determine which schools are better than others.

If the most important thing about a college is educational quality, then the *Report* is deeply flawed. Schools are ranked based on factors—such as acceptance rate, faculty compensation, and average alumni donation rate—that have little to do with educational quality. The rankings don't measure whether the students are learning anything or whether they're otherwise satisfied with their educational experience.

For students, the rankings provide an easy way to outsource their thinking. Many of them make one of the most expensive investments in their life based on rankings that tell them very little. Instead of thinking through what program is the best fit for them, they let the rankings decide. The price they pay for outer prestige is inner anguish when they attend a school that they end up hating.

What's more, schools game the system to get a higher spot. They reverse-engineer the formulas and attempt to move the needle on metrics that boost their ranking, instead of focusing their energy on what matters for educational quality.[11] They add faculty members they don't need. They lower admissions standards for transfer applications who don't count toward the rankings. They pour a ton of money into admissions recruiting to increase application numbers just so they can reject more students and lower their acceptance rate.

Those who can't game the system try to cheat it. Numerous schools—including reputable institutions like George Washington and Emory—were caught misreporting data in an attempt to move to the top.

There's a famous saying attributed to Peter Drucker: "What gets measured gets managed." The principle makes sense on the surface: It's only when you quantify outcomes that you can see whether your actions move the needle toward those outcomes.

But what gets measured doesn't just get managed. What gets measured also gets our attention and alters our behavior.[12] And if you're not careful, numbers can replace thinking. They can become *the thing*.

Business leaders often take their hands off the wheel and hand control over to a set of numbers. And even when they veer off the road—even when the numbers lead them astray—they keep driving because they're trained to myopically measure miles per hour, not to lift their gaze to see if the car is taking them where they want to go.

Wells Fargo fell into this trap. The bank put its employees under immense pressure to sell additional financial products to existing customers. The only way to meet impossible quotas was to defraud the system and fake new accounts. Wells Fargo employees "opened more than 1.5 million deposit accounts and more than 565,000 credit-card accounts that may not have been authorized."[13] The company had to pay $480 million to settle a class-action lawsuit for securities fraud.[14]

When we're too focused on the things we measure, we can lose sight of everything else—including common sense.

Measurement has another downside. It prompts us to focus on outcomes that are easy to measure. Lawyers count billable hours in six-minute increments. Computer programmers count lines of code. Social-media influencers count likes and retweets as evidence of tangible achievement. Many people track the number of zeros at the end of their bank account balance or the number of emails still sitting in their inbox. We track what's easy to track—not what's important—and falsely assume that if we hit certain metrics, we've accomplished something valuable.

Consider writing. Creativity requires connecting the dots, and connecting the dots requires allowing time for my subconscious to consolidate my ideas and make associations. From time to time, I need to just stare out the window and do nothing.

This doesn't *feel* productive, even though it is. But when I measure my output by the number of words I moved down the assembly line, I don't feel like I accomplished anything and feel lousy as a result.

The output of a modern knowledge worker is often hard to measure. Knowledge workers assemble decisions. They sell influence. They make change happen. What's more, there's often a long lag between the input of a knowledge worker and the output. They may work for days, weeks, months, even years, without seeing anything that can be quantified.

In fact, the most valuable qualities in life often don't come with measurable units. Values like honesty, humility, beauty, and play are more shapeless, so they get ignored. It's hard to measure whether you're a better parent or a better colleague now than you were last year. As a result, these immeasurable qualities turn into afterthoughts.

So be careful what you measure. Regularly ask yourself, *What is this metric for? Am I measuring the right thing? Is this metric serving me, or am I serving the metric?*

Because the metric isn't an end in itself. It's a means to an end.

And if it's no longer serving that end, it's time to get rid of it.

## This doesn't work for me

That's the thought that kept swirling in my head as I browsed through the Cornell course catalog.

*This doesn't work for me.*

I was a college freshman planning out my next four years. But there was a problem: None of the available majors appealed to me. There were a few that came close, but none of them quite captured what I wanted to study.

And then I asked myself, *What if I created my own major?* Instead of adjusting my preferences to fit the predetermined curriculum menu, I wondered if the menu itself could be changed.

I trekked over to the registrar's office and asked them if I could design my own path of study. The answer, shockingly, was yes. There was a little-known program that gave free rein to a small group of freshmen to create their own major.

I applied and was accepted. I got to design my own four-year adventure, picking exactly the classes that I wanted to take—not what someone else thought would be good for me.

Most people go through life walking through the most convenient door. We follow the path of least resistance and get pulled around by strings we didn't attach. We tell ourselves, *Sure, I could do that job. Sure, I could major in that program. Sure, I could contort myself to fit through that tiny door that someone else created.*

But those doors may not be the best ones for you. There's immense power in intentionally creating and opening the doors that accommodate you—instead of shrinking yourself in order to squeeze through the ones already there.

Once you've decided what you want from life, go off-menu.

Ask for it. Create it.

Because the best things in life aren't on the menu.

## You're in a jail cell of your own making

*Birds born in a cage think flying is an illness.*
—ATTRIBUTED TO ALEJANDRO JODOROWSKY

Imagine you're in a jail cell.

You grip the bars. You kick and scream. You curse the guards to let you out.

But no one comes to help you because the jail cell was designed by you. You're the master architect of your own prison, the iron bars that constrain your thinking, and the chains that hold you back.

You are the jailor. And you are the jailee.

To be sure, life comes with real limitations—your place of birth, your social class, and structural discrimination, to name a few. But then there are the self-imposed limitations where you stand in your own sunshine and block your own wisdom. You close doors before the universe even has the opportunity to open them. You turn into your own gaslighter—the one who manipulates you, misleads you, and makes you question your reality.

We often make things worse by defending our jail cells and self-imposed limitations. We don't launch a new business because we think we don't have what it takes. We hesitate to apply for a promotion, assuming that someone far more competent will get it.

Our expectations change our reality and become self-fulfilling. As the saying goes, argue for your limitations and you'll get to keep them.

It's not the dark inside the cell that scares us. It's the light outside. We complain about being in jail, but deep down we find our cell safe and comfortable. After all, we built it. The world outside is a scary place—once we venture out, we don't know what we'll find.

The older the jail cell and the rustier the bars, the harder it becomes to escape. Often, we don't even notice that we're living in a jail cell. Over time, as our outdated ideas of what's possible continue to hold us back, the iron bars become invisible to us. We keep pacing the same confined space, unaware that there's a way out.

That discomfort you've been feeling with where you are in life? It might be a sign that you've unwittingly confined yourself in a jail cell—and that there's a different life waiting for you that's greater than what you can even imagine.

Ask yourself, *What are the jail cells I've constructed for myself? How am I complicit in creating the conditions that hold me back? Where can I go further than I have before? What do I believe I'm not good enough for, smart enough for, worthy enough for, fill-in-the-blank enough for?*

To expose your self-imposed limitations, take extreme action. Go for a moonshot you don't think you'll achieve. Ask for a raise you don't think you deserve. Apply for a job you don't think you'll get.

You can't always get what you want, as the Rolling Stones remind us, but by expanding your vision, you'll expand the boundaries of possibility. What you assumed were immovable bars will often reveal themselves to be illusions.

In the end, the door to your prison cell is unlocked.

Stop banging on the bars and cursing the guards.

Stop stopping yourself.

Open the door and leave.

## The three stages of change

1. You think you can't do something.
2. You're forced to do it (or you're brave enough to try).
3. You find out that you actually can.

## Stop shoulding all over yourself

There's a word that I decided to drop from my vocabulary.

It's the word should. It comes from the word shall, which in Old English meant "to be under an obligation" or "to owe." Should often represents something I've obligated myself to do—without even realizing it.

The shoulds are the belief systems I unwittingly adopted. The shoulds are the expectations of other people about how I'm supposed to live my life. The shoulds are my own prison, the iron bars that constrain my thinking, and the chains that hold me back.

Some of these "shoulds" sound familiar:

- You should start meditating.
- You should be more active on social media.
- You should get married and have kids—before it's too late.
- You should speak only when spoken to.

It's easy to lose ourselves in the tide of shoulds. When I find myself using the word should, what I'm about to do is usually unaligned with me. I'm being steered by someone else's expectations instead of looking to my internal compass for guidance.

Take a moment and write down the shoulds of your life. Examine each bar of your prison cell. For each should, ask yourself:

*Where did this sense of obligation come from? Who put it there? Does it belong to me? Is this what I want? Or is it what I think I should want?*

If one of your shoulds really does belong to you—if it's aligned with who you are—change your vocabulary to reflect that shift, so it's less of an obligation and more of a desire. Instead of saying, "I should . . .," say, "I get to . . ." or "I want to . . ." or "I'm privileged to. . . ."

But if it doesn't belong to you—if it's constraining your thinking, limiting your potential, or holding you back from the life you want to live—let it go.

Stop shoulding all over yourself. Live up to your own expectations instead of being trapped by someone else's.

## The email that changed my life

*To send or not to send?*

That was the question swirling through my mind as I sat in front of my computer as a 17-year-old high school senior in Istanbul.

The cursor was blinking at the end of an email I had just typed to a professor at Cornell, where I had recently been admitted.

I had discovered that the professor was the principal investigator for a planned mission to Mars. What's more, back in the day, he had worked as a graduate student for Carl Sagan, a childhood hero of mine. This was too good to be true.

The email I'd just written shared my résumé and expressed my burning desire to work for him on the mission. But when I thought about hitting Send, a chorus of voices filled my head, reminding me of the boundaries of my jail cell.

*There's no job posting. Why would you apply for a job that doesn't exist?*

*What could you possibly contribute?*

*If you send this email, you'll make a fool of yourself.*

I had grown up in a society that reinforced these boundaries. When I told my friends that I wanted to work on a NASA space mission one day, many of them said: "You can't do it. You were born into modest circumstances in a developing country. People like you don't work on space missions. Maybe in another life."

But I wasn't willing to postpone my dreams for another life.

When other people say you can't do something, they're often revealing what they haven't allowed themselves to achieve. Their advice is a projection. Seeing you walk out of your jail cell reminds them of theirs. *I'm stuck in this jail cell, and you're out there? Doing things? How dare you!*

They may know the odds are low. But they don't know you.

And a closed door isn't necessarily a locked door. Sometimes you just have to push.

I decided to push. I took a deep breath and I sent the email. Less than a week later, I got a response. The professor invited me for an interview upon my arrival at Cornell. Thanks in part to the coding skills I had picked up in high school, I landed a job on the operations team for the 2003 Mars Exploration Rovers mission.

Little did I know at the time, but that email catalyzed a series of events over the ensuing two decades that led to the publication of my book *Think Like a Rocket Scientist* and the launch of my career as an author. If I hadn't sent that email, you most likely wouldn't be reading this book.

I still struggle from time to time with breaking out of my jail cell. When I find myself afraid to make a move—when that chorus of voices comes roaring in telling me that I can't do something— I think back to the email that changed my life.

And I click Send.

## You can't do it

"She's acting odd. What got into her?" they'll say.

"Nothing got into me," you'll respond. "Things finally started to come out. And it's just the beginning."

"She's so full of herself," they'll say.

"What else can I be full of, if not my own self?" you'll respond.

"She changed," they'll say. "She's not who she used to be."

"Good," you'll respond. "I'm growing and evolving."

"She's going through a midlife crisis," they'll say.

"It's not a midlife crisis," you'll respond. "It's a midlife blossoming."

"You can't do it," they'll say.

"Watch me," you'll respond.

Visit ozanvarol.com/genius to find worksheets, challenges, and exercises to help you implement the strategies discussed in this part.

# *The Inner Journey*

Part III has three chapters:

1. **Unlock the Wisdom Within:** On igniting creativity by tapping into your inner wisdom
2. **Unleash the Power of Play:** On using play to generate original insights
3. **Dare to Create:** On creating art that matters, for yourself and for the world

Along the way, I'll reveal:

- A simple practice used by the best thinkers to generate original insights
- The fascinating story of how playing with plates in a cafeteria produced a Nobel Prize
- Why shutting down your mind is the key to thinking better
- What you can learn from Netflix's biggest mistake
- Why you should stop calling your office an office
- The power of strategic procrastination
- The nonsense of "shameless self-promotion"
- The surprising strategy that the writers of *The Office* used to boost their creativity

# 6

# Unlock the
# Wisdom Within

*The powerful play goes on, and you may contribute
a verse.*

—WALT WHITMAN, "O ME! O LIFE!"

## How to think for yourself

There's a scene in the movie *Good Will Hunting* where Will and his friends walk into a Harvard Square bar. None of them are Harvard students—a point made clear by the clothes they're wearing and the way they talk. In the bar, Will's friend Chuckie starts chatting with a Harvard student named Skylar.

Then another Harvard student named Clark shows up and begins to mock Chuckie's intellect. He asks Chuckie for some insight into the "evolution of the market economy in the southern colonies." He continues:

CLARK: *My contention is that prior to the Revolutionary War, the economic modalities—especially in the southern colonies—could most aptly be characterized as agrarian precapital—*

In one of the best smackdown moments in film history, Will jumps in:

> WILL: *Of course that's your contention. You're a first-year grad student. You just got finished reading some Marxian historian, Pete Garrison probably. . . . That's gonna last until next year, you're gonna be in here regurgitating Gordon Wood, talkin' about, you know, the prerevolutionary utopia and the capital-forming effects of military mobilization.*
>
> CLARK: *Well as a matter of fact I won't, because Wood drastically underestimates the impact of—*
>
> WILL: *"Wood drastically underestimates the impact of social distinctions predicated upon wealth, especially inherited wealth. . . . " You got that from Vickers,* Work in Essex County, *page 98, right? Yeah, I read that too. Were you gonna plagiarize the whole thing for us or do you have any thoughts of your own on this matter?*

This scene is a microcosm of our current reality. The world is littered with Clarks, but there's no Will to call them out.

We may lack Clark's pretentious attitude, but we find ourselves in his position far more often than we realize. "We enjoy the comfort of opinion without the discomfort of thought," as John F. Kennedy put it.[1] We regurgitate what we hear from sources that pop up on our algorithm-manipulated feeds. We retweet what the Gordon Woods of the world say without pausing and reflecting. We infuse so much external junk into our internal world that it becomes hard to know where other people's thoughts end and ours begin.

We don't think with a pen and paper. We "think" with Google. It feels better to start from a known place and leverage someone else's ideas than it does to stare at a blank page and form our own. We don't even have to complete the search query ourselves.

Google's auto-complete function takes that momentous burden off our shoulders by telling us what we *should* be searching for and what we *should* be thinking. We then sift through SEO-optimized results to find the answer to life, the universe, and everything. This process gives us the illusion of thinking—when, in reality, we just surrendered control of our precious synapses to manipulative algorithms.

Glennon Doyle, the best-selling author of *Untamed*, once found herself in this position.[2] Sitting in bed at 3 am, she typed the following question into the Google search bar: "What should I do if my husband is a cheater but also an amazing dad?" In a moment of clarity that escapes many people, she stared at that question and thought: "I've just asked the internet to make the most important and personal decision of my life. Why do I trust everyone else on Earth more than I trust myself? WHERE THE HELL IS MY SELF?"

I've been in Doyle's position more times than I care to remember. In fact, when I was writing the chapter you're reading right now, I found myself Googling *Why is my book so hard to write?*—as if a faceless crowd of strangers and bots I've never met could find a solution to my writer's block.

We've lost touch with one of the most basic of human experiences—thinking. We beg for answers from others, like Tolstoy's fabled beggar pleading for pennies from passersby—while unaware that he's sitting on a pot made of gold. Instead of digging deep into our core to find clarity, we outsource life's most important questions to others and extinguish the fire of our own thoughts. These suppressed thoughts then come back to haunt us: In works we admire, we see ideas that we crushed because they were our own.

As Bob Dylan reminds us in "Subterranean Homesick Blues," "You don't need a weatherman to know which way the wind blows." When we look to the weatherman to figure out answers we can find ourselves, we lose the ability to think for ourselves.

Thinking for yourself isn't just about reducing external inputs, in the ways that I described in the *Detox* chapter. It's about making thought a deliberate practice—and thinking about an issue *before* researching it. It's about unlearning the habit—programmed into us in school—of immediately looking to others for answers and instead becoming curious about our own thoughts.

Let's say you're curious about where good ideas come from. Instead of jumping on Google right away, or even reading relevant books, think about the question first on your own. Search inside your own mind, mine it for relevant ideas, and jot them down. If you reverse the order—if you think *after* you read—other people's opinions will exert too much gravitational pull on your own. Captured by their orbit, you won't reach escape velocity. Your own ideas will end up deviating only marginally, if at all, from what you've read.

When you begin exploring your depths, the initial thoughts you encounter often won't be your best. These will be the stories you've told yourself or the conventional wisdom on the subject. So resist the tendency to settle on the first answer and move on. Deep thinking requires time. It's only by concentrating on the problem or question long enough that you'll dive deeper and locate better insights.

Most of us resist setting aside time for deep thinking because it doesn't produce immediate tangible results. With every email you answer, you make visible progress toward inbox zero. With every minute you think, nothing seems to happen—at least not on the surface. As a result, most people don't stay with their thoughts long enough before reaching for the nearest available distraction.

"I don't have time to think" really means "Thinking is not a priority for me." A commitment to deep thinking is shockingly rare even in professions where the value of original ideas is clear. But shallow thinking produces shallow ideas—along with bad decisions and missed opportunities. Breakthroughs don't happen in 60-second bursts of thought between meetings and notifications.

Pop culture exacerbates shallow thinking. When it comes to explaining how breakthroughs happen, storytellers focus on the "eureka" moment when a fully formed insight seemingly appears in an effortless flash. A clip of someone thinking for a long time doesn't make for exciting television. It's not thrilling to read: "And then she thought some more."

But epiphanies are the product of a long, slow burn. Ideas, as the filmmaker David Lynch puts it, are like fish: "If you want to catch little fish, you can stay in the shallow water. But if you want to catch the big fish, you've got to go deeper."[3]

Diving deeper requires sustained focus on one idea, one question, or one problem. It's called "top of mind" for a reason: This question has to be where your mind drifts when it's allowed to drift. If you clutter your brain-attic with junk, important ideas will get crowded out by the rest and won't have the room they need to expand.

After you've gone deeper on a question by thinking about it yourself, turn to reading what others have written about it. But don't pause your own thinking. When we read, we often don't engage with what we read. We see through the author's eyes, instead of our own. We passively absorb their opinions without thinking for ourselves. As a result, reading becomes a way of shirking responsibility.

Underlining or highlighting passages in what you read isn't enough. It's also not enough to ask, *What does the author think?* You need to also ask, *What do I think? Where do I agree with what I'm reading? Where do I disagree?* Just because Gordon Wood wrote it doesn't make it right—and his perspective certainly isn't the only one. In addition to reading between the lines, also write between them—scribble in the margins and hold imaginary dialogues with the author.

The goal of reading isn't just to understand. It's to treat what you read as a tool—a key to unlocking what's inside of you. Some of the best ideas that come up when I'm reading a book aren't from the book. An idea I read will often dislodge a related thought in me that was previously concealed. The text will act as a mirror, helping me see myself and my thoughts more clearly.

Your own depths aren't a place to escape reality. They're a place to discover it.

Breakthroughs lie not in absorbing all the wisdom outside of you but in uncovering the wisdom within you.

## The magic of talking to yourself

*Abracadabra.*

Meaning: *I create as I speak.*[4]

It's the key, not just to magic, but to creating anything that didn't exist before.

By creating as you speak, I don't mean speaking to other people. I mean speaking to yourself. Self-talk is considered taboo in society. Only children and characters in a Shakespearean sonnet are supposed to talk to themselves. If you search *Talking to yourself is a sign of . . .* on Google, one of the top auto-complete predictions is "impending mental collapse."

But it's quite the opposite. Self-talk is critical to mining deeper insights. "It's not thought that produces speech but, rather, speech is a creative process that in turn generates thought," literary scholar Nana Ariel writes.[5] Self-talk helps us discover what we think. It allows us to locate and retrieve preexisting ideas by giving tangible form to our intangible thoughts.

For many thinkers, self-talk takes the form of freewriting—writing down what you think without publishing it. We walk around with numerous unsorted thoughts in our heads. Some are half-baked, some are contradictory, and a lot of them are completely wrong. They stay that way in one big mush because we don't take the time to sort them out.

Something magical happens when a thought takes shape in words. Freewriting connects you to your intuition and opens a channel between the subconscious and the conscious. It links the depths of your mind directly to your fingers. With nowhere to go—facing only your thoughts and a blank page—a process of self-actualization begins to take place. You begin to find out who you are, what you know, and what you think. It's the closest thing to splitting open your head and watching your own ideas from a distance.

By letting yourself freewrite, you also let yourself freethink. The suppressed big fish in your subconscious break out of their nets and begin to swim around in your cerebral ocean. The more you release these thoughts—the more you open up your stream of consciousness—the more they come.

In writers' circles, this freewriting practice is called "morning pages," a term coined by Julia Cameron in her book *The Artist's Way*.[6] There's some value to making freewriting a morning practice—before you turn on your phone and begin to pollute your mind. But morning pages can be any-time-of-the-day pages. It's more important that you do it and less important when you do it.

I have a document open throughout the day on my computer where I jot down thoughts as they come. An idea for a book? I put it down. What kept me up the night before? I write about it. The unfinished nature of this document keeps my thoughts flowing. Nothing is final—and nothing is perfect. Anything goes.

Start writing and put down whatever comes up. On some days nothing of interest will show up, or what comes out will be nonsense. But on other days unexpected insights will appear out of nowhere. Remember: You're writing, not to publish or get credit for what you write, but to discover what you think.

If the idea of a free-flowing thought dump is too intimidating, try adding some structure to the practice. You can connect your freewriting, at least loosely, to a particular goal. Ask yourself, *What should I title my book? How do we introduce delight into our customer service process? What should my next career be?*

For your thoughts to flow unimpeded, two things need to happen.

First, your words must be private. If you fear that your thoughts might be discovered by someone else, you won't have a safe playground. You'll have a hard time lowering your inhibitions and shutting down your self-censoring systems. The process of creation is embarrassing. Ideas, in their initial stages, are fragile. If you expose them to others too early—before they begin to blossom—you might crush out unconventional or half-baked insights. Eventually, you'll want to share your ideas with a trusted group (more on that later). But for now, treat these thoughts like Fight Club and don't talk about them.

Second, you must be honest with yourself. This is harder than it sounds. When I first started freewriting, I found myself lying—to myself. I would come up with a polished narrative to justify a misstep or write a curated account of what happened instead of revealing the truth.

For your creations to be true to yourself, you must yourself become true. Your notebook is not Instagram. Present yourself in all of your imperfect glory. If you have doubts, don't bury them. Acknowledge them. Hold your thoughts up to the light and examine them. By airing these thoughts on the outside, you also ensure they don't eat you alive on the inside.

When you freewrite, you also generate a historical record of your thoughts. Over time dots connect and trends begin to emerge. A repetitive negative thought. A lesson that keeps presenting itself. An idea for a book that keeps nagging you (you're reading the one that nagged me). If these thoughts were to remain unrecorded and isolated, you might overlook them, but with repetition, they form a pattern that becomes hard to ignore.

Ideas may not come during the freewriting session itself. But once you set up your antenna and start to consider a question through self-talk, epiphanies buried in your subconscious will start popping up in random moments—like magic.

## The power of procrastination

I have a confession: I'm a master procrastinator.

I don't mean the type of procrastination where I repeatedly clean my desk instead of writing this book (though I did plenty of that in my younger and more vulnerable years).

It's a strategic type of procrastination that I use to generate breakthroughs regardless of what I'm working on.[7]

Here's how it works. When I'm working on a new project, I start as quickly as possible. For a book, I jot down ideas and examples—anything that's already on my mind that might be relevant. After I plant these seeds, I walk away and wait to see what blossoms. I resist planning everything out far in advance to prevent rigidifying my thinking and closing off creative possibilities.

This waiting may look passive, but it's not. When I start a project and deliberately stop after an initial period of focus, I ignite the thought factory in my brain. Even as I wait, the project is active in my subconscious, which is churning behind the scenes and cooking up insights. During this process, ideas mature, become richer, and pick up new associations, like wine aging in a barrel. I move away from shallow waters to the depths where David Lynch's big fish swim.

If you stay focused for too long, your thinking will stagnate. So follow a period of focus with a state of unfocus. Let your mind wander. Don't turn to social media or email, which won't give you the break you need. Instead, stare out the window, take a shower, listen to music, or meditate.

My high school soccer coach had a saying that I love: *If you're not in possession, get in position.* If you don't have the ball, move to a different place on the field where you'll be open to receive the ball. The same principle applies to ideas. If you're not in possession of them, physically move to a different place to encourage their flow. I find it helpful to move outside of the room where I normally write—which is associated with the same old thought patterns—to different parts of my house. The shift in location brings a shift in perspective and creates a blank space onto which I can project new ideas.

Walking also helps. Research shows that movement and cognition are activated in the same region of the brain and that walking improves creativity.[8] In one study—cleverly titled "Give Your Ideas Some Legs"—Stanford researchers divided participants into two groups and gave them a divergent creativity test. One group sat for one hour before the test, and the other group walked on a treadmill. On average, walking boosted creativity scores by 60 percent.[9]

Quentin Tarantino's procrastination practice involves floating in a swimming pool. When he's working on a movie script, he writes for a few hours during the day and then goes into his heated pool. "[I] just kind of float around in the warm water and think about everything I've just written, how I can make it better, and what else can happen before the scene is over," Tarantino says.[10] He then gets out of the pool and writes down the insights that came up while he was floating. Those insights become his work for the next writing day.

In my own strategic procrastination process, I keep the circuit open by regularly returning to the project and revisiting the main themes and ideas. I also consciously mine my thoughts for new golden insights and write them down as soon as they come up. Like Tarantino's notes, these insights provide a creative compost pile for my next writing session. I'm no longer staring at a blank page, not knowing where to begin. The pool is no longer cold. It's been heated with ideas that invite me to dive in.

Something else happens when I start a project and then deliberately step away from it. I turn into a magnetized rod that attracts ideas. I begin to notice relevant insights in everything I read, watch, and observe. Seemingly random events, stories, and even song lyrics transform into ideas that I can use. But if I hadn't started the project, the relevance of these nuggets would have been lost on me.

This is an intentional, not impulsive, type of procrastination. It's a way of walking away from the project to grow the project—not to avoid it. Which means, you'll need to return to your desk to finish it.

This rhythm—focus and unfocus, float and write—aggregates over time to something that may have seemed undoable at the start.

A small thing, repeated, becomes a big thing.

## Lose your mind

Carl Sagan was the voice of scientific reason.

His creative process, however, was anything but reasonable.

He had a practice of letting his thoughts run wild at night, often with the aid of marijuana.[11] He'd smoke a joint, start talking to himself, and record his thoughts on a tape recorder so he wouldn't forget what he said. In the morning, he'd listen to the tape and examine his wild ideas from a more skeptical perspective.

There was a Jekyll and Hyde quality to Sagan's practice. His rambling "evening" self had to convince his doubtful "morning" self that he wasn't out of his mind. So the evening Sagan would record messages to the morning Sagan specifically to dispel his skepticism. For example, he'd recite hard-to-remember facts to demonstrate feats of memory only associated with high intelligence. These facts generally turned out to be accurate.

When this approach failed, Sagan would resort to intimidation. In one particularly memorable tape, the evening Sagan berated the morning Sagan for being too judgmental about his ideas. "Listen closely, you sonofabitch of the morning!" he yelled to his future self on the tape recorder. "This stuff is real!"

You don't need controlled substances to emulate Sagan's approach to creativity. The key is to separate the idea generation phase from the idea evaluation phase—your evening self from your morning self.

During idea generation, you must protect your thoughts from, well, you.

Ideas that make a big impact initially seem unreasonable. If they were reasonable, someone else would have thought of them already. Unreasonable often refers to reasonable not yet made reality. Unreasonable often means untried or unfamiliar. Unreasonable suggests that an idea deviates from your preconceived benchmark of what is reasonable. But, in many cases, it's not your idea that's misplaced. It's your benchmark.

Your inner critic, if left unconstrained, will snuff out all seemingly unreasonable insights and crush valuable ideas while they're still incubating. And generating a new idea is far more difficult than toning down an unreasonable one.

This approach is backed by research. In one study, researchers used functional magnetic resonance imaging (fMRI) to track the brain activity of six musicians while they were playing jazz.[12] They found that during improvisation—when musicians generate new music instead of performing old music—the regions of the brain linked to evaluation and self-censoring decreased in activity. "The ability to suppress your own brain may be one of the real hall-marks for what makes somebody great," said Charles Limb, one of the researchers and a trained jazz musician himself.[13] Limb's statement was echoed decades before by Walt Whitman, who attributed his best creative work to his ability "to stop thinking at will, and to make his brain 'negative.'"[14]

So when you're generating ideas, ask your inner critic to leave and instead invite your inner child to play. Don't censor, evaluate, or critique. Inside your own mind, all ideas—however foolish or outrageous—are welcome. The goal is to leave them unjudged in the curiosity cabinet where they can germinate as your imaginative inner child turns them over.

Most people prematurely cut off idea generation by immediately judging whether an idea belongs in the cabinet in the first place—by evaluating what's reasonable, what's probable, or what's doable.

That's like driving a car while simultaneously pressing on the gas and brake pedals. No wonder you can't move. No wonder you get blocked. Just as you begin to speed up, your inner critic slams on the brakes by telling you *That's a terrible idea* or *That sentence you just wrote—it's no good*. A terrible idea is "often the cousin of a good idea, and a great one is the neighbor of that," as Astro Teller says.

The inner critic—like Sagan's morning self—serves a critical function. And its services will be needed when you switch from generating to evaluating ideas. But when you're still playing around with thoughts, put the inner critic in the backseat where it can't reach the brake pedal.

In the end, creativity isn't about forcing ideas to come.

Whether you realize it or not, the big fish are already swimming in the depths of your subconscious.

You just need to unblock the obstacles that prevent their natural flow.

## Follow your body

*It is by logic that we prove, but by intuition that we discover.*

—HENRI POINCARÉ, *SCIENCE AND METHOD*

*Whoosh! BANG! Miss.*

The same cycle kept repeating itself.

At the time, I was in Dublin to give a keynote. A nearby farm offered skeet shooting, which I had never tried before, so I decided to give it a shot. The clay target would launch with a *whoosh*, I'd mentally calculate velocity and distance, and then I'd pull the trigger at what I thought was the perfect moment.

And I would miss. Every. Single. Time.

After about 10 misses in a row, the instructor took pity on me and came over. He leaned in and gave me some advice that I've been turning over in my mind ever since.

"You're overthinking it," he said.

"I have no other type of thinking available," I responded.

"Follow your body," he said. "Your mind is getting in the way."

"I see," I said, not seeing at all.

"Your body knows what to do," he reiterated. "Pull the trigger when you *feel* it's the right moment—not when you *think* it is."

I decided to take his advice and give it a try. I shut down the incessant chatter of my overcalculating mind. When the clay target launched, I sank into my core and pulled the trigger when my body signaled it was the right moment.

And I nailed it dead center.

This was a new way of operating for me. For decades, I prided myself on my mental acumen. My brain was by far my most important organ. My body had no purpose other than transporting my head around and creating fuel for my mind to do what it does best—think.

The instructor's advice jolted me out of this traditional mode of operating. After I left the farm that day, I thought about how many times in my life my body had known the right thing to do but my mind had gotten in the way and led me astray.

I remembered that time when my intuition screamed, *There's something fishy about this guy—don't do business with him!*, and I overrode it with pro-and-con calculations. It ended up being a terrible deal.

I remembered that time when I knew deep down the candidate wasn't the right person to hire, but I hired them anyway because they looked great on paper. It ended up being a terrible relationship.

I remembered that time when I knew I should break up with a girlfriend but continued the relationship assuming I could fix things. It prolonged what should have ended.

You've probably had similar experiences. You knew something was right *in your gut*. Or you recognized, *deep down*, that something was wrong but you couldn't rationally explain what. Airplane pilots call this "leemers," the "vague feeling that something isn't right, even if it's not clear why."[15] They're trained to pay attention to leemers instead of dismissing them.

Here's the thing about your body: It's ancient. From an evolutionary perspective, it dates back hundreds of millions of years. Your brain is much younger.[16] It's a magnificent machine, but its experience is more limited. Your body houses all of that ancient wisdom that's waiting to be uncovered.

But we obscure that wisdom by constantly directing our attention away from our bodies—to our spreadsheets, notifications, and emails. We're so disconnected from our bodies that we don't hear its signals even when it's screaming. There's now a condition called "email apnea"—the increasingly common habit of holding your breath while emailing or texting.

Paying attention to your body doesn't mean ignoring your mind. It means treating thinking as a whole-body activity, not just something narrowly limited to your brain. It means paying closer attention to the signals from your body—the feelings, sensations, and instincts that come from a deeper place inside you.

If you keep missing the proverbial targets in your life, your mind might be getting in the way. Align your mind with your body and watch next-level magic happen.

## Great minds don't think alone

When the bubonic plague struck England in 1665, among those who retreated to the countryside was a young scholar named Isaac Newton. During his quarantine, Newton would go on to invent calculus, theorize gravity, and discover the laws of motion. (On a less glamorous note, he would also stick a needle in his own eye to understand how lenses work.)[17]

This story went viral during the Covid-19 pandemic as a testament to the power of isolation. The message was clear: If Newton could change the world during the plague, could you at least *consider* getting out of your pajamas and doing something besides doom scrolling?

The truth turns out to be more complicated than the viral story. Yes, Newton did theorize gravity when he was in isolation. But without access to a library, he got one of the constants in the equation wrong. He concluded that the theory didn't work and stuck his notes in a drawer. It was years later that he dug them up and showed them to a friend, who spotted the error. Working together, and with library access, they fixed the math and finalized the theory. Two eyes produced a more accurate picture of the world.

Our society fetishizes the lone genius and celebrates the hero's journey. Alexander Hamilton. Isaac Newton. Steve Jobs. Elon Musk. In popular culture, one superstar—usually a man— is pushed to the forefront. We're made to believe that they sort it all out by themselves and deliver brilliant answers to a largely ungrateful world. Their achievements then become like tickets to *Hamilton* on Broadway: out of reach for most people. The story—really, the myth—of the lone genius leaves no room for the unrecognized constellations of people who collaborated with that person to make their achievements possible.

Optimal creativity doesn't happen in complete isolation. The one thing you can't do, even if you're as brilliant as Newton, is to see what you can't see—what lies in your blind spot. It often takes other people—with different life experiences and viewpoints—to see possibilities that you've missed and point out the mistakes you've made in your constants. From Renaissance Italy to Xerox PARC to X, Alphabet's moonshot factory, diverse personalities and talents in one place create sparks that burn down obsolete ideas and generate breakthroughs.

People who don't live in our self-constructed jail cells can see the iron bars constraining our thinking. Without the distortions of our own biases and assumptions—our own internal funhouse mirrors—they help us see ourselves more clearly and reveal the wisdom within.

Organize your own community of diverse thinkers. Find like-hearted people who share your values—but not your thoughts. Here are some questions I ask in deciding who to allow into my inner circle: *Is this person transparent? Do they enjoy diving deep to catch the bigger fish instead of remaining in shallow waters with small talk? Will they listen to what I say without judging me or shaming me? Will they share honest feedback intended to improve my work?*

Your community will be a mirror for you. Some of your best insights will emerge while problem-solving for others in the group. The ideas you generate for others will unlock ideas within yourself. The advice you give to others will often be advice you need to follow yourself. This mirroring effect is one reason why Alcoholics Anonymous assigns sponsors to new members—the system helps both the new member and the sponsor.

In addition to tapping your community to gain clarity, you can try some of these thought experiments. Imagine an open chair in front of you and invite your 90-year-old self to sit down there. Picture yourself in detail—the gray hair, the wrinkled hands, the decades of additional wisdom. Ask your elderly self, *What advice do you have for me? What would you do in this situation?*

Alternatively, imagine that your best friend is struggling with the same problem you have. Ask yourself, *What advice would I give to my best friend?* Then take your own advice.

These thought experiments can help you rise above your own biases, but they can't replace actual interactions with actual people. There's a reason why the best artists of the Renaissance went to Florence. And there's a reason why Newton needed input from his friend to finalize his theory. "If I have seen further," Newton famously wrote, "it is by standing on the shoulders of giants."[18]

Find or create your own Florence—your own community of the *un*-like-minded who can help you spot the big fish swimming in your depths.

## Great minds don't think alike

Imagine a courtroom.[19] There's a prosecutor, a jury, and a judge.

The prosecutor presents convincing evidence and uses polished arguments to show beyond a reasonable doubt that a crime has been committed.

The defendant has no lawyer. He's not even allowed to present arguments. He sits silently as the prosecution paints a clear picture of him as guilty as charged. The jury, moved by the prosecution's argument, votes to convict unanimously.

This scenario would be unconstitutional in most democratic systems. A defendant normally has the right to present a defense.

Yet this scenario happens frequently in organizations across the globe.

When ideas are pitched in most institutions, there's only one team arguing for only one side of the case: "We should pursue this marketing strategy." "We should launch this new service." "We should acquire this promising start-up."

The team has done its research and has seemingly convincing data and fancy PowerPoint slides where Decision A invariably leads to Outcome B. No one else is present to offer other perspectives or muddy the waters with nuance and uncertainty. Even if there are defense attorneys on the team, they've often been forced to choose between honesty and loyalty. They disguise themselves by putting on a prosecutor's hat and saying what others want to hear.

Confirmation bias often looks like scientific data collection. But instead of looking for data that refute our hypothesis, we fish for support. We collect data that support only our side. We cook the books and rig the trial so we can win—often without realizing it.

Paradoxically, the smarter you are, the worse this tendency can be. You'll be better at finding evidence and arguments to support your position. "The first principle is that you must not fool yourself and you are the easiest person to fool," as Richard Feynman reminds us.

Netflix found itself in this position when it decided to launch the ill-fated Qwikster service in 2011. This, says Netflix CEO Reed Hastings, was "the biggest mistake in Netflix history."[20] Before the announcement, Netflix offered a single service that combined streaming and mailing DVDs. Hastings saw the writing on the wall—DVDs would soon become obsolete—and decided to spin Netflix's DVD business into a separate company called Qwikster.

This plan would have allowed Netflix to focus on building its future in streaming without getting weighed down by its past.

The announcement provoked one of the biggest consumer backlashes in corporate history. "Not only was our new model way more expensive," Hastings writes, "but it also meant customers had to manage two websites and two subscriptions instead of one." As a result, Netflix lost millions of subscribers and its stock dropped by more than 75 percent. Hastings was humiliated. He describes his decision to launch Qwikster as "the lowest point in my career."[21] Even *Saturday Night Live* made fun of him in a skit.

The humiliation resulted in part because—despite all the talk inside Netflix about the importance of transparency—dissent wasn't always welcome. The defense attorneys were notably absent from Qwikster's launch. They kept quiet even though they had serious misgivings about the idea. One Netflix vice president told Hastings: "You're so intense when you believe in something . . . that I felt you wouldn't hear me. I should have laid down on the tracks screaming that I thought it would fail. But I didn't."[22]

After the failure, Netflix decided to adopt a culture of actively farming for dissent. Multiple systems are now in place throughout the organization to make sure that dissent is unearthed and voiced before a major decision is made. For example, a Netflix employee with a proposal will often distribute a spreadsheet asking colleagues to rate the idea from –10 to +10 and provide comments. This isn't a democratic vote. It's a way to make it easier to collect feedback, gauge the intensity of dissent, and start a candid conversation. "To disagree silently is disloyal," as the now-reformed Hastings puts it.[23]

The film director Mike Nichols took a similar approach. Meryl Streep, who worked with him on several movies, says that Nichols would accept ideas from anyone on the set. "He wasn't threatened by other people, and many, many directors are—when you say something, you can just see them bracing themselves." Nichols would actively seek to unearth dissent by asking, "'What's the dead whale?' Meaning, what's the thing under this scene that's stinking up the whole room that no one is talking about?"[24]

Identical sounds create an echo chamber. You have nothing to learn from someone who thinks exactly as you do. Yet we surround ourselves with our intellectual clones. We befriend people who think like us. We hire people who followed the same path that we did. It's like putting two mirrors together that reflect each other into infinity.

Intellectual friction shouldn't be avoided. When offered in good faith to improve outcomes, dissent should be embraced. If people are free to think for themselves—and free to point out the dead whales in the room—you're far less likely to produce an echo chamber. An opposing view, even if it turns out to be wrong, can reduce overconfidence and insert nuance into a one-sided conversation.

Before you make any major decision, ask yourself, *Is there an attorney on the other side?* If so, court their dissent. If not, actively look for one (*Who will disagree with me?*). If you're surrounded by people who always agree with you, consider it a warning sign. It means they aren't being honest with you or thinking critically.

Above all, stop fishing for support. And start farming for dissent.

# 7

# Unleash the Power of Play

*We don't stop playing because we grow old;*
*we grow old because we stop playing.*

—UNKNOWN

## The problem with deliberate practice

Peter was tired of playing the electric guitar.[1]

His band had been on tour for 10 years. They were a decent indie band from a small college town in the South, but they'd never had a mainstream hit. They were all in a rut—including Peter. He had been strumming the same melodies on the same instrument for eight hours a day.

On a whim, he traded his electric guitar for an acoustic mandolin, an instrument he had never played. Playing the mandolin forced him to do chord changes that he wouldn't do on the guitar. He set up a musical sandbox, experimenting with new scales, trying new chords, and creating new riffs—all with the playful mindset of a curious child.

Other band members joined him in the sandbox. The bassist switched to keyboards, and the drummer picked up the bass. The lead singer, who normally wrote lyrics with political themes, began to play around with other topics.

One of the riffs on the mandolin struck a chord with Peter. He played it during a band practice, and the rest of the group loved it. The drummer and the bassist joined the game and added more oomph to the acoustic melody from the mandolin.

The final player to go on the field was the lead singer, Michael. As the band played the new melody, he picked up his Dictaphone and began walking around the room in a meditative state. The lyrics slowly poured out of him.

> *Oh life, is bigger.*
> *It's bigger than you.*
> *And you are not me.*

As he improvised the lyrics, Michael had no predetermined outcome in mind. He didn't go into the practice session thinking, *This is the song I'm going to write today.* To him, this was a good sign. The lyrics "just kind of flew out of me," Michael explained later.[2]

This playful environment generated a song that became a massive hit. The album that featured the song topped the charts, selling more than 18 million copies and winning the band three Grammys.

The song, as you may have guessed, was "Losing My Religion" by R.E.M.

The secret to this creation story was the band's ability to infuse play into their practice.

You may have heard the term deliberate practice. The goal is to practice a skill in a deliberate way, get immediate feedback, correct what's not working, and iterate and improve over time.

Deliberate practice is terrific for honing a specific skill that can be performed the same way. That's how you fine-tune your golf swing, hit the right notes on your guitar, or play a great opening move in a game of chess. You hit the same golf shot, play the same melody, and practice the same opening until you get it right.

As the saying goes, practice makes perfect. And that's part of the problem.

With repeated practice, we perfect one way of doing things. We play the same types of songs on the electric guitar and launch the same types of marketing campaigns. We explore only well-trodden paths and avoid games we don't know how to play. As a result, we grow stagnant. We can't adjust to the curveballs the universe throws at us or spot new opportunities.

In one study, researchers analyzed all previous studies covering the relationship between deliberate practice and human performance.[3] Deliberate practice explained 21 percent of performance in music and 18 percent in sports. But the number dropped to less than 1 percent for professions like sales and computer programming.

These professions, like many others, involve games of constant change. Just when we think we've mastered the game—just when we think we've figured it all out—the rules, the board, and the pieces all suddenly change. Yet we remain stuck playing yesterday's game with yesterday's rules, even as the world around us changes—and even as *we* change.

With practice, there are two outcomes: You either get it right or you get it wrong.

But with play, there's no right or wrong. The process is far more important than the outcome. We ski, not to get to the bottom as fast as possible, but for the sake of skiing. We pick up the mandolin, not to write the next breakthrough hit, but to fiddle around with the instrument. We play fetch with our dog, not to win at the game of fetch, but for the sake of playing. The play is its own reward.

Practice hones one skill, but play diversifies your skills. Unlike a journey, which has a set destination, play is an odyssey into the unknown. There are no scripts or manuals. You go where your internal wind directs you in a loose and free-flowing manner.

If practice is performance, play is improvisation. When you play, you let your subconscious take over. You explore paths that your prudent self would normally avoid. You temporarily set aside daily constraints and rules that imprison you. You rise above your well-worn neural pathways just enough to create new connections that didn't exist before.

Interrupting your patterns through play makes them visible. The moment you set aside your guitar and pick up the mandolin, you introduce a variation to your pattern. You create a glitch in the matrix that exposes the matrix—one that jolts you out of your established ways of being.

Play also allows you to set aside your inner judge and be yourself. This is why, during holidays, otherwise quiet older members of the family all of a sudden become extroverted when you bust out Cranium. You're allowed to sing, dance, hum, improvise, draw— behaviors that your regular self might find completely irrational or embarrassing.

Unlocking your full potential often demands bending established practices, not reinforcing them.

It requires cultivating openness, not just focus.

It requires diversifying what you do, what you read, and who you talk to.

It requires play, not just rote application.

## All work and no play

"When we are at work we ought to be at work," wrote Henry Ford in his autobiography. "When the work is done, then play can come, but not before."[4] The Ford Motor Company lived by this principle. In the 1930s and 1940s, laughter at work was considered insubordination and subject to discipline.[5]

It wasn't just Ford. This was the dominant ideology of the Industrial Age. The work-play separation stemmed from the idea that play was antithetical to business. It got in the way of productivity. It distracted workers on the assembly line. It slowed things down.

We no longer penalize people for cracking a joke during work meetings. But there's still a huge stigma attached to play in the workplace. If something has no obvious purpose—if it's not in a manual somewhere—we assume it doesn't belong in a never-a-wasted-moment workday. The "work hard, play hard" mentality reinforces the same idea from Ford's time that work and play take place at different times.

Play isn't an escape from work or a reward for making it through work. It's a better way of working. "A master in the art of living draws no sharp distinction between his work and his play, his labour and his leisure, his mind and his body, his education and his recreation," the author L. P. Jacks wrote. "He hardly knows which is which. He simply pursues his vision of excellence through whatever he is doing and leaves others to determine whether he is working or playing. To himself he always seems to be doing both."[6]

In *The Checklist Manifesto*, surgeon Atul Gawande wrote about the importance of using checklists that guide experts through the different steps involved in a complicated procedure.[7] Checklists can ensure that surgeries are performed properly, airplanes are ready for flight, and skyscrapers are constructed safely.

Checklists are critical where people need to replicate the same set of actions every time in a structured, sequential way. A checklist ensures that they don't miss a step or make an error in the pressure of the moment.

But what if your goal isn't idea execution but idea generation? What if, instead of trying to repeat what you've done in the past, you're trying to imagine the future? In that case, a backward-looking checklist that describes how things *should* be done won't be useful. Instead, you need a forward-looking playlist that opens up possibilities for how things *could* be.

Play-deprived workers are unoriginal workers. Imagination isn't a car part. There are no "seven steps" that you can follow to engineer creativity. You can't generate new ideas if you're in autopilot mode, constrained by made-up rules and boundaries. You can't see the possibilities around you if your nose is stuck to the grindstone and if you're repeatedly performing the same routine tasks. You can't reach the highest levels of your profession if you don't enjoy what you're doing.

All work and no play really does make Jack a dull boy.

Research shows that play is a catalyst for creativity.[8] After watching a funny five-minute film, people generate more original word associations and integrate seemingly unrelated concepts.[9] In a different study, watching the same funny film improved participants' ability to solve problems.[10]

As the researchers explained, "small everyday events" can generate these benefits. Just a little play infused into the workday can make all the difference. A short funny movie to start a meeting. A quick game to kick off a brainstorming session and put people in a playful mindset. The positive use of humor to relieve workplace tension.

When I take a break from writing, I jump on a trampoline in our backyard. I play tug-of-war with our dogs. My inner child loves me for it. The more I'm aligned with him, the more creative my work gets.

When I find myself getting stuck, I pick up a book or an article from a writer who I know is playful with their writing. Seeing them play gives me permission to play. At the sight of his counterpart in another, my inner child comes alive.

Symbols also matter. Just as a box of tissues on the coffee table of a therapist's office gives the client permission to let it all out, symbols can remind people to come out to play. Pixar animators work in wooden huts.[11] Robert Langdon, the protagonist in Dan Brown's novels, wears a Mickey Mouse watch. Although its juvenile appearance often draws odd looks from people, the watch serves as Langdon's reminder to stay playful. I keep figurines on my desk from *Back to the Future*, one of my favorite movies of all time. Marty, Doc, and Einstein serve as little reminders to be playful with my own work.

You might be thinking: My job is too complex, too serious, too fill-in-the-blank for play.

Think again.

Space flight is as serious as a business can get. One wrong step, one miscalculation, and you can expect the worst. This is why astronauts play more than just about any other professionals. By the time an astronaut sits on top of a rocket, she's gone through years of training and played with thousands of failure scenarios in a simulator.

These simulations aren't just about deliberate practice—training the astronauts to follow the same process to tackle the same problems they'll encounter in space. Space is a deeply uncertain environment. In many cases, the universe will throw them curveballs they've never seen before.

The purpose of the training is to get astronauts to play in this state of uncertainty. As astronaut Megan McArthur explains, the purpose is to "build you up" and prove to "yourself that you have the ability to work when maybe some really terrible things are happening."[12] It's to make astronauts more resilient and provide the skills and flexibility they'll need to tackle any problem that might arise in the unforgiving environment of space.

So it's not that you can play when the stakes are low. It's that you *must* play when the stakes are high.

This doesn't mean creating a corporate free-for-all or playing at the expense of work. The goal is to be intentional about when to transition into play and when to transition out of it. Play is most helpful when we're generating new ideas and exploring different options. But when it's time to execute, it makes sense to get more serious.

This is what R.E.M. did with "Losing My Religion." Each band member played around with new instruments to generate the melodies and lyrics for the song. But when it came time for execution—to record the song—they went back to their native instruments.[13]

Over to you: When you start strumming the strings of your own life, how can you incorporate more play into your work? What games could go on your playlist for generating new insights? In the next few sections, I'll give you some ideas to get you started.

## Follow the trail of curiosity

After his wife died, the physicist Richard Feynman went into a deep depression. He found himself unable to work on research problems. So he told himself that he'd instead *play* with physics— not for immediate practical results, but for its own sake.[14]

One day he was eating in a cafeteria at Cornell University, where he was teaching at the time. He noticed someone "fooling around" and throwing a plate in the air. "As the plate went up in the air I saw it wobble, and I noticed the red medallion of Cornell on the plate going around," he explained. "It was pretty obvious to me that the medallion went around faster than the wobbling."

Just for fun, he decided to calculate the motion of the rotating plate. He shared his discovery with his colleague Hans Bethe, a Nobel laureate and nuclear physicist.

Bethe said: "Feynman, that's pretty interesting, but what's the importance of it? Why are you doing it?"

"Hah!" Feynman replied. "There's no importance whatsoever. I'm just doing it for the fun of it."

Undeterred by Bethe's reaction, Feynman went on to work out the equations of the wobbles in the plate.

That, in turn, got him thinking about how electron orbits wobble in relativity.

That, in turn, led him to pursue his work on quantum electrodynamics.

And that, in turn, won him the Nobel Prize in Physics in 1965.

"[What] I got the Nobel Prize for," Feynman explains, "came from that piddling around with the wobbling plate."

There might have been no Nobel Prize for Feynman if he had abandoned playing with the wobbling plate in order to be more "productive."

Extraordinary thinkers pursue knowledge with no obvious utility. They explore for the sake of exploring. They calculate the rotation rate of wobbling plates, not knowing it might lead to a Nobel Prize one day. They read textbooks on economics and geology, not knowing that their insights may help them formulate the theory of evolution, as happened with Charles Darwin.[15] They follow their interest in botanical exploration, not knowing it will produce a *New York Times* best-seller, as it did for Elizabeth Gilbert.[16]

Make room in your life to do *some* things for their own sake. If you love how French sounds, learn French. If you like working with your hands, put on your overalls à la Demi Moore and bust out that pottery wheel. If you're curious about physics, spend your Sunday watching the Feynman lectures.

If you keep doing what's "productive," you'll stick to the familiar.

To find unfamiliar insights, follow the trail of curiosity to unfamiliar places.

## Solve someone else's problem

*The Office* is one of my favorite comedy shows of all time. The series ran for over 200 episodes. It's not easy for the writers of a show to maintain momentum and generate good ideas for that long. When the writers inevitably found themselves in a rut, they'd do something highly unusual.[17]

They'd stop working on *The Office*. And they'd start playing—on someone else's show.

Instead of trying to write another episode of *The Office*, they'd start plotting a future episode of *Entourage*, a comedy series about the film star Vincent Chase and his close group of friends. There was only one requirement: Every episode had to end with Chase winning the Oscar for Best Actor.

With that guardrail in place, the *Office* writers would begin to play. This was their way of putting down their electric guitar and picking up the mandolin.

*Entourage* wasn't their baby—and that was precisely the point. They had no stake in the outcome, so they could throw around seemingly ridiculous ideas. It didn't matter whether the structure was right or the scenes were funny. They could let their guard down and play.

This might seem like an enormous waste of time. Why spend your precious time writing an episode of someone else's show—one that will never air?

But there's genius at work—or really, at play—here.

Generating ideas for *Entourage* in a low-stakes setting sparked the writers' creativity and put them in a playful mindset. That mindset would carry over to their work on *The Office*. Once they got back to their own show, they could look at it with renewed energy and fresh perspective. Pieces of the puzzle would suddenly fall into place.

Play increases creativity in part because it reduces our fear of failure. Even if you fail—even if the *Entourage* episode you plotted sucks—nothing bad is going to happen. That feeling of safety can shut down the inner critic that often gets in the way of imagination.

In your next marketing meeting, try kicking things off by spending 15 minutes coming up with a campaign for a competitor's product. If you write nonfiction, write an outline for a novel. Design your best friend's career from scratch.

Think of these thought experiments as warm-ups before exercising. If you skip the warm-up and go right to running fast or lifting heavy, your body won't perform at its best. The same idea applies to creativity. It helps to warm it up first with a low-stakes game before you turn to what matters.

You can also try the approach that former Intel president Andy Grove followed when he took over the company.[18] At the time, Intel was stuck in a rut. The company had become a giant based on the success of its memory chips. By the early 1980s, however, Intel's dominant position in that market was being challenged by Japanese competitors making better memory chips. Between 1978 and 1988, Japanese competitors doubled their market share in memory chips from 30 to 60 percent.

As president, Grove had to decide: Should Intel double down on memory chips, making bigger factories to leapfrog the competition in manufacturing? Or should the company kill memory chips and move instead into making microprocessors—a promising product line Intel had begun to manufacture? Memory chips had brought Intel to where it was, so the weight of history and the company's identity were tied to them.

One day in 1985 Grove was discussing this quandary with Intel's CEO Gordon Moore. Instead of thinking through the pros and cons or pulling out the whiteboard, Grove decided to play. He asked Moore: "If we got kicked out and the board brought in a new CEO, what do you think he would do?"

The two then walked out the door and walked back in as their replacements. Their own problem became someone else's problem. This moment of playful make-believe loosened the grip of ego and historical practice on their beliefs. It provided distance, and distance in turn provided clarity.

They decided to get out of the memory chip business and steer Intel toward making microprocessors. The company eventually became the dominant force in that market.

The lesson is simple: Sometimes the best way to find a solution to your problem is to solve someone else's—to drop *The Office* and pick up *Entourage* or to drop your guitar and pick up the mandolin.

## Stop calling your office an office

There's a room in our home that I've called my "home office" since we first moved in. I had no good reason for the name—other than an "office" is what people conventionally call a room where work is supposed to get done.

But in my mind, an office is where good ideas go to die. An office conjures up images of cubicles, mind-numbing water-cooler conversations, personal attacks, half-empty cups of awful coffee, and headache-inducing fluorescent lights.

Creativity, in other words, hates offices.

So instead of calling my room an office, I started calling it an idea lab. An idea lab is where innovative ideas are born. An idea lab involves experimentation. An idea lab is for daydreaming. I love my idea lab (and I hated my office).

You might be wondering: What's in a name? Who cares what a room is called?

Names matter, much more than you might assume. This is called priming.[19] Mere exposure to a word or an image can have a powerful influence on your thinking. And the importance of naming extends far beyond your office.

Don't call it a status meeting. Call it something that inspires the attendees to show up in a way that will move the needle—a visioning lab, a collaboration cave, or an idea incubator.

Don't call the position Senior Director of Operations. Call it Head of Getting Moonshots Ready for the Real World (which was the real title of my friend Obi Felten when she worked at X, Alphabet's moonshot factory).

Don't call it a to-do list. When I hear "to-do list," I want to run as far and fast as possible. Call it a playlist or a design list—a title that will delight you and pull you in.

Don't call your staff employees. The word employee reinforces the notion of a top-down bureaucratic system where the employer tells the employees—the cogs in the machine—what to do. Instead, follow the lead of Brasilata, a can-manufacturing firm that's at the forefront of innovation in Brazil.[20] There are no employees at Brasilata. There are only inventors, the title given to all staff. When they join the firm, the inventors sign an "innovation contract." Brasilata then reinforces these names by actively encouraging its employees—sorry, inventors—to take ownership of their work and submit original ideas.

If you want unconventional results, pick an unconventional name. Find your own words that ignite your imagination and prime you for what you're trying to achieve.

Because that's you in the corner.

And that's you in the spotlight.

Playing this game of life.

# 8

# Dare to Create

*Daniel: How do I know if my picture is the right one?*

*Mr. Miyagi: If come from inside you, always right one.*

*—THE KARATE KID*

## Write one of your own

There were two secrets to Stephen King's success: measles and comic books.[1]

The six-year-old Stephen spent nine months bedridden at home instead of attending the first grade. His problems started with the measles and progressed to repeated ear and throat issues.

To entertain himself, he'd read comic books—tons of them. Sometimes he'd copy the books he read panel by panel. But he wouldn't just copy them. He'd add to them. As he copied, he'd modify the stories to introduce his own ideas, twists, and plotlines.

The young Stephen once showed one of these copycat hybrid books to his mother. She was impressed. She asked him if he had written the story himself. Stephen said no—he had copied most of it from another book.

"Write one of your own, Stevie," she said. "I bet you could do better. Write one of your own."

"I remember an immense feeling of possibility at the idea," King recalls, "as if I had been ushered into a vast building filled with closed doors and had been given leave to open any I liked." He took his mother's advice and wrote one of his own. He then wrote another. And another. And another.

He went on to publish over 50 books that have sold more than 350 million copies.[2]

What started King's writing career was a seemingly simple insight from his mother: Creating is more valuable than consuming.

We talk about information as if it's food. We focus on how we can *consume* more of it and how we can *process* it faster. While we're busy stuffing ourselves with morsels of information from the outside, we lose sight of the nourishment already inside. The internal nuggets of wisdom get crowded out by the high-decibel voices crashing into our eardrums. Learning becomes an excuse for not creating.

This was a problem long before the internet came along. "Just as a coiled spring finally loses its elasticity through the sustained pressure of a foreign body, so too the mind through the constant force of other people's thoughts," the 19th-century German philosopher Arthur Schopenhauer wrote. This was "the case of many scholars," according to Schopenhauer. "They have read themselves stupid."[3]

This doesn't mean you skip *all* the reading and completely ignore the insights of people who came before you. But it does mean getting comfortable with imperfect information, with not clearly seeing the path before you start walking the path. There'll always be one more book you could read, one more podcast you could listen to, one more credential you could acquire, and one more course you could take. Some awareness—not too much, not too little—can be a good thing.

It also means striking a balance between consumption and creation—between reading other people's thoughts and generating your own. If you're like most people, this ratio is skewed heavily on the consumption side (even if you call responding to routine emails "creative," which it is not).

Work on balancing the ratio. You can start, as Stephen King did, by improving what others have created. Take one page from *The Great Gatsby* and improve it. Instead of complaining about the ending of *The Sopranos* or *Lost* or your favorite TV show, write a better ending. Take one piece of dialogue from *The West Wing* and make it snappier than Aaron Sorkin did.

And don't stop there. Move on, as Stephen King did, to creating beautiful things that are unmistakably yours—whether it's your own business, your own nonprofit, or a new strategy at work that reimagines the status quo.

There's a scene in the movie *Rocketman* where a young Elton John plays the piano for an American band. After the show, Elton asks the lead singer, "How do I get to be a songwriter?" The lead singer replies, "Write some songs."[4]

This deceptively simple advice is also profound. The author Austin Kleon calls it "doing the verb." We often want to be the noun (a songwriter) without doing the verb (writing songs). We tell ourselves we're going to be an entrepreneur, but we don't build anything. We tell ourselves we're going to be a novelist, but we don't write a novel.

The key is to forget the noun and do the verb instead.

If you want to be a blogger, start blogging every week.

If you want to be a stand-up comedian, start performing at open-mic nights.

If you want to be a podcaster, start podcasting.

A final note: Criticism isn't creation. It's easy to point fingers. It's easy to complain and then wonder why things don't magically get better. It's easy to jump on Twitter to argue with people you don't know and tell them to "do better" (while secretly telling yourself to do just that).

Criticism, in other words, is cheap. Creation—that's what's valuable.

People who raise their hand and lead the way.

People who say, "Let's go over there," and blaze a trail into the unknown.

People who write one of their own.

## Can one person really make a difference?

Back in the 1940s, a 14-year-old boy lived in a small village in Turkey. He had grown up in poverty and helped support his family as a shepherd, tending sheep.

The boy heard that a school had opened up in a nearby village for training future elementary school teachers. He applied and was accepted. He walked 50 kilometers (roughly 30 miles) from his village to the school to register—a trip he'd have to make back and forth on a regular basis.

During his first week, the school nurse noticed that the boy's shoes were falling apart. Students (and teachers) were required to do manual labor around the campus, building classrooms and dorms. They also worked the fields that supplied food to the school, and the field work left his feet soaking wet and his shoes filled with mud.

The nurse bought the boy a new pair of hobnail boots. Those boots transformed his life: Without this gift, he probably would have dropped out of school.

The boy graduated, returned to his village, and became an elementary school teacher. Over the next few decades he taught thousands of students, becoming an inspirational leader in his community.

He also taught me.

That boy was my grandfather—and my first teacher. He opened my eyes to the magic of reading and writing and encouraged my sense of wonder about the world.

If that nurse hadn't given him those boots, my grandfather might have dropped out of school. And I would have grown up without his influence—which set me on the path I'm on today.

In other words, a butterfly flapped its wings in a small village in Turkey and created a ripple effect that radiated outward for decades to come.

We often assume we must "do something big" to make a difference. We think our individual actions aren't enough. If we don't have a "large following" or if we lack the ability to create change on scale, we don't even bother.

A huge splash—a big best-seller or a runaway hit—is what's visible, and we assume what's visible is what's important.

But a tiny drop can create ripples that extend far beyond what's visible. We often don't see those ripples, so we assume they don't exist. The nurse who gifted my grandfather that pair of boots doesn't know about the impact she had on my life and on the lives of the thousands of students he later taught. And the effect rippled out from there to all the people my grandfather's students were able to impact because of his guidance—all radiating from a single act of generosity.

I often get a version of this question when I give keynotes: "How do I get others to change?" My answer? Embody the change you want to see. Stop waiting for others to act. The nurse didn't wait for "the authorities" to help my grandfather. Instead, she did what she thought was the right thing to do.

"The arc of the moral universe is long," as Martin Luther King Jr. reminded us, "but it bends toward justice."

But it doesn't do that automatically.

It doesn't bend toward justice if you wait for someone else to show up and take action.

It bends toward justice when people make individual contributions that build up over time to something extraordinary.

## What you don't know can help you

Before she founded Spanx, Sara Blakely made a living by selling fax machines door to door.[5]

She lived in Florida. It was scorching hot. The pantyhose she was forced to wear were old-fashioned and uncomfortable—particularly because the seamed foot stuck out of her open-toe heels.

Frustrated, she took her $5,000 in savings, moved to Atlanta, and began developing plans to produce footless pantyhose.

She had never taken a business class. She had zero experience in fashion and retail. She was laughed out of the hosiery mills she visited to pitch her product. Undeterred, she used that $5,000 to launch Spanx and turned it into a billion.

People often ask her, "How did you do it, Sara? What was your business plan?"

Her reply? "I never had a business plan."

She had no idea how business was supposed to work, so she kept it simple. "I focused on 3 things: Make it, sell it, build awareness," she explains. "I made the product, sold it to as many stores as I could and spent the rest of my time building excitement and awareness. Then I would repeat the cycle."[6]

That's it.

Blakely knew that spending all her energy developing the "right branding" or a well-crafted business plan could become an elaborate excuse for not doing the essentials. She explains: "I see a lot of entrepreneurs with really great ideas freeze in their tracks because of their 'lack of experience' or knowledge. But what you 'don't' know could be the very thing that sets you apart from all the rest."

Let me repeat that: What you don't know can set you apart from others.

Beginners don't have a muscle memory. Too much knowledge can hamper your imagination by focusing your attention on how things *are* rather than how they *could* be. As Kevin Kelly, founding executive editor of *Wired*, says, imagination is "the one skill in life that benefits from ignoring what everyone else knows."[7]

Philip Glass, one of the most influential composers of the 20th century, would agree. "If you don't know what to do," he says, "there's actually a chance of doing something new. As long as you know what you're doing, nothing much of interest is going to happen."[8]

The world's best baseball players relentlessly keep their eyes focused on the ball they need to hit. They don't get distracted by the crowds around them or by what other players are doing. The same applies to you. If you're not focused on what's in front of you—if you're distracted by what your peers are doing, or if you're too busy looking behind at what you've done in the past—you can easily lose sight of what matters.

This mindset doesn't require retreating to an isolated monastery. But it does require approaching knowledge with caution. Knowledge should inform, not constrain. It should enlighten, not obscure.

You can't hit a home run unless you can see the ball.

## The article that changed my life

*This whole thing is so obvious.*

I was shaking my head in self-loathing at what I'd just written. It was an article about why facts don't change people's minds. The insights in it were obvious to me. As a former rocket scientist, I had spent much of my life trying to convince people using objective, irrefutable data.

I eventually discovered a significant problem with this approach: It doesn't work. If someone has made up their mind, facts often won't be enough to change their mind.

I was tempted to leave the whole article on the cutting room floor. But my newsletter was due out the next morning, and I had nothing else in the works. I asked my inner critic for a pass and reluctantly hit Publish.

This was in 2017. At that point I had been writing online for less than a year. I had only about 1,000 subscribers on my email list, and the word viral didn't appear anywhere in my vocabulary.

After I published the article, a series of strange events occurred in rapid succession.

People started sharing the article on social media. These weren't just friends or regular readers. They were complete strangers who had somehow come across the article and liked it enough to share it.

Then an editor from the website Heleo—the predecessor to the Next Big Idea Club—asked if they could share the article on their website.

"Really interesting and well written," the editor said.

"I see," I said, not seeing at all.

A few days later, I got a message from my web developer. "Something strange is happening," she said. "Take a look at your website stats."

You know the scene in *The Matrix* where Keanu Reeves goes "Whoa"? That was my reaction as I looked, jaw dropped and head cocked, at the hockey stick–shaped graph depicting the exponential rise in traffic to my website—most of it coming from the article published on Heleo.

My article had gone viral. It quickly became the most popular article ever published on Heleo, drawing hundreds of thousands of people to my website. All those new readers eventually played a key part in the success of my last book, *Think Like a Rocket Scientist*.

The moral of the story? You are a terrible judge of your own ideas. You're too close to them to evaluate them objectively.

This happens to me often. I publish an article that I think is brilliant, and it gets crickets. I publish an article that I think only states the obvious, and it goes viral.

The Oscar-winning screenwriter William Goldman had it right: "Nobody knows anything."[9] In the movie industry, as in life, no one knows what will be a hit and what will be a flop.

That is, until you try. I can spend days mulling over the pros and cons of an idea—which my overthinking mind is prone to doing—or I can just give it a shot.

So if you have an idea, don't hoard it. Raise your hand and speak up, even if you think the idea is "obvious." Just remember how close I came to *not* sharing the article that changed my life.

What's obvious to you could be groundbreaking for someone else.

## And yet it moves

Mothers and their newborn infants were dying—at a horrific rate.

This was the tragic situation in what I'll call Clinic No. 1, one of two maternity clinics at the Vienna General Hospital in the 1840s.

Life in Clinic No. 2 was drastically different. Even though both clinics were in the same hospital, mortality rates in Clinic No. 2 were far lower than in Clinic No. 1—a fact so well known that desperate mothers would beg on their knees not to be admitted to Clinic No. 1.

The two clinics were identical in all relevant respects, except for one. In Clinic No. 2, midwives attended births, whereas in Clinic No. 1, doctors and medical students delivered infants. It wasn't that midwives were better at delivering babies. The maternal deaths were happening from childbed fever following delivery, not during it.[10]

The car had not yet been invented, and in the large city of Vienna, women would often deliver their babies on the streets and then carry them to the maternity clinics. Counterintuitively, the mortality rate for mothers who gave birth on the street was significantly lower than for those who delivered in Clinic No. 1.

This discrepancy escaped the notice of most doctors—except a physician named Ignaz Semmelweis. He was a stranger in a strange land, a Hungarian working in a top Austrian hospital in a xenophobic era.

Working on the front lines, Semmelweis was deeply troubled and puzzled by the pattern he was observing. What explained the drastic difference in mortality rates between the two clinics? Why were well-educated doctors and medical students losing more patients than the midwives working next door? Why were mothers who delivered their babies on the streets—in far less favorable conditions than a medical clinic—far more likely to survive once they arrived at the clinic?

The death of his friend and colleague Jakob Kolletschka provided a clue. Kolletschka was a professor of forensic medicine. During an autopsy, his finger was pricked by a contaminated knife, and he died from the resulting infection. "Day and night I was haunted by the image of [his] disease," Semmelweis recalled. He realized that the disease that took Kolletschka might be the same disease that was claiming the lives of countless maternity patients.

Dots began to connect, and the disturbing answer eventually revealed itself. The same hands that healed patients were also transmitting disease to them. Unlike the midwives in Clinic No. 2, the doctors and medical students in Clinic No. 1 routinely performed autopsies. They'd go from dissecting cadavers in the morgue to delivering babies in the maternity ward—without properly washing their hands. Semmelweis suspected that they would then infect their patients with particles they picked up from corpses.

This suspicion might seem obvious now, but at the time it was a wild idea. This was before Louis Pasteur formulated germ theory. People didn't yet believe that microbes could spread disease.

To test his theory, Semmelweis devised an experiment. He asked doctors to wash their hands with chlorinated lime after autopsy work and before they examined patients. It worked. The deaths slowed down—significantly. In just a few months, mortality rates in Clinic No. 1 dropped from over 18 percent to below 2 percent.

Semmelweis was stunned, in part because he felt responsible. "I have examined corpses to an extent equaled by few other obstetricians," he wrote. "Only God knows the number of patients who went prematurely to their graves because of me." Yet "no matter how painful and oppressive such a recognition may be, the remedy does not lie in suppression," he continued. "If the misfortune is not to persist forever, then this truth must be made known to everyone concerned."

Semmelweis's battle to find a solution turned into a battle to be heard—which he quickly lost. The rigid Viennese medical establishment rejected his simple solution to wash their hands, despite clear evidence supporting the practice. Doctors took offense at his suggestion that their lack of personal hygiene could cause death. A gentleman's hands, they believed, couldn't possibly transmit disease.

Imagine standing in Semmelweis's shoes. To discover this simple, yet earth-shattering, insight—wash your hands and save lives—and fear that the answer may die with you because no one is willing to listen to you. So you kick and scream—as Semmelweis did, louder and louder, writing one letter after another—only to be forced out of your hospital.

In Semmelweis's mind, each preventable death became a murder.[11] Haunted by all the lives he couldn't save, he eventually suffered a nervous breakdown. He was committed to an asylum, where he was severely beaten by the guards and died two weeks later from an infected wound.

Years after Semmelweis's death, handwashing gained widespread acceptance as a way to prevent the spread of germs. His idea saved countless lives—including perhaps yours and mine. He is now known as "the savior of mothers."

Today the Semmelweis reflex refers to the instinctive rejection of ideas that buck the status quo. The names differ, but the narrative is the same. The step was a first, the road was new, the vision their own, and the response received: rejection and backlash.

You may not end up in an asylum, but when you challenge conventional wisdom, convention will balk. When you separate from the herd, the herd will call you out. Those with a stake in the status quo will resist and resist hard.

When you create anything meaningful, someone, somewhere, will try to make you feel lousy about it.

Nicolaus Copernicus's discovery that the Earth orbits the Sun, rather than the other way around, was banished for almost a century. Books supporting this insight were banned, and Galileo was famously put on trial for endorsing it.[12] The Roman Inquisition declared Galileo's ideas "foolish and absurd in philosophy, and formally heretical since it explicitly contradicts in many places the sense of Holy Scripture."[13] He was forced to recant his theory and sentenced to house arrest, where he remained for the last nine years of his life.

Stephen King routinely finds himself on the receiving end of bitter criticism. "Not a week goes by," he writes, "that I don't receive at least one pissed-off letter (most weeks there are more) accusing me of being foul-mouthed, bigoted, homophobic, murderous, frivolous, or downright psychopathic."[14]

When Walt Whitman published *Leaves of Grass*—one of the most influential and original works of American poetry—the reviews he received were scathing. "It is impossible to imagine how any man's fancy could have conceived such a mass of stupid filth, unless he were possessed of the soul of a sentimental donkey that had died of disappointed love," wrote one particularly colorful reviewer. He went on to call the book "a gathering of muck . . . entirely destitute of wit."[15] Another compared Whitman to a "pig" rooting "among a rotten garbage of licentious thoughts."[16]

There's only one way to avoid criticism: Stop doing meaningful work.

Fear of criticism is a dream slayer. It slays dreams by preventing us from getting started, from taking on a challenging project, or from raising our hand during a meeting to voice dissent.

Don't get me wrong: Criticism is helpful when it's given in a spirit of generosity, with the intention of improving your work. A generous critic will deliver her feedback without personally attacking you and with the intention of making your work better. That kind of feedback is precious. But the conformist criticism from the peanut gallery—the type of criticism that tells you that you have no business doing what you're doing and that you should go back to coloring between the lines—should be ignored.

Conformist criticism says more about the criticizer than the creator. When people appear to judge you, they're often revealing a part of themselves that they've judged into silence—a part they hammered down to conform and fit in. When that part sees its promise fulfilled by you, the tendency will be to attack rather than to praise.

So, yes, you will be misunderstood. They will attack you, insult you, and drag your good name through the mud. When that happens, do what Elizabeth Gilbert advises: "Just smile sweetly and suggest—as politely as you possibly can—that they go make their own fucking art. Then stubbornly continue making yours."[17]

Galileo continued to stubbornly make his art after he was placed under house arrest. He spent much of his time writing his magnum opus, *Two New Sciences*, which earned him the title "father of modern physics."

And he never lost the courage of his convictions. Legend has it that after he was forced to recant his belief in heliocentrism, his response was *Eppur si muove*.

And yet it moves.

This was a fact. The Earth moved around the Sun. Authorities could ban his books or imprison him, but they couldn't move that fact.

"Care about other people's approval, and you become their prisoner," as Lao Tzu writes in *Tao Te Ching*.[18] When you don't act because you fear criticism, you elevate other people's thoughts above your own. The less external approval you need—the less you fear criticism—the more original ideas you can explore.

It's a great act of human courage to create with no need for constant validation—for being loved, respected, and understood by everyone. If you depend on external sources for power, that power can be withdrawn at any time. But if your fuel is internal, there's nothing they can take away from you.

Internal fuel burns clean. It's renewable. If you run out, you don't need to turn to foreign sources to replenish it with more validation, more approval, and more likes. You have an infinite supply of it within.

In the end, criticism, however painful it may be, is often validation that you're doing meaningful work.

If you stick with it long enough, the trolls and the critics will move on. They'll find someone else to sneer at.

And your art will speak for itself.

## Happy accidents

As a young boy growing up in Istanbul, my vision of America was put together from an eclectic set of American TV shows selected for translation to Turkish.

America's ambassadors to Turkey included Cousin Larry in *Perfect Strangers*, the Tanner family in *ALF*, and Al Bundy in *Married with Children* (who strongly reinforced every stereotype that people ever had about Americans).

But another ambassador stands out and deserves special mention.

His name was Bob Ross—the host of the iconic show *The Joy of Painting*. In every episode, Ross would sport the same blue-collar look, sit on a chair, and oil-paint on a canvas.

When I first came across the show on Turkish TV, it stopped me in my tracks. I remember thinking that Americans must be so bored that they resort to watching a man paint landscapes. This made me reconsider the magic of America.

But something about the show proved strangely addictive. It pulled back the curtain on the creative process, letting the audience see how a creator could make something out of nothing.

For Ross, it was important for the audience to see the entire creative process, warts and all. Instead of editing out his mistakes, he documented them. He embraced them. And most importantly, he reframed them. "We don't make mistakes," he would say. "We have happy accidents."[19]

Ross knew what most of us neglect: Mistakes are intrinsic to creation. If you're not making mistakes, you're playing it too safe. You're not aiming high enough or moving fast enough.

A canvas isn't there to be protected from smudges. A canvas isn't there to be stared at, enjoyed for its perfect whiteness. It's there to be painted on—wildly and beautifully.

People who are prolific in success are also prolific in failure.[20] They succeed more because they do more—they paint more canvases, take more shots on goal, and launch more businesses than others. Babe Ruth was the home run king, but he was also the strikeout king.[21] Michael Jordan made more last-minute baskets to win the game than any other NBA player in history. But he also missed the most last-minute baskets to lose the game.[22]

Most of your attempts will fail. Many will be less than spectacular. A few will succeed and compensate for everything else.

Failure is knowledge. The ground will teach you more about flight than clouds ever can, to paraphrase the poet Rudy Francisco.[23] I haven't had a single failure that didn't lead to some learning. You can fail and still win if you view what you do as an opportunity to learn—and not only as an opportunity to achieve.

Perfectionism is primarily fueled by a desire for external approval. It's an indulgence. We're afraid that if we expose our smudges, we'll stop getting our daily dose of approvals.

If you're human, you are imperfect.

When you strive for perfection, you're searching for some ideal that just doesn't exist. So you procrastinate because if you avoid doing the work, you also avoid making mistakes. You misdirect your creations toward what's easy and what's safe—into a zone where you're likely to minimize smudges. You conform rather than contradict. You finesse rather than finish. You stand rather than dance.

Many Navajo rugs have mistakes in them—distortions in the patterns, lines, and shapes. Some say that these mistakes are intentionally crafted as a reminder of human imperfection.[24] But others suggest that the mistakes aren't intentional. What's intentional is the decision not to fix them but to leave them in place, woven into the fabric.[25]

These rugmakers know what's obvious: An imperfect, handcrafted rug with a story is far more beautiful than one manufactured to perfection in a factory.

I'm not talking about the type of fake imperfection that makes blue jeans look weathered or a Crate & Barrel chair look antique. Manufactured imperfections are easy to spot. You know them when you see them.

When you cover up your authentic imperfections, you also conceal what makes you interesting. People who pretend to be perfect are good for about 10 minutes of conversation. If I want to spend time with airbrushed humans, I can do that on Instagram.

And remember: You're not Bob Ross. You don't have a camera pointed at your canvas at all times, recording every smudge. So don't worry about what others think of you—because most of the time they're not thinking of you. Everyone else is stuck in their own universe, too busy worrying about their own smudges to notice yours.

Yes, mistakes can sometimes be painful. The pain of making a mistake is the price of admission to a courageous life, and I'm happy to pay it. But there's another type of price you pay—not for failing, but for failing to try at all. I've felt that pain before, and I never want to feel it again.

In the end, the only way to have a smudge-free canvas is to never paint.

So go ahead and make mistakes. Make amazing mistakes. Make mistakes that only you can make—the type of smudges that have your signature on them.

Good mistakes won't make you perfect. But they will help you stop thinking that you must get it perfect.

## How professionals make it look easy

In June 1976, a 22-year-old Jerry Seinfeld took the stage to perform publicly for the very first time at an amateur night in a New York City comedy club.[26] He grabbed the microphone to deliver his well-rehearsed routine and . . . nothing happened.

"I couldn't even speak," Seinfeld recalls, "I was so paralyzed in total fear." When he finally mustered the strength to move his lips, he could only rattle off the subjects he was going to cover: "The beach. Driving. Dogs," Seinfeld said into the microphone, his voice unraveling. The whole performance lasted for 90 seconds.

When I first started public speaking, I was spectacularly awkward. I would write out everything I planned to say and deliver it, word by word, in a monotonous tone that never changed—except to register the palpable tension in my voice. As I read from my mental teleprompter, I could sense boredom wafting from the audience. There was *zero* connection between my listeners and me.

The same was true in the classroom. The first time I ever taught a class as a professor, I was so nervous that I tripped over some computer wires, nearly producing an unhappy meeting between face and floor.

Over the next decade, I showed up again and again and again, marching to the decisive beat of effort-result, effort-result, effort-result. Each class I taught, and each speech I gave, was a little bit better than the one before. Along the way, I discovered how to build a connection, how to tell a good story, and how to conceal missed beats so the audience doesn't even notice. I'm now often rated the top speaker at conferences and company events.

Gloss reflects more than it reveals. Lionel Messi, one of the best soccer players of all time, says it took him "17 years and 114 days to become an overnight success."[27] Steve Martin echoes the same sentiment: "I did stand-up comedy for eighteen years," he says. "Ten of those years were spent learning, four years were spent refining, and four were spent in wild success."[28]

The actors Al Pacino and Ben Shenkman starred together in the miniseries *Angels in America*. Pacino was Shenkman's hero, so Shenkman watched Pacino on the set to learn what made his hero so great. One day, after Pacino did 10 takes for a particular scene, the director Mike Nichols turned to Shenkman and asked, "So what have you learned?" Shenkman replied, "Keep it simple." Nichols said: "No, that's not the right answer. The right answer is: see how hard it is? Even for the master, even for your idol? See how many times he has to try it? You've just watched ten takes, and I know you can see it was great here but not there, and then great again but not great right at that important moment."[29]

We can learn from the professionals, as Shenkman did by watching Pacino on the set. But when we compare ourselves to them—when we measure the distance between where we are and where they are—we assume we're not good enough or talented enough, so we don't even bother trying. Or we quit too soon, assuming we don't have what it takes. But when you compare yourself to a more experienced professional, the comparison isn't apples to apples. You're the beta version, and they're the finished product. They've been doing this for years, if not decades, and you're just starting out.

And we don't all start from the same place. Privilege, opportunity, and luck combine to give some people a head start or a Mario Kart–type rocket boost. This isn't an excuse for failing to try or for giving up. It's simply an acknowledgment of reality—that you might run the same distance at the same speed as someone else but still remain behind them. In life, there's no one-size-fits-all timeline. "It's never too late to be who you might have been," as George Eliot purportedly said. So honor where you are right now and how far you've already come.

If you watch a rocket take off, at first it looks like the rocket is barely moving. It ignites in a thunderous roar and begins to inch up really, *really* slowly from the launchpad. Even though there's massive thrust, the rocket is too heavy to move fast. Take a snapshot of a rocket right after ignition and you might assume it's going to fail. Progress becomes visible only if you watch the rocket over a longer time period.

Life works the same way. When you first start a new project or launch a new business, you'll often feel like you're pushing, pushing, and pushing—and nothing much is happening.

The founder of Pinterest, Ben Silbermann, says it took him four years to build a successful company after leaving Google. "That's a four-year period where things weren't going awesome," he says. "But I thought: That's not that long. That's like medical school before you go into residency."[30]

Most people don't even get on the launchpad because they fear creating something lousy. And that's a valid fear: At early stages, your creations will be unimpressive. Despite appearances, nothing springs into existence perfectly formed. You're not seeing the earlier versions of that stand-up routine that elicited boos from the audience, the tens of takes it took to get that Oscar-worthy monologue, and the earlier drafts of that book chapter that would make any self-respecting writer cringe. Every creator must push through these early, embarrassing stages to reach the great work that lies beyond them.

If things feel heavy at first, it's because they *are* heavy. You've just ignited your rocket—and it's going to take a while for you to find your way to your destination. Things will start slow and then gain momentum over time.

So stop comparing yourself to other rockets that have already reached escape velocity. Focus on your own trajectory. Move up one inch. And then another. And then another. The higher you climb, the lighter things will feel.

And before you know it, the distance behind you will be longer than the distance ahead.

## The myth of shameless self-promotion

I never got the concept of "shameless self-promotion."

The phrase presumes that self-promotion is shameful. And that if you're promoting yourself—if you're putting your ideas and your work into the world—you must be shame*less*.

But if you don't promote your creations, no one else will. Life isn't *Field of Dreams*, and you're not Kevin Costner. If you build it and do nothing to promote it, no one will come. You'll just be a weirdo who built a baseball diamond in the middle of a cornfield in Iowa.

We often play small to make others comfortable. We shrink ourselves so we're invisible, even to our own self.

Here's the thing: Your art enables other people's art. Your wisdom unlocks other people's wisdom. Your expansion inspires others to expand. Your voice can change the way that people think and act. But it can't do any of that if you keep your mouth shut.

This doesn't mean you spam people or take advantage of them. It means you promote with kindness. It means you promote with respect. It means you promote to people who've given you permission—who've raised their hands and said, "Yes, I want the thing."[31]

If you don't promote your book, the readers won't come.

If you don't promote your product or your service, the customers won't come.

If you don't promote yourself, the job offers won't come.

Self-promotion is not an act of shame. It's an act of love—for others who want what you created.

It's also an act of courage. It's to say, "Here, I made this," and take the risk of being rejected. It's to be vulnerable—and to be *un*-selfish. It's quite selfish to refuse to promote your creations to protect your own ego.

The alternative to self-promotion is hiding. Coming up with ideas and not executing them. Writing poems and not sharing them. Creating things and hoarding them.

It's time to take the shame out of self-promotion.

If there's any shame, it's in *not* promoting something that can move others and enrich their lives.

Visit ozanvarol.com/genius to find worksheets, challenges, and exercises to help you implement the strategies discussed in this part.

# PART IV

# *The Outer Journey*

Part IV has three chapters:

1. **Detecting Bullshit:** On filtering misinformation and spotting the truth
2. **Look Where Others Don't Look:** On escaping the tyranny of the new, the convenient, and the popular in order to see what others don't see
3. **I Am Not Your Guru:** On why success stories fool us, how well-meaning advice often misleads us, and what you can do to stop comparing yourself to others

Along the way, you'll learn:

- The eye-opening origins of the "breakfast is the most important meal" adage
- Why there are stupid questions (and how to ask better ones)
- A counterintuitive way that a Pulitzer-winning journalist spotted the extraordinary in the ordinary
- What the George Clooney effect can teach you about starting your next project
- How we're being intellectually imprisoned (and what to do about it)
- What you can learn from the world's most misunderstood poem
- Why competition and comparison are a form of conformity

# 9

# Detecting Bullshit

*To doubt everything or to believe everything are two equally convenient solutions; both dispense with the necessity of reflection.*

—HENRI POINCARÉ, *SCIENCE AND HYPOTHESIS*

## How we fool ourselves

*My battery is low and it's getting dark.*

Those were the final words of the Martian rover Opportunity, as reported by numerous media outlets. The rover, lovingly nicknamed Oppy, fell silent in June 2018 after getting stuck in a massive dust storm. NASA officials beamed up hundreds of commands to the little rover, asking it to call home, but with no success. Oppy was officially pronounced dead in February 2019.

What got most people's attention wasn't the fact that Oppy operated on Mars for over 14 years—well past its 90-day expected life span. Nor was it the record-breaking 28 miles it traversed on the red planet—far more than any other extraplanetary rover.

No, what took the world by storm was the rover's final transmission to Earth, reported with a tweet from a journalist.

*My battery is low and it's getting dark.*

The tweet went viral, generating a media frenzy across the globe. Designers on Etsy jumped on the bandwagon, rushing to sell T-shirts, mugs, and coasters emblazoned with Oppy's final words. Numerous people had the words tattooed on their body.

Oppy's message resonated with us in part because we all feel, from time to time, like our batteries are low and it's getting dark out there. To have the same sentiment expressed by a nonhuman gave us all the feels. For 14 years, the little rover had dutifully obeyed her humans' commands while getting whipped around by fierce Martian winds and dust storms. As the dust slowly swallowed Oppy, she beamed to Earth a final goodbye that summed up the courage of the little rover that could.

*My battery is low and it's getting dark.*

Here's the problem: The story is false.

Right before it went silent, Oppy beamed a bunch of routine code to Earth that reported, among numerous other things, its power levels and the outside light reading. A journalist—who didn't let facts get in the way of a good story—took a small part of this random code, paraphrased it into English, and tweeted to the world that these were "basically" the rover's last words.[1]

Millions of people then hit the retweet button and a chorus of media outlets published stories about the rover's final transmission—all without pausing, contemplating, or bothering to ask, "How does a remote-controlled space robot spit out fully formed English sentences designed to tug at people's heartstrings?"

I spent four years serving on the operations team for Oppy. Yet, for a brief moment, even I fell for the story. When I first read Oppy's supposed final words, I let out an instinctive "Awww!" and began to scroll through the press coverage digging for more.

"Old George Orwell got it backward," Chuck Palahniuk, the author of *Fight Club*, writes. "Big Brother isn't watching. He's singing and dancing. He's pulling rabbits out of a hat." He's telling you powerful stories that overwhelm you until your imagination becomes "as useful as your appendix."[2] We fall for the story, throw logic and skepticism to the wind, and rush off to get Oppy tattoos.

This is a common phenomenon. A study by MIT scholars examined true and false news stories shared on Twitter from 2006 to 2017.[3] During that period, false stories were 70 percent more likely to be retweeted and they spread six times faster than true stories—which is particularly concerning because Twitter is the main source of news for many people. What author Jonathan Swift wrote in the 18th century still applies today: "Falsehood flies, and the truth comes limping after it."[4]

The next time you instinctively start to hit that retweet button or feel tempted to accept conventional wisdom, pause for just a moment. Ask yourself, *Is this right?* Question everything, from the supposed emotional farewell of a dying rover to a marketer's confident claims. When you make a regular practice of asking *Is this right?*, you'll be surprised how often the answer isn't an immediate yes.

Skepticism isn't denialism. The denialist is Grampa Simpson shaking his fist at the clouds. The denialist is the person who writes seven-paragraph-long Facebook posts that begin with "I've done my own research," but whose "research" involves simply regurgitating misinformation from manipulative sources. The denialist is certain—now and forever. In contrast, the skeptic has an open mind that can change with the right evidence.

But skepticism by itself isn't enough. It's easy to say, "That's bullshit." It's easy to shoot down your colleagues' ideas at a work meeting. It's much harder to express skepticism in a constructive way.

The solution is to be skeptically curious. This requires striking a delicate balance between being open to ideas—even those that seem controversial or wrong at first—and being equally skeptical of them. The goal isn't skepticism for the sake of skepticism. It's to reimagine the status quo, discover new insights, and figure out where you may need to think again.

The curious skeptic might respond to the Mars rover story by asking, "How does the reporter know what the rover said?" That might lead to additional questions like: "How does a Martian rover communicate with Earth in the first place? Does it speak in fully formed English sentences? How do we know what the rover is doing at any moment?" These questions are guided both by skepticism of the reporter's claims and, more importantly, by curiosity about the underlying truth.

They will lead you to places that few others dare to go and reveal gems that few others see.

## Is breakfast really the most important meal of the day?

This adage is so well known that it's become a cliché—repeated by parents across the globe to get their kids to eat their breakfast: "Breakfast is the most important meal of the day."

What's less known is the origin of this mantra: a 1944 marketing campaign that General Foods created to help sell more cereal.[5]

The campaign was named "Eat a Good Breakfast—Do a Better Job." During the campaign, grocery stores distributed pamphlets touting the benefits of breakfast, and radio advertisements declared that "nutrition experts say breakfast is the most important meal of the day." The campaign was key to the rise of cereal as a staple breakfast food.

Breakfast cereal, in turn, had been invented at the turn of the century to promote health and well-being—paired with a specific moral agenda. Dr. John Harvey Kellogg, who gave his name to the Kellogg cereal brand, co-developed cereal to suppress sexual desire and prevent people from masturbating—which Kellogg believed was "the most dangerous of all sexual abuses." In his book *Plain Facts for Old and Young*, Kellogg wrote that flavorful foods have "an undoubted influence upon the sexual nature of boys, stimulating those organs into too early activity, and occasioning temptations to sin which otherwise would not occur."[6]

To curtail this rampant immorality, Americans needed a more bland breakfast.

And that's how cornflakes were born.

More than 75 years have passed since the marketing campaign that cemented breakfast as the most important meal of the day. And the same adage continues to be repeated and retweeted as if it were breaking news.

Repetition breeds false confidence. "A lie told once remains a lie, but a lie told a thousand times becomes the truth," as the popular saying goes. If you repeatedly hear that bats are blind, or that we use only 10 percent of our brains, or that breakfast is the most important meal of the day, you'll tend to believe it's true.

These long-standing myths continue to be repeated even when scientific evidence disprove them. Bats aren't blind. In fact, some species of bats see better than the average human.[7] And the 10 percent figure about the brain "is so wrong it is almost laughable," notes neurologist Barry Gordon. Over the course of a day we use virtually 100 percent of our brains.[8]

In the case of breakfast, however, there appears to be a scientific basis for its claim to fame as the most important meal. A 2019 study published in the *Journal of the American College of Cardiology* found that skipping breakfast "significantly increased risk of mortality from cardiovascular disease."[9] Here's a sample of the news headlines that reported the study:

- "Eating Breakfast Every Morning May Be Better for Your Heart" (*Healthline*) (This article has a reassuring "Fact Checked" label at the top.)[10]

- "Eating Breakfast? Skipping a Morning Meal Has Higher Risk of Heart-Related Death, Study Says" (*USA Today*)[11]

- "Study: Skipping Breakfast Increases Risk of Heart Disease Mortality by 87 Percent" (FOX 11 Los Angeles)[12]

- "Skipping Breakfast a Bad Move for Your Heart?" (WebMD)[13]

Maybe you should eat those cornflakes after all?

Not so fast. An association between two things—skipping breakfast and risk of heart disease—doesn't mean one is responsible for the other. Put differently, correlation isn't causation.

Here are a few ridiculous examples to illustrate the point. There's a correlation between the number of films Nicolas Cage appears in and the number of people who drown by falling into a pool.[14] There's also a correlation between the consumption of margarine and the divorce rate in Maine. But this doesn't mean Cage movies *cause* people to drown, or that the consumption of margarine is bad for relationships in Maine. There may be good reasons to stop eating margarine or watching Cage movies, but preventing divorces or drownings isn't one of them. In both cases, other factors are responsible for the results.

Back to the breakfast study.

It turns out that people who skipped breakfast also engaged in all sorts of unhealthy behaviors, any one of which could have caused heart disease. As the breakfast study researchers acknowledged, the participants who didn't eat breakfast were more likely to be "former smokers, heavy drinkers, unmarried, physically inactive, and with less family income, lower total energy intake, and poorer dietary quality, when compared with those who regularly ate breakfast." In other words, the breakfast skippers may have gotten heart disease because they smoked too much or drank too much or didn't exercise—not because they skipped breakfast. Although the study tried to control for some of these variables, "it's extremely difficult (actually it's impossible) to accurately and appropriately adjust for what amounts to fundamentally different people," explained Dr. Peter Attia, who first critiqued the study.[15]

Yet the headlines morphed correlation into causation and distorted these scientific claims for public consumption. Why? Correlation doesn't sell newspapers. Confidence does. Sensational headlines draw more clicks and retweets. In a world that demands instant gratification, we just want the conclusion, the life hack, the silver bullet—without the nuances that complicate, well, everything. Instead of explaining the nuances and limitations of the study, the media doled out prescriptive advice: *Eat breakfast or risk heart disease.*

Sensationalist articles like these then quickly spread from one media outlet to another. When people see the same information repeated across different venues, their confidence in its accuracy increases. What's more, their friends also read the same sources, so there's no one to dispute their perspective. This quickly leads to a flawed consensus.

Fact-checking doesn't solve the problem. For starters, most publishers depend on writers to fact-check their own work. If the material is fact-checked at all, the process is often used to catch the most obvious mistakes—such as dates, names of people, and libelous claims that could result in a costly lawsuit.

Sometimes, particularly with a deadline looming, fact-checking ends up being sloppy. I once picked up a book that spent several weeks at number one on the *New York Times* best-seller list that repeated as fact the laughably wrong cliché that we use only 10 percent of our brains.

What's more, fact-checking isn't necessarily objective. Fact-checkers and journalists are human beings who live in the real world. Like the rest of us, they bring their own political and ideological biases into the process. Liberal sources tend to scrutinize the right, and conservative sources tend to scrutinize the left—while cutting their own tribe serious slack.

Most of us can't take the time to read and digest scientific studies that concern every aspect of our lives. And even if we read the study, we may not know what to look for or what to ask.

So we turn to the opinions of experts. Unfortunately, the internet is chock-full of supposed experts who claim to have discovered the truth. On the internet, expertise has become a self-proclaimed qualification. Experts become experts by calling themselves that.

News outlets desperate for attention resort to a trusted roster of "experts" who favor consistency over accuracy and confidence over nuance.

In the face of rampant misinformation, who do we trust? How do we detect misleading information and separate the useful from the useless?

All great thinkers must have what Ernest Hemingway called a built-in, shockproof crap detector.[16] In the next section, I'll share the crap-detecting process I follow. This is my process—which means it's not the right one for everyone. Take what works for you and modify or leave out the rest. And don't treat this like an intellectual hygiene protocol—sterile and boring. Instead, treat it like a fun puzzle. The goal is to question what you read with curious skepticism and discover gems buried under outdated conventional wisdom.

## Built-in, shockproof crap detector

*Exercise skeptical curiosity.* What are the supporting facts? Where did the author get these facts? Beware of sentences that begin with "Science says" or "Research shows" and that end with no citations. Filter out low-quality citations (and yes, by low quality I mean that "8 Surprising Superfoods You Should Eat Every Day for a Long Life" article that tops your Google search results).

Ask yourself, *If I were speaking with the author, what questions would I ask? If I were debating the author, what points would I raise?* Some questions for the authors of the breakfast study might include: What does it mean to "skip" breakfast? If someone doesn't have breakfast until noon, does that count as skipping? What did the participants eat, and how might that have affected the rates of heart disease?

*Watch out for sources that speak in absolutes.* Scientific facts exist on a spectrum of truth. When scientists make statements, "the question is not whether it is true or false but rather how likely it is to be true or false," as Richard Feynman explains.[17] Beware of never-in-doubt experts who attempt to drown all uncertainty with a flood of confidence and exaggerated hand gestures. Beware of one-size-fits-all claims ("Breakfast is the most important meal for everyone" or "Meditation is a universal remedy"). Beware of authors who don't acknowledge the limitations of their arguments, add nuance to their claims, or address studies that call their conclusions into question.

*Watch out for sources that use clichés or speak in generalities.* Here's an example from a company shareholder letter: "Our talented people, global presence, financial strength and massive market knowledge have created our sustainable and unique businesses."[18] That's a whole lot of *nothing*. What makes the people talented? In what ways is the company's market knowledge massive? What exactly does "financial strength" mean? In what way are its businesses unique?[19]

Generalities like these are often used to cover up gaps. That was the case for Kenneth Lay and Jeffrey Skilling, the Enron executives who wrote the above sentence in 2000—the year before the company went bankrupt and Lay and Skilling later found themselves indicted for federal crimes.

*Does the author have a vested interest in the outcome?* Are they promoting a product they've invested in—like a cereal brand touting the virtues of breakfast or an internet doctor peddling his own "health tonic"?

Medical research, for example, is often sponsored by pharmaceutical companies. Take the *New England Journal of Medicine*, one of the most prestigious medical journals in the world. Of the 73 studies of new drugs published by the *Journal* over a yearlong period, "60 were funded by a pharmaceutical company, 50 were co-written by drug company employees and 37 had a lead author, typically an academic, who had previously accepted outside compensation from the sponsoring drug company in the form of consultant pay, grants or speaker fees."[20]

Conflicts of interest aren't confined to academia. They're also found in government organizations. Consider, for example, the US National Cholesterol Education Program, which creates official guidelines for target cholesterol levels. In 2008, eight out of the nine members serving on the panel responsible for creating those guidelines had direct ties to statin manufacturers—who stood to make a handsome profit if the panel set lower target cholesterol levels.[21]

These ties don't necessarily influence results. But people tend to be reluctant to bite the hand that feeds them. As Upton Sinclair famously said, "It is difficult to get a man to understand something, when his salary depends upon his not understanding it."[22]

*Beware of relative risk values.* The breakfast study reported that skipping breakfast increases the risk of heart disease mortality by 87 percent. Sounds huge! But the raw numbers tell a very different story. Among the breakfast eaters, 415 out of 3,862 died from heart disease (10.7 percent). Among the breakfast skippers, 41 out of 336 died from heart disease (12.2 percent). The media reporting of a *relative* risk reduction of 87 percent blows out of proportion what's in fact a much smaller *absolute* risk reduction (1.5 percent).[23] Mark Twain had it right: "There are three kinds of lies: lies, damned lies and statistics."[24]

*Who disagrees with these arguments?* Many sources present only one perspective on an issue. For example, none of the news articles cited earlier that reported the breakfast study mentioned any counterarguments. You need sources that present multiple perspectives, which can mitigate the creation of false beliefs.

One trick is to research the opposite of the claim you're checking (after doing your own thinking). Instead of researching "breakfast is the most important meal of the day," or even a question like "Is breakfast the most important meal of the day?," search for "breakfast is *not* the most important meal of the day." The results will give you some missing perspectives.

*Don't fool yourself.* Do you want to believe what you're reading? If so, be careful. Be *very* careful. If you enjoy eating breakfast every day, you're more likely to believe it's the most important meal of the day—and to disregard any arguments to the contrary. If something jives with what we believe, we subconsciously activate our confirmation bias and call it proof. We then call any challenge to our belief system fake news.

In the end, André Gide had it right: "Believe those who are seeking the truth; doubt those who find it."

Seeking the truth is a continuous process. It won't generate any immediate answers. In many cases, you'll find conflicting conclusions and greater uncertainty about the answers.

But it's better to be uncomfortably uncertain than to be comfortably wrong.

## The truth is a living thing

"Smoking or nonsmoking?"

This could have been a question from a maître d' at a European restaurant.

But it wasn't. The year was 1999, and my parents and I were checking in for a Turkish Airlines flight.

*Smoking or nonsmoking?*

My parents picked the nonsmoking section. Wise choice, I thought.

Two things then revealed themselves in rapid succession. First, smoke doesn't remain stationary. It moves. Second, smoke moves particularly fast on an airplane designed to create a continuous circulation of air.

Airline smoking protocols seem ridiculous to us now. How did we possibly think it was a good idea to allow smoking on flights—as recently as 20 years ago? Setting aside the immense amount of secondhand smoke imposed on travelers seated in the nonsmoking section, an in-flight fire started by someone lighting up a cigarette could be unhealthy for everyone on board.

Let's go back even further.

In the early 20th century, doctors and dentists were some of Big Tobacco's most enthusiastic salespeople, endorsing cigarettes to help with digestion, physical fitness, and stress. "Leading nose and throat specialists suggest Philip Morris," read one ad. "More doctors smoke Camels than any other cigarette!" read another.[25] (Take that, Trident!)

Many of today's controlled substances were once common household items. As Ayelet Waldman writes, "Up through the early twentieth century, opioids and cocaine were readily available and frequently used. The Sears Roebuck catalogue, the amazon.com of the time, featured kits with syringes and vials of heroin or cocaine, complete with handy-dandy carrying cases. . . . In fact, it wasn't until 1929 that Coca-Cola became free of [cocaine], thereafter relying solely on caffeine to invigorate its customers."[26]

Consider also the theory of continental drift—which says that continents were one big mass that broke up into smaller masses that drifted apart over time. The theory is the brainchild of Alfred Wegener, a meteorologist and an outsider to geology. When Wegener first proposed the theory—which bucked the established wisdom of the day—he was ridiculed by geological experts, who assumed that continents were stable and didn't move. They accused Wegener of peddling pseudoscience through his "delirious ravings" and "moving crust disease and wandering pole plague."[27] The prominent American geologist Rollin Thomas Chamberlin refused to even consider it. To believe Wegener's theory, he wrote, "we must forget everything which has been learned in the past 70 years and start all over again."[28]

That's how science works, Rollin. Over time "the untrue becomes true, the true untrue," as the Russian painter Wassily Kandinsky put it.[29] Some see this natural rhythm as a reason to distrust science, but I see it as a reason to embrace it.

Embracing science doesn't mean treating it as dogma. Those who claim to speak in the name of science can be some of its most damaging enemies. I cringe every time I hear someone say, "Because science says so." This is a form of intellectual tyranny—a way of shutting down curious skepticism rather than igniting it.

There's no science with a capital S. Science is not a set of perfectly known and immovable facts. Facts, like continents, drift over time. What we're told this year may change next year. Even after a theory gains acceptance, new facts often emerge that require the refinement or complete abandonment of the status quo. This is why the biggest rewards in science, like the Nobel Prize, are handed out to those who can successfully move facts and disprove established theories.

Science, as Carl Sagan put it, "is a way of thinking much more than it is a body of knowledge."[30] It's a process of curious skepticism, a doctrine of doubt, a method of discovering the truth—not the truth itself.

In science, we decide whether something is true or false based on research, not on authority. It doesn't matter how many titles follow your name. It doesn't matter how many Ivy League credentials you hold. It doesn't matter that you're triple board-certified. You're still subject to the same scientific process. You must show your work, prove your case, and let others attempt to replicate and disprove your conclusions.

Richard Feynman once received a letter from an undergraduate student who got an answer wrong on a physics exam.[31] Her answer was based on a statement she found in a textbook authored by Feynman, so she wrote a letter to him. Feynman wrote back admitting that he made a mistake: "I am not sure how I did it, but I goofed." Then he added: "And you goofed, too, for believing me."

Feynman's point was simple: Don't accept anything as true simply because you read it in a textbook—even if the author was Feynman himself. Your responsibility as a learner includes questioning what you read, not simply regurgitating it. "Science," Feynman said in a 1966 address, "is the belief in the ignorance of experts."[32] He warned of the "danger of belief in the infallibility of the greatest teachers of the preceding generation."

This isn't anti-intellectualism or an assault on reason. Ignorance is not a virtue. But when we completely outsource our civic responsibility to the authorities, when we don't bother to evaluate the evidence or arm ourselves with facts and nuance, we disempower ourselves. Our critical-thinking muscles atrophy over time from disuse.

No one has a monopoly on science. Science is a process, not a profession. Scientific inquiry doesn't take place only in laboratories. It's not confined to lecture halls. It's not limited to those who hold the right pedigree. The only requirement is a nimble mind willing to exercise skeptical curiosity toward all ideas—especially your own.

The pseudoscientist focuses on proving himself right, instead of finding what's right. He denies ideas without objectively considering them. He thinks everything is settled, once and for all. He has no laboratory, no place where his ideas can be tested, and no hypotheses that can be falsified by others.

You don't find pseudoscientists only on obscure YouTube channels. Every politician who refuses to hear dissent is a pseudoscientist. Every CEO who believes disagreement is disloyal is a pseudoscientist. Every person who's unwilling to change their mind even in the face of conflicting evidence is a pseudoscientist.

Consistency is not a virtue in science. Self-confirmation leads to self-deception. I haven't really learned a subject until I've changed my mind about it at least once. If you're still regurgitating what you learned five years ago—or even last year—it's time to pause and reflect. As Timothy Leary purportedly said, "You are only as young as the last time you changed your mind."

This isn't just about being open to changing your mind. It's about being eager to do so. Eagerness means you prod and poke at your ideas. It means you search for information that proves yourself wrong. It means you don't feel bad when you find yourself in error. You actually feel good about it.

This should feel liberating. You don't need to waste mental energy on protecting your ego or fooling yourself by continuing to be wrong going forward. You get to act like a curious scientist and experience the delight of finding the unexpected.

The truth is a living thing. It doesn't have a final resting place. Some of the truths you now hold dear will turn out to be wrong.

Do you want to know what those wrong answers are? Or do you want to be validated?

You can't have both.

## Yes, there are stupid questions

When I first became a professor, I'd pause from time to time during class and ask, "Does anyone have a question?"

Nine times out of ten, no one would raise their hand. I'd move on, confident that I'd done a stellar job of explaining the material.

I was wrong. The exam answers made it clear that there were plenty of students who weren't getting it.

So I decided to run an experiment. Instead of asking, "Does anyone have any questions?," I began to say, "I'll now take your questions," or even better, "The material we just covered was confusing, and I'm confident there are plenty of you with questions. This is a great time to ask them."

The number of hands that went up increased dramatically.

I realized that "Does anyone have any questions?" was a stupid question. I had forgotten how hard it is for students who pride themselves on their intellectual powers to admit that they didn't understand something in front of a crowd of their peers.

My reframed question made it easier for students to raise their hands. It made it clear that the material was difficult and I expected questions. With this reframing, my desired outcome (more questions from students) became the norm, not the exception.

We ask stupid questions all the time outside the classroom.

If you ask a new employee, "Everything going well so far?," you're not really asking for their opinion. You're making a statement: What you really mean is, "I trust everything is going well." In most cases, this "question" will produce a response from the new hire that parrots your assumption instead of revealing how they really feel.

If you ask a team member, "Are you facing any challenges?," most will say no. They might fear that their admission will be seen as a weakness. You're more likely to get an honest response if you ask: "What challenges are you facing right now?" That question presumes that challenges are the norm, not the exception.

Research supports this approach. In one Wharton study (cleverly titled "There Is Such a Thing as a Stupid Question"), participants were asked to play the role of a salesperson selling an iPod.[33] They were told the iPod had crashed twice in the past, wiping out all the music stored in it. The researchers were curious about what types of questions in a role-played negotiation would lead the sellers to come clean about the problem. They tried three different questions from potential buyers.

"What can you tell me about it?" prompted only 8 percent of the sellers to disclose the problem.

"It doesn't have any problems, does it?" increased the disclosure to 61 percent.

"What problems does it have?" led 89 percent of the sellers to disclose the crashing issue. Unlike the others, that question presumed that there were problems with the iPod and led the sellers to open up.

Werner Heisenberg, the brains behind the uncertainty principle in quantum mechanics, had it right: "What we observe is not nature itself, but nature exposed to our method of questioning."[34]

When we reframe a question—when we change our method of questioning—we also change the outcome.

## Live the questions

I wanted to drop what I was doing, stand up on the podium, and applaud her in front of 90 students. At the time, I was teaching a constitutional law class in a big lecture hall. As we were discussing the intricacies of the Commerce Clause, a hand shot up in the air.

"I didn't get anything from that," the student said, with visible trepidation. "I'm completely lost."

I wanted to give her a standing ovation.

This was an act of courage. She did what most of us don't dare do: admit that we don't know or we don't understand.

This was an act of humility. When we utter those three dreaded words—I don't know—our ego deflates, our mind opens, and our ears perk up.

This was also an act of compassion. By raising her hand, she was standing up not only for herself, but also for her fellow students who were just as confused as she was.

Many of us already feel inadequate in life, and admitting our ignorance seems to confirm that fact publicly. Instead of acknowledging that we don't know, we pretend to know. We smile, nod, and bluff our way through a makeshift answer.

This response is in part a relic of our education system. If you wrote "I don't know" on an exam, you'd fail. In school, we were led to believe that "all questions have answers, and it is a good thing to give an answer even if there is none to give, even if you don't understand the question, even if the question contains erroneous assumptions, even if you are ignorant of the facts required to answer," as Neil Postman writes.[35]

"Quick on your feet" is one of the highest compliments of intellectual achievement. But speed doesn't equal credibility, and confidence doesn't equal expertise.

Malcolm Gladwell traces his inquisitive nature to his father's intellectual humility:

> My father has zero intellectual insecurities. . . . It has never crossed his mind to be concerned that the world thinks he's an idiot. He's not in that game. So if he doesn't understand something, he just asks you. He doesn't care if he sounds foolish. [If my father had met Bernie Madoff, he] never would have invested money with him because he would have said, "I don't understand" a hundred times. "I don't understand how that works," in this kind of dumb, slow voice.[36]

Even though his questions might have made Gladwell's father appear foolish, the questions themselves weren't foolish. For Gladwell's father, "I don't understand" didn't mean "I don't want to understand." As Isaac Asimov writes, "Uncertainty that comes from knowledge (knowing what you don't know) is different from uncertainty coming from ignorance."[37] Don't turn into the cardinal from the play *Galileo*, who refuses to look through a telescope to avoid finding out that the planets revolve around the Sun.

And remember: The goal of asking a question isn't to find an answer as fast as possible. Some questions shouldn't go away.

Their job is to linger with you, to unmake you, and to work you from the inside out.

*Are you, you?*

*Is this the life you want to live?*

*If you were to die tomorrow, what would you regret not doing?*

Can you be patient with these questions—and not rush to the answers? Saying "I don't know" allows transformative questions like these to stay with you—and gives them the time they need to be the teacher that they are.

"Live the questions now," as Rainer Maria Rilke put it. "Perhaps you will then gradually, without noticing it, live along some distant day into the answer."

10

# Look Where
# Others Don't Look

*If you're not inspired by life, you're not paying*
*attention.*

—IN-Q, "ALL TOGETHER"

## The tyranny of the obvious

On November 24, 1963, Clifton Pollard woke up at 9 am.[1] It was a Sunday, but he knew he would probably need to go in to work.

His wife cooked him breakfast—bacon and eggs—but a phone call interrupted the meal. It was Pollard's supervisor from work— a call that he had been expecting.

"Polly," his supervisor said, "could you please be here by eleven o'clock this morning? I guess you know what it's for."

He knew exactly what it was for. He quickly finished breakfast and left his apartment. He then went to the Arlington National Cemetery, where he spent the day digging a grave for President John F. Kennedy.

JFK's assassination had made headlines across the globe. Who was Lee Harvey Oswald? Why didn't Jackie Kennedy take off her blood-stained pink suit for the rest of the day? What role did communists play in the plot? What would Lyndon B. Johnson do as president?

For most journalists, these were the obvious questions to pursue.

But one journalist thought better than to ask the obvious. Jimmy Breslin was a college dropout turned newspaper columnist. He had a knack for looking where others don't look and spotting nonobvious perspectives.

On the day of JFK's funeral, Breslin went to the White House like most other journalists reporting the assassination. There were thousands of reporters there, all being fed the same narrative from the official mouthpiece of the executive branch. "I can't make a living here," he thought to himself. "Everybody's gonna have the same thing."

So he decided to leave the White House and go across the river to Arlington National Cemetery. There he found Pollard the grave-digger. He interviewed him and wrote a column telling the story of the assassination from the perspective of the man who prepared JFK's final resting place. From this unique angle, Breslin crafted a masterful story that stood out from the flood of nearly identical news stories coming to nearly identical conclusions.

"He was a good man," Pollard said, referring to JFK. "Now they're going to come and put him right here in this grave I'm making up. You know, it's an honor just for me to do this," he added.

Pollard didn't get to attend JFK's funeral. When the procession began, he was already hard at work in another part of the cemetery, digging graves for $3.01 per hour and preparing them for their future occupants. (Pollard himself later became one of those occupants: He was buried at Arlington National Cemetery about 100 steps away from the grave he dug for JFK.)

The column about JFK's gravedigger became a signature piece for Breslin. His knack for spotting the nonobvious made him a household name. He went on to win the Pulitzer Prize and host *Saturday Night Live*.

Talent hits a target no one else can hit, but genius hits a target no one else can see, to paraphrase the philosopher Arthur Schopenhauer.[2] The best thinkers look for inspiration in unconventional places. They intentionally step outside their version of the White House press briefing room and seek their version of the cemetery.

Until 1970, suitcases were missing an ancient invention: wheels.[3] People had to physically lug their monstrous bags from car to terminal to airplane to destination. Wheels were ubiquitous on other objects, but no one thought to attach them to suitcases until Bernard Sadow came along. Inspired by the sight of a worker using a wheeled skid to roll a heavy machine, he decided to do the same for baggage. And the wheeled luggage was born.

Consider the birth of Netflix.[4] Back in 1997, Netflix cofounder Reed Hastings was a software developer. He had racked up a big late fee when he misplaced a copy of *Apollo 13*. On his way to the gym, Hastings had an epiphany. His gym, like most other gyms, used a subscription model. "You could pay $30 or $40 a month and work out as little or as much as you wanted," he recalls. That epiphany was the seed that created Netflix.

Don't just look *where* no one else is looking. Also look *how* no one else is looking. There were other people who knew wheels can help move heavy objects and other people who knew about the subscription model prevalent in the fitness industry. But none of them saw the same utility that Sadow and Hastings did. They saw what others missed in part because they weren't just passive observers of the world. They were actively asking themselves how ideas from one field could be relevant in an entirely different one. "Knowing how to look is a way of inventing," as Salvador Dalí put it.[5]

To find nonobvious ideas, search for the extraordinary in the seemingly ordinary. Life is filled with sources of inspiration, but we're too busy spending all our time in our own version of the White House press briefing room to notice them. Leave the briefing room and engage with the world. Find your version of the gravedigger that everyone else is ignoring.

Every single person you meet is your teacher. Unfamiliar people embody unfamiliar wisdom. They know something interesting that you don't, and it's never obvious what that is. Search for it. Treat it like a game of hide-and-seek. Skip the small talk and try some of these questions: "What's one thing that's been exciting you lately?" "What's an unusual hobby or interest that you have?" "What's the most interesting thing you're working on right now?" (*I'm digging JFK's grave.*)

It's only in the unconventional places that you'll find the connections—and ultimately the targets—that no one else can see.

## The tyranny of the convenient

*Think for yourself, or others will think for you*
*without thinking of you.*
—UNKNOWN

These days, we're assaulted with suggestions for media consumption tailored for maximum appeal by sophisticated algorithms.

Instead of broadening our horizons, these algorithms cater to our supposed preferences. We can dig around for other options, but our time and energy are limited. Instead, we jump right into the "most popular" list on Netflix and start bingeing *Tiger King*. Over time the breadth of our inputs dwindles and our intellectual vista narrows.

We often don't even have to decide what to consume next. Our streaming services take that burden off our shoulders by automatically queuing up a new show that the algorithms think we'll love. Hello, *Indian Matchmaking*.

These algorithms don't care about quality. They only care about your attention—getting it and retaining it. Some of the best minds of our generation spend most of their time ensuring that you keep watching, keep clicking, and keep refreshing.

Algorithms don't just report trends. They also create them. They generate a customized reality for you that affects not just how you see the world but also how you see yourself. By prioritizing certain more profitable suggestions over others—by deciding what song, movie, book, or podcast to put on the front page—they shape what you see, what you read, and what you pay attention to.

The price we pay for this convenience is our freedom to choose. We're being intellectually imprisoned, but we're not even aware of it.

Our imprisonment goes beyond algorithms to every convenient shortcut. In the face of an overwhelming deluge of content, we turn to top-10 lists, best-sellers, and blockbusters. We look for what's hot—the hottest stock, the hottest job, the hottest cryptocurrency. We assume that popularity indicates quality—something that's in demand must be better than something that's not in demand.

But popular doesn't mean better. Popular simply means the majority prefers that thing over something else.

In many cases, it's not even the majority that determines what's popular. Publishers predetermine which books have a good chance of success before they hit the stands, spend marketing dollars on those books, and make sure they're displayed front and center in your local bookstore. Record companies preordain which songs get the most radio play, leaving little choice to the DJ. When you search for media online, algorithms primarily show you books, movies, and albums that are already selling well, so more people buy them and they sell even better.

The result is a vicious cycle. "Best sellers sell the best because they are best sellers," as journalist Alexandra Alter puts it.[6]

Newspapers operate in a similar way. They closely track which articles are being read and shared and which ones prompt people to purchase a subscription.[7] Articles that are less popular get sidelined in favor of those with a higher click-through rate—or CTR, in industry lingo. Andrew Gorham, a former editor for one of Canada's most popular newspapers, *The Globe and Mail*, explains the prevailing approach: "You're looking at your analytics and you're saying, Holy shit, this story's got a high CTR, let's move it forward. Surface it—share it on Facebook, put it on the home page, release a news alert, put it in the newsletter." He adds, "If we don't juice it, it just evaporates."

This ruthless juicing of the popular comes at a serious cost. Life turns into a middle school popularity contest that makes the popular kids even more popular. The more we are exposed to what's popular, the more skewed our reality becomes. Unpopular arguments that challenge conventional narratives all too easily disappear from discourse. Independent journalists get demonetized. Authors without big platforms have a hard time getting a book deal.

By the time an idea becomes popular, it's no longer scarce. You see the same idea, the same story, the same one-liner regurgitated—with a different clickbait headline—on every platform to maximize the number of clicks and eyeballs. Popular ideas spread like fashion until you see the same T-shirt on every corner. This is why best-selling books have now become fashion statements. People sometimes buy a book, not to read it, but to convey the message that they're the type of person who buys that type of book. The book then becomes bookshelf décor.

To paraphrase Haruki Murakami, if you consume what everyone else is consuming, you'll think what everyone else is thinking. If you head over to the White House with a thousand other journalists to get the same answers to the same questions, you'll write the same story as everyone else.

Extraordinary ideas often grow out of overlooked ideas. And overlooked ideas don't make a grand appearance on the front page of the *New York Times*. (If they did, they wouldn't be overlooked.) If you want to stand out from other chefs, you need to either cook with different ingredients or combine them in a way they haven't been combined before.

Escaping the tyranny of the convenient doesn't require drastic changes. You don't have to put on a beret, listen only to snob-approved music, or watch only art-house cinema. (*It's got subtitles. It must be art.*) It simply requires being intentional about what you consume—and making your own choices instead of letting others choose for you.

This, in turn, requires you to answer simple questions that most algorithm-nurtured people find exceedingly difficult to answer: *What do I actually want to learn? What am I—not other people—interested in?*

Once you've figured out what you want to learn, turn to less flashy sources of information. Search for groundbreaking ideas that have yet to break through. Academic papers on the cutting edge. Scientific findings still in need of a champion. Movies that have fallen out of mainstream awareness. Once-influential books now out of print—the type of books you can find only in libraries and used bookstores, not on Kindle Unlimited.

Have you always wanted to learn more about country music? Ken Burns has an excellent documentary about that. Do you want to learn more about the creative process of filmmaking? Watch *The Director's Chair*, where director Robert Rodriguez interviews filmmakers about their craft. It's one of my favorite shows of all time, but you've probably never heard of it because it airs on an obscure television network called El Rey.

Walk into an independent bookstore, skip the best-sellers section, and follow the trail of curiosity and serendipity to find your next read. Pick random books from the shelves, skim through them, and buy the ones that jump out at you.

Follow independent journalists publishing on Substack.

Go to a newsstand and buy a magazine you've never bought before.

Yes, these actions are inconvenient. But it's only through the inconvenient that you'll find diverse inputs that will expand your thinking and spur your imagination.

## The tyranny of the new

In 2019, Instagram dropped a bombshell. It announced that it would experiment with hiding "like counts."[8] Users would no longer see the little heart-shaped indicator that displays how many people liked their latest selfie.

The reason for the change? To create "a space that feels much less pressurized," Adam Mosseri, the head of Instagram, explained. "We don't want Instagram to feel like a competition." On a less altruistic level, the move would also encourage more people to post more frequently on Instagram by reducing the pressure to maximize likes for each post—thereby increasing daily activity among potential sources of revenue.

Unhappy barely begins to describe the reaction of many Instagram influencers to this news. For an influencer, likes are money. It's the outward display of likes that makes an influencer attractive to brands for sponsorship deals. And this experiment would conceal that display.

The announcement brought many Instagram influencers to the brink of despair. They threatened to boycott Instagram and posted angry videos of themselves (ironically, on Instagram). "I've put my blood sweat and tears into this for it to be ripped away," one Melbourne-based influencer wrote. "It's not just me suffering too, it's every brand and business I know."[9]

When you sign up for a platform like Instagram, you make a Faustian bargain. In exchange for a snazzy design and a convenient audience that frequents the platform at all hours of the day, you agree to relinquish all control to an intermediary. This intermediary can unilaterally change policies, hide like counts, and generally do whatever it wants—even if it puts an end to your business or influence.

We're highly attuned to what's new. From an evolutionary perspective, this makes sense. Changes in our environment can indicate a potential threat. This is why you'll immediately notice a sketchy white van parked in front of your house but ignore the familiar tree you've walked by a thousand times.

Many people assume that progress requires embracing the new: "Build your following on Twitter! That's where all the action is." "Make sure you sign up for Clubhouse and drop some wisdom bombs." "You can't afford not to be on Snapchat." "Facebook and Instagram are dead. TikTok is where it's at."

What's new is visible, and what's visible is largely assumed to be effective. But social media rarely makes people famous. It reflects how famous they already are.

And new often doesn't last. Of the 95 million photos and videos posted every day on Instagram and the 500 million tweets shared every day, how many linger beyond a fraction of a second?[10] We look, like, and promptly forget. And yet, we keep chasing these fleeting ideas that have the shortest of lives.

What's hot today turns cold tomorrow. If you let the latest fad dictate what you do, your work will have a short expiration date. There's tremendous value in investing in things that age well.

I call this the George Clooney effect: For some things in life, aging is more of an asset than a liability.

This is a mantra that Amazon's Jeff Bezos lives by. "I very frequently get the question: 'What's going to change in the next 10 years?'" he observed. "I almost never get the question: 'What's not going to change in the next 10 years?'"[11] It makes more sense to invest in what's *not* going to change—what people will still care about and will still use even 10 years from now.

Back in 2016, when I started my own online platform, I asked myself the same question: What's *not* going to change? It was tempting to invest my time in building a social-media following. After all, social media is very public, and people tend to equate likes and followers with popularity. It's also exponentially easier to get a new follower on social media than it is to get the same person's email address.

Forgoing the ease and visibility of social media, I decided instead to launch a blog and invest in growing an email list. I host this blog on my *own* website—and not on a third-party platform like Medium. I send a weekly newsletter to my own email list—and don't allow an intermediary to dictate the terms of my relationship with my audience (or worse, take it away altogether).

Here's the thing: The services I use to host my platform—primarily the web and email—aren't going anywhere anytime soon. Both have been popular since the 1990s. American users are quitting Facebook by the millions, but no one is quitting email.[12]

Some of today's hottest services might feel like permanent fixtures, but they're not. Remember Friendster, AOL Instant Messenger, Myspace, or Vine? All these services were huge—until they weren't. Now we can hardly recall why people were so entranced by them.

The here-today-gone-tomorrow nature of these technologies and their fickle business models make them poor candidates for an all-in investment. You can still use them as long as you diversify your investments and invest primarily in services that have stood the test of time. But relying entirely on Instagram to access your followers is the social-media equivalent of investing all your money in a single stock. You're courting catastrophe.

There's another false assumption that attracts us to the new: For an idea to be "innovative," to use that buzzword, it must be new. When I first started writing, this assumption was paralyzing. Whenever I thought I'd come up with a "new" idea, I'd eventually discover that someone else had already written about it. I'd scrap the idea and go back to searching for that elusive originality unicorn (which vanished the moment I thought I spotted it).

But original doesn't mean new. "It's not where you take things from—it's where you take them to," as Jean-Luc Godard says.[13] Once you put your own take on existing ideas—once you bring your own quirky perspective to them—they will be original. No one can look at the world through your two eyes. "Write one true sentence" was Ernest Hemingway's remedy for writer's block.[14] It's also the key to finding your voice. If you speak your truth—if you share what you *really* see, feel, and think—it will be uniquely yours.

You've heard the term *déjà vu*—being in a strange place or circumstance yet feeling like it's familiar, like you've been there before. There's also the reverse, *jamais vu*—seeing something familiar but experiencing it in a new way.

*Jamais vu* is key to creativity. Many original ideas come from looking backward for inspiration and finding the new in the old— from seeing something in a way that others haven't. Older works of art "stand against the conventional wisdom of today simply because they're not *from* today," as William Deresiewicz says.[15] Older books, for example, will give a different perspective on a topic than the hottest read in the best-sellers section. So instead of reading the newest book on evolution, pick up Charles Darwin's *On the Origin of Species*. You'll find insights that others have missed because they're focused on what's shiny and new.

Looking backward also means rereading books you've read in the past. Rereading is not a waste of time. Every time I return to a book, it's a new person reading it. The book hasn't changed. But I have changed. I pick up on subtleties that I missed the first time around, and ideas become relevant because of where I am now in life.

So don't just ask, "What's new?" Also ask, "What's old? What will still be around 10 years from now?"

If your goal is to create ideas that last, remember the George Clooney effect: Focus on things that age well.

## The tyranny of sound bites

Robert Frost's "The Road Not Taken" is one of the most popular poems of all time. If the title doesn't ring a bell, the last stanza should:

> *I shall be telling this with a sigh*
> *Somewhere ages and ages hence:*
> *Two roads diverged in a wood, and I—*
> *I took the one less traveled by,*
> *And that has made all the difference.*[16]

This poem is quoted everywhere from bumper stickers to Skymall posters as a testament to individualism and self-determination. We choose our own path—not the path that others choose for us.

What's surprising about the poem isn't its popularity. What's surprising is how a poem this popular can be this misunderstood.

A close inspection of the poem reveals important nuances that are often missed. Earlier in the poem, Frost writes that the foot traffic had worn down the two paths "really about the same." In the next stanza, he writes that the paths "equally lay in leaves no steps had trodden black." In other words, neither path was more or less traveled, and the choices were just about equal. The traveler's hindsight belief that he took the superior, less traveled path is nothing less than self-delusion.

In one of the greatest ironies of all time, a poem that's partially about self-delusion has generated widespread delusion.

I was once part of the problem: I remember selectively quoting the poem in my freshman-year English class, only to be put in my place by a professor who suggested (nicely) that I should first bother to read the poem and give it a moment of thought before quoting it with misguided confidence.

I, like many others, hadn't bothered to read the poem, but chose to quote snappy lines without context. This is how misinformation about the poem—and misinformation in general—often spreads.

Instead of bothering to listen, read, or even skim the facts, we rely on sound bites that inevitably distort the content. Each distortion, once reported and retweeted, gets magnified. We rely on one author's interpretation of another author's interpretation of another author's work—with each level adding its own distortions.

A satirical website once published an article with the following headline: "Study: 70% of Facebook Users Only Read the Headline of Science Stories Before Commenting."[17] What did nearly 200,000 people do? They shared this article on social media, and many of them probably didn't bother to read it. How do we know? Those who bothered to click through to the article would have noticed that the article is fake. There are only two English sentences in it. The rest of the article is paragraph after paragraph of meaningless filler.

Failing to read the full text ignited one of the worst opioid epidemics in American history. In 1980, Dr. Hershel Jick wrote a five-sentence letter to the editor of the *New England Journal of Medicine*.[18] Jick, a doctor at Boston University Medical Center, had a database of hospital records that included information on how many hospitalized patients developed addictions after being treated with pain medication. In the letter, he reported that addictions were rare.

As far as research goes, Jick's report was informal and his findings were narrow—limited to hospitalized patients with no history of addiction. The letter was published in the journal's correspondence section and wasn't peer reviewed. Jick himself didn't think much of the letter, explaining that it was "very near the bottom of a long list of studies that I've done."

The letter initially didn't attract much attention. But then, 10 years after it was published, it took on a life of its own. In 1990, an article published in *Scientific American* cited the five-sentence letter as an "extensive study" to support the proposition that morphine isn't addictive.[19] In 1992, *Time* magazine cited the same five-sentence letter as a "landmark study" that showed that fear of opioid addiction was "basically unwarranted." Purdue Pharma, which manufactures OxyContin, began to cite the letter to assert that fewer than 1 percent of patients treated with opioids became addicted. Based on that assertion, the FDA approved a label for OxyContin that described the development of addiction as "very rare" if used legitimately in pain management.[20]

This game of telephone mutated and grossly misrepresented the findings in Jick's letter. Those findings were based on patients prescribed opioids in a hospital setting for a short amount of time. They had no bearing on long-term use by patients at home. Drug manufacturers used the letter to convince front-line doctors, not only that opioids were safe for chronic pain, but that those who failed to prescribe them were leaving patients in unnecessary agony.

No one bothered to read the letter.

From 1999 until 2015, a reported 183,000 people died from prescription opioid overdose.[21] Millions more became addicted. Jick, the author of the letter, said, "I'm essentially mortified that that letter to the editor was used as an excuse to do what these drug companies did."[22]

The solution?

Read the poem.

And if you didn't read the poem, don't quote the poem.

In a world of clickbait—where most people focus on the title and ignore the content—reading the poem is one of the most subversive things you can do.

It will give you a distinct advantage over all others who don't bother to dig up the original source.

You'll be able to see what others miss.

# 11

# I Am Not Your Guru

*Not I, not any one else can travel that road for you,*
*You must travel it for yourself.*

—WALT WHITMAN, "SONG OF MYSELF"

## How success stories fool us

It's World War II.[1]

You've been tasked with determining how to protect American warplanes flying over enemy territory. The planes are taking serious fire, with some returning home and others crashing and burning. Armor can be added to the warplanes, and your job is to determine where on the plane that extra armor should go.

Here's one relevant fact: In the planes that safely return home, the bullet holes are clustered mostly on the fuselage, not on the engines.

Knowing this information, where would you put the extra armor?

The answer might appear obvious. Put more armor in places that have shown visible damage because that's where the planes appear to be taking the most flak.

But a mathematician named Abraham Wald thought the right approach was the exact opposite. The extra armor, he argued, should go where the bullet holes are missing—not where they are present.

Wald saw something concealed in everyone else's blind spot. He realized they were looking only at the planes that had survived enemy fire and safely returned home—not at the planes that crashed and burned.

In other words, the bullet holes on the surviving planes showed where the planes were strongest, not weakest. After all, these planes could survive having their fuselage turned into Swiss cheese. The most vulnerable part of the plane was the engine, which showed no damage at all on the surviving planes. They weren't seeing any holes through the engines—not because the planes weren't getting shot there—but because the planes that were hit there didn't return home.

So Wald proposed bulking up the armor on the engines. His proposal was quickly implemented with success in World War II. The same approach was also later used in wars in Vietnam and Korea.

This story holds important lessons that extend far beyond warfare. In our daily lives, we focus on success stories—the surviving airplanes—and try to emulate them. In school we're taught best practices based on how others succeeded in the past. Pick a random business book from the nonfiction aisle, and chances are that you'll find a formula for winning the business game by following the lead of today's mega successful entrepreneurs.

Formulas for success satisfy the popular craving for heroes, but they also mislead. We're seeing only the survivors—not the failures who took bullets to their engine and never returned home. The aspiring entrepreneur who moved to Silicon Valley to pursue a start-up only to fail doesn't make the cover of *Fast Company*. The man who tried and failed to lose weight on the Jenny Craig diet doesn't appear on the infomercial. The college dropout who was mesmerized by Branson, Jobs, and Zuckerberg and left behind a promising education only to get stuck in a dead-end job doesn't make the news.

It's also possible that some of these titans became successful despite the path they took, not because of it. Perhaps Steve Jobs would have been even more successful if he hadn't dropped out of Reed College. Perhaps the woman in that fitness commercial has a six-pack, not because of the workout program or supplements she's peddling, but in spite of them. Perhaps the man who put on 20 pounds of muscle in one month by working out once a week has superhuman genes that you lack.

The gatekeepers often show you limited information that leads to one conclusion. They drown you in hard data, stellar testimonials, and references that look convincing but provide only part of the story. Who are the people that took that online course but didn't benefit from it? Who are the people that didn't enjoy working at that company and quit? Who are the references that will give you more accurate information about the job candidate than the references carefully curated to appear on a résumé?

Success stories also discount the role of luck. The pilot may have gotten lucky and never took a bullet in the engine. This is the guy who smokes like a chimney, drinks like a sailor, and still lives to be 95. If you follow his approach—but take one bullet in the wrong place—you'll crash and burn.

Keep in mind: What's called the "industry best practice" isn't necessarily the best practice. It often consists of people putting extra armor in the most obvious spots.

Catch yourself when you're about to be captivated by a success story. Remind yourself that you're not seeing the entire picture. Apply the same scrutiny to the success stories you're reading about in this book.

Above all, don't get distracted by the obvious bullet holes. The vulnerabilities are often hiding under a deceptively untarnished surface.

## Thoreauly misleading

In 1845, Henry David Thoreau made a famous pilgrimage to Walden Pond in Massachusetts to live in a tiny cabin that he built in the woods. He went to the woods "to live deliberately," as he wrote, "to front only the essential facts of life, and see if I could not learn what it had to teach, and not, when I came to die, discover that I had not lived." Thoreau would live like a Spartan and on his own means, with no electricity and no running water. He would "suck out all the marrow of life" and "reduce it to its lowest terms."[2]

Thoreau recorded his experiences in a book called *Walden*, which is assigned in high schools and quoted in Hollywood movies to illustrate the virtues of self-reliance and humankind's connection with nature.

I've envied Thoreau ever since I read about his pilgrimage into the woods. His story reminds me of my own inadequacies. You see, I'm a city boy, raised in the urban sprawl of Istanbul, home to 15 million people. I have the soft, uncalloused hands of a writer. My work injuries consist of paper cuts (they *can* be nasty). If you put me in a cabin by Walden Pond and cut off electricity, running water, and wi-fi, I wouldn't survive. So I admire people like Thoreau who can deliberately expose themselves to rough conditions and thrive.

But my attitude began to change after I read Amanda Palmer's book *The Art of Asking*, where she reveals a few more details about Thoreau's experiment with "self-reliance."[3] It turns out that the cabin Thoreau built was less than two miles from his house—not in some remote woodland, as the story might imply. Almost every day he took trips back to civilization, which was within walking distance in nearby Concord. He regularly had dinner at his buddy Ralph Waldo Emerson's house. My favorite part: Every weekend Thoreau's mother brought him fresh pastries. The historian

Richard Zacks sums it up well: "Let it be known that Nature Boy went home on weekends to raid the family cookie jar."[4]

I don't tell this story to poke fun at Thoreau (okay, maybe a little bit). I tell it because it highlights an important lesson: The people we put on a pedestal often don't live up to their own legend. The best-selling low-carb diet book author shoves his face with foods that make your cheat meals look healthy. (I've seen this firsthand numerous times.) The famous productivity guru wastes an hour every day scrolling through social media.

This doesn't mean their advice is wrong. It means they're human. It also means you take what they say with a grain of salt and remember the African proverb: "Be careful when a naked person offers you a shirt."[5]

Influencers are paid to make their lives appear glamorous—to cover up their bullet holes with social-media spackle. If Thoreau had lived in the age of Instagram, he might have been shooting selfies in front of his self-made cabin while neglecting to snap photos of himself devouring his mother's fresh-baked goods.

This book, for example, represents years of work distilled into roughly 250 pages. The words you're reading didn't just pour out of me. The book went through countless revisions. Most of the bad ideas were thrown out, and the remaining ideas have been polished and repolished by several capable hands.

This is why I get slightly terrified meeting readers in person. There's no way I can live up to your expectations. I'd rather have you meet my far better-looking, smarter, and funnier doppelgänger who lives only on these pages.

Teddy Roosevelt purportedly said, "Comparison is the thief of joy." Comparison does more than that: It also robs your confidence. When we compare ourselves to others, we often come up short. That's because we're comparing ourselves to an illusion—a curated, airbrushed, seemingly perfect version of a deeply imperfect person.

The internet has exacerbated this tendency by reducing the distance between us and our role models. It allows us to track their every movement, constantly reminding ourselves of how we fall short. But what you envy is their social-media feed—which, as shocking as this may sound, is different from their actual life. No one spends that much time looking at impressionist sunsets or sunbathing with models.

Much of what you see on the internet is fake. You can purchase 5,000 Instagram followers for $40 or get 5,000 YouTube views for $15.[6] There are click farms, which are businesses where hundreds of computers and smartphones play the same content over and over to drive up fake engagement.[7] People even post fake sponsored content on social media, pretending to be brand ambassadors without getting paid. Why? "In the influencer world, it's street cred," said one influencer. "The more sponsors you have, the more credibility you have."[8]

If you're hungry for influence or fame, you might be seeing only the doors that it opens and not the doors that it closes. There's a relevant scene in *Miss Americana*, a documentary about Taylor Swift.[9] She's rich, famous, and at the top of her field, having sold over 100 million albums. In the scene, she's begging her team to let her endorse a political candidate in her state. They resist, worried that her endorsement may alienate some of her fans. She eventually breaks down in tears struggling to do something—publicly support a politician—that most people can do without thinking twice.

"I marvel at how unexciting it is to be famous, how mundane famous people are," the tennis champion Andre Agassi writes in his refreshingly raw memoir *Open*. "They're confused, uncertain, insecure, and often hate what they do. It's something we always hear—like that old adage that money can't buy happiness—but we never believe it until we see it for ourselves."[10]

We fall into a trap when we pick only snippets from someone else's life as a basis for comparison. You may want her money, but you probably don't want her grueling 80-hour workweek. You may want to look like him, but you probably don't want the intense diet and workout regimen behind those looks. If you wouldn't want to swap your life *completely* with someone else, there's no need to envy them.

Competition and comparison are a form of conformity.

When we compete with others, we measure ourselves against their metrics. We try to be like them—but better. As a result, our lives turn into a miserable zero-sum game of never-ending one-upmanship. We end up behaving like six-year-olds looking around to see who got more candy. In so doing, we give away our power to others. We let the gap between us and them decide how we feel about ourselves.

I once came across this post from the best-selling novelist Taffy Brodesser-Akner: "I just read a book that's so good I can't get out of bed. Did great books make me feel this terrible before I started [writing] novels? Is writing a competitive sport?"[11] I understand where she's coming from. *My book will never be as good as* _____ is a frighteningly recurring thought for me. But then I remind myself: The author of that book also felt that way about other books. And I'm so glad that feeling didn't stop them from writing their book. And it won't stop me either.

The best way to escape comparison is through authenticity. "Authentic" has become so overused that it has lost much of its meaning. When I say authentic, I mean living a life according to your own metrics, not someone else's. If you're pursuing your own goals—and avoiding ego-driven vanity contests—comparison becomes futile.

In fact, the more unique your life is, the more comparison loses its meaning. If you crave what others also crave, you're more likely to get caught up in a rat race. There are a limited number of rungs on that corporate ladder, so someone else's gain becomes your loss. But if you invent your own ladder—if you're pursuing an idiosyncratic bundle of activities—then it becomes harder to make an apples-to-apples comparison.

I envied Thoreau until I realized I don't want his life. I have no interest in living in a cabin with no running water or heat. Nor do I want mosquito bites, Lyme disease, and poison ivy. The grass around Walden Pond, as elsewhere, is a lot browner than it might seem.

The next time you're tempted to put someone on a pedestal because of the story they tell to the world, just picture Thoreau— not sucking on the marrow of life—but feasting on his mom-made donuts.

## The problem with most advice

Back in 2016, I started thinking about launching a podcast.

At the time, a trusted friend and mentor cautioned me against it. He said, "Please don't start a podcast. Everyone and their cousin is launching one. There are already too many podcasts out there. Do something different instead."

I followed his advice. Instead of launching a podcast, I started a written interview series. I recorded interviews with my guests, transcribed them, edited them down, and published them on my website.

This might sound straightforward. It wasn't.

People speak differently than they write. Good grammar, proper word choice, and other niceties go out the window. Converting these oral conversations into interviews that made sense in a written format required *days* of work. What's more, in publishing the material only as written interviews, I lost countless audience members who would rather have listened to the raw, unedited conversation on their podcast app.

Yet I stuck with the written format because I trusted my mentor's advice. It was only after 15 grueling interviews that I gave up and launched a podcast.

Here's the problem: We give advice like an air traffic controller lands flights—with a strong dose of certainty. "United 135, descend and maintain 10,000." "Ozan, don't start a podcast." We don't even bother to qualify our advice with "Take what I say with a grain of salt" or "Your mileage may vary."

We're led to believe that there's one surefire way to launch a product, one surefire way to set up a business, and one surefire way to create a marketing funnel that's guaranteed to work.

But there is no surefire way to do anything. The myth of the silver bullet is just that—a myth.

Certainty is a virtue when all airplanes must follow a predetermined traffic pattern to land safely. But our traffic patterns in life are all different. What works for one person may not work for another.

Some people should start a podcast, but others shouldn't.

Some people should go to college, but others shouldn't.

Some people need to take more risks, but others shouldn't.

Some people need to work harder, but others are already flirting with burnout.

In conditions of uncertainty—in other words, in life—we often assume that others know something we don't. If the powers that be already decided that starting a podcast is a bad idea, we can move on. There's no reason to second-guess their seemingly informed conclusions.

But their conclusions often aren't informed. They're shaped primarily, and sometimes exclusively, by their own experience. They're a sample size of one—a single case study that represents the entire foundation for their well-meaning yet disturbingly confident advice.

Consider a popular blog post that the entrepreneur and venture capitalist Marc Andreessen wrote in 2007, entitled "A Guide to Personal Productivity." In it, Andreessen shares his strategies for getting things done. His advice includes: "The best way to make sure that you are never asked to do something again is to royally screw it up the first time you are asked to do it." He also advises readers to "start the day with a real sit-down breakfast" because "study after study [has] shown that breakfast is, yes, the most important meal of the day."[12]

For most people, the first piece of advice is indeed effective—for losing your job. And the second, as I discussed earlier in the book, is far more dubious than the "study after study" claim makes it out to be. (Andreessen notably cites no studies after that sentence.)

There's a logical fallacy called *post hoc, ergo propter hoc.* That's a fancy Latin phrase that means "After it, therefore because of it." A person did a, b, and c and became a billionaire. Therefore, a, b, and c must have led to their success. Not necessarily. Other factors like x, y, and z could also be the cause.

This fallacy partially explains why morning-routine stories have become a core part of the self-help genre. These stories provide voyeuristic glimpses into how titans "crush" their morning and perform at their best. They do yoga, meditate, run several miles, do a cold plunge, and warm up some raw milk from their pet goat—all before 9 am.

This obsession with morning routines gives the false impression that if you just copy and paste someone else's choreographed pregame routine—if you do a, b, and c—you'll be on the path to success. But life doesn't work that way. Using the same type of pen that Stephen King uses won't make you a better writer.

We're often given a single plot about what makes life worth living. Just follow this one path, the story goes, and you'll get your

happy ending. But the paths and the plots are multiple. In attempt-
ing to duplicate someone else's seemingly happy ending, we end
up extinguishing the possible plots of our own life. We become a
silent extra in the background of someone else's movie.

Blindly following another person's path isn't just an innocuous
exercise. In so doing, we also let ourselves off the hook. We tell
ourselves that if we only had the right tactic, the right pen, or the
right process, we'd be all set. We pretend that copying from success
stories is an acceptable strategy, so we don't bother to pave our
own path.

Before you act on advice—even from a trusted source—take a
moment and pause. Seek opinions from multiple people, particularly those who disagree with each other. Remember that their
advice is just that—theirs. It's based on their own experience, their
own skills, and their own biases. That advice may not be right for
you or the work you're doing right now.

Be informed by other people's advice, but don't be constrained
by it. Test their advice, but don't blindly follow it. See if it holds up
to scrutiny in your own life. What people claim as gospel is often
nothing more than their experience.

And remember: The best advice doesn't dictate precisely what
path you should take. Instead, it helps you see the many possible
paths ahead and illuminates what's in your blind spot—so you can
decide what to do yourself.

When you give advice, situate it in your own personal context.
Explain your own experience, and avoid turning your advice into
universal wisdom. Use "I" statements (*Here's what I did . . .*). Add
the necessary nuance and caveats. Encourage others to think for
themselves and find their own path forward. Ask, *What do you
think? What feels aligned for you? When you faced this type of
problem in the past, what worked for you?*

In the end, starting a podcast was one of the best decisions I've
made in recent memory. It led me down a path that eventually

culminated in a dream book deal and introduced me to people who've been deeply influential in my life.

And that mentor who told me not to start a podcast?

He later started one of his own.

## No one is coming

*No one is coming*
*To rescue you*
*Mend you*
*Pick you out of the crowd*
*Tell you it's your turn*
*Say you've made it*
*Carry you on their back*
*Give you the formula*
*Or travel the path for you*

*You're not a damsel in distress.*
*You are the hero in your own story.*
*You are your own knight in shining armor.*

Visit ozanvarol.com/genius to find worksheets, challenges, and exercises to help you implement the strategies discussed in this part.

# *The Transformation*

Part V has two chapters:

1. **Let Go of Your Future:** On opening yourself to new possibilities, letting go of trying to control what can't be controlled, and leaning into the beauty of not knowing

2. **Metamorphosis:** On continuously reimagining who you are

Along the way, you'll learn:

- Why experts are terrible at predicting the future
- How planning for the future can blind you to better possibilities
- Why your safety net might be a straitjacket
- How to start walking before you see a clear path ahead
- Why quitting can be an act of love
- How a life lived carefully is a half-dead life
- What the transformation of the caterpillar into a butterfly can teach you about discovering who you are

# 12

# Let Go of Your Future

*Deep in the human unconscious is a pervasive need for a logical universe that makes sense. But the real universe is always one step beyond logic.*

—FROM *THE SAYINGS OF MUAD'DIB* IN *DUNE* BY FRANK HERBERT

## The secret to predicting the future

"No airship will ever fly from New York to Paris. That seems to me to be impossible," wrote Wilbur Wright, the co-inventor of the airplane, in 1909.[1] Just 10 years later, in 1919, a British airship crossed the Atlantic.[2]

"The growth of the Internet will slow drastically," wrote Paul Krugman in 1998. "Most people have nothing to say to each other! By 2005 or so, it will become clear that the Internet's impact on the economy has been no greater than the fax machine's."[3] That one may have *slightly* missed the mark. Krugman went on to win the Nobel Prize in Economics.[4]

Predictions are popular because they appeal to human nature. They create an illusion of certainty in an uncertain world. But predictions are wrong far more often than we assume.

University of Pennsylvania professor Philip Tetlock designed a study to determine the accuracy of predictions. The study comprised

284 experts whose professions involved "commenting or offering advice on political and economic trends."[5] Their credentials were impressive: Over half of them had doctorates, and almost all had graduate degrees. On average, they also had 12 years of relevant professional experience.

The study asked these experts to make forecasts about a variety of events—for example, whether the incumbent party in the United States would retain control in the next election or whether GDP growth rates would accelerate, decelerate, or remain the same in the next two years. Between the mid-1980s and 2003, Tetlock collected over 82,000 predictions.

The experts performed terribly. They failed to beat a simple algorithm that assumed that what happened in the past would continue in the future—for example, that the current GDP growth rate of 1 percent would remain the same in the next two years. The experts also failed to beat sophisticated dilettantes—people Tetlock calls "attentive readers of the *New York Times*." The experts' only victory was over UC Berkeley undergraduates, "who pulled off the improbable feat of doing worse than chance," Tetlock writes.[6]

Extra education or experience made no difference. Experts with a doctorate failed to outperform experts without one. Seasoned experts failed to outperform the amateurs.

There was, however, one variable that affected accuracy: media acclaim. Experts who attracted media attention—the type of pundits you see on TV—performed *worse* than their lower-profile colleagues. The more media appearances an expert made, the greater was their temptation to offer overconfident sound bites and quotable predictions that turned out to be wrong.

The problem with predictions isn't limited to political science or economics. It cuts across domains. Another study—cleverly subtitled "How Can Experts Know So Much and Predict So Badly?"—identifies the same problem in fields as diverse as medicine, accounting, and psychology.[7]

Yet the experts who make inaccurate predictions aren't called out. They often get away with it. People rarely say, "Maybe you should sit this one out, Dr. Stu, since 90 percent of your economic predictions have been proven wrong." By then, we've already moved on to the next, shiny, exciting piece of breaking news.

Every now and then, Dr. Stu will get a prediction right, but not because he's got divine levels of foresight. It's because he got lucky. If you take shots all day, you'll eventually hit the target. But that doesn't make you a good marksman.

Don't get me wrong: Experts serve critical functions. Only experts can program computers or design aircraft. I wouldn't want a dentist who learned how to perform a root canal by watching YouTube videos. Experts have experience, and with experience comes great domain knowledge. They're terrific at telling you what happened in the past in their field. But they aren't good at predicting what will happen in the future.

The problem isn't just with experts. *No one* is great at predicting the future. Much of life can't be forecasted, diagrammed, or reduced to a PowerPoint deck. When the future doesn't match our expectations, our projections get thrown out (or worse, they're still followed).

We spend so much psychic energy trying to predict things outside of our control and worrying about what might happen. We suffer preemptively, living out the bad economy, the bad weather, the bad fill-in-the-blank.

Worrying is a giant waste of your imagination. Think about all the time and energy you've spent worrying about the future and brooding over predictions—political predictions, stock market predictions, Covid-19 predictions, to name just a few.

Surrender can be liberating, not defeating. Surrender doesn't mean giving up responsibility or walking away from problems. It means focusing on what you can control and letting go of what you can't.

It all boils down to one question: Will it help?

Will it help to worry about the future?

Will it help to refresh your favorite news site for the umpteenth time this hour?

Will it help to hand over agency and responsibility for your state of mind to self-proclaimed prophets spewing comforting yet misleading predictions?

If the answer is no, let it go.

Stop trying to predict the future. Create it instead.

## The problem with planning

*The eye that looks ahead to the safe course is closed forever.*

—PAUL ATREIDES IN *DUNE* BY FRANK HERBERT

*Done with the Compass!—*
*Done with the Chart!*

—EMILY DICKINSON, "WILD NIGHTS—WILD NIGHTS!"

In the 1800s, the peppered moths in Britain experienced a strange transformation.[8]

Before the transformation, 98 percent of the moths were light-colored. Only 2 percent were dark. But over the next five decades the ratio completely flipped. By 1895, 98 percent of moths were dark and the rest were light.

The transformation can be traced to a cataclysmic event whose ripple effects transformed not only the moths but also life as we know it.

The Industrial Revolution.

Before the Industrial Revolution, the light-colored moths enjoyed a significant advantage over the darker ones. The light-colored lichen that grew abundantly on tree bark camouflaged the light-colored moths from predatory birds, making them more difficult to detect.

When the Industrial Revolution arrived, coal-burning factories began to spew immense amounts of sulfur dioxide and soot into the air. The sulfur dioxide killed the light-bodied lichens growing on tree bark, and the soot painted the bark darker.

With these changes, the light-colored moths stuck out against the dark background and became easy lunch for hungry birds. In contrast, the darker moth population, which now blended in with the bark, skyrocketed.

The old advantage became a new liability, and the old liability became a new advantage. The light-colored moths withered. The darker ones blossomed.

The world is evolving at dizzying speed. Tomorrow refuses to cooperate with our best-laid plans. A promising new product fails, a seemingly stable job disappears, and the disrupter becomes the disrupted. Thriving businesses begin to wither as change chips away at their competitive advantage, exposing them like light-colored moths against a darkening bark.

Although people yearn for a return to "normal" or try to predict the "new normal," there is no such thing as *normal*. There's only change. Never-ending, constant change. Sometimes slow, sometimes fast, but constant nonetheless. Once we realize that the ground beneath us isn't stable—and never has been—we can relax, open ourselves to new possibilities, and lean into the beauty of not knowing.

It's fine to have a general sense of direction—to want to start your own business, write a book, or open a yoga studio. It's not fine to be held victim to those plans and the precise way that you think they'll come into being. When you plan, you're pulling ideas from what you know *now*. But the foresight of your current self is limited. If you don't remain open, you'll get in your own way.

There's a famous story about how to catch a monkey. You put nuts in a jar. The monkey reaches into the jar to grab the nuts and finds that he can't get his fist full of food out of the narrow opening. If he lets go of the nuts, he can escape and be free. But he refuses. Instead of detachment, he chooses attachment—to what he can't have.

The firmer our plans, the more we attach to them, even when things don't go as planned. We close our eyes when we need to look. We remain seated when we need to move. We see what we expect to see instead of what's actually there. If you're a light-colored moth hell-bent on confirming your belief that the Industrial Revolution hasn't arrived, you'll end up as food for hungry birds.

We're in a constant struggle to figure everything out. But "everything all figured out" is the end. That's when the credits roll. The movie of your life isn't over yet. You're still in the middle of the action, constantly evolving and expanding. If you knew what came next, you would disrupt what's unfolding. You wouldn't learn the lessons you need to learn.

We try to control the future in part because the future is uncertain, and uncertainty is scary. We don't know what's going to work or what's going to come next. So we try to eliminate uncertainty by looking for certainty. We cling to our old skin, we attach to our plans for the future, and we look for a proven formula, a recipe, a process. We search for a map to uncharted territories and to paths that have yet to be trodden.

What we cling to defines us—and confines us.

We become hostage to our vision of the future. We end up fixating on one set of circumstances, one path, or one person. We act like the Great Gatsby throwing one party after another, waiting in vain for Daisy to show up. We forget that the possibilities awaiting us might be even better than the Daisys of our current imagination.

Think back to the most noteworthy moments of your life. If you're like most people, these moments weren't carefully charted and planned. They transpired precisely because you relaxed into possibility and kept yourself open to mystery. They unfolded in ways far more magical than you ever could have predicted.

When the tree barks change color, we have a choice. We can cower in dread. We can live in denial and cling to the darkening trees, desperately hoping that our old ways of doing things will magically start working again. We can spend our days shaking our fists at the gods in a futile attempt to force the universe to deal us a better hand.

Or we can ease our grip on our plans for tomorrow, just like we shed the skin of yesterday. We can play the hand we were dealt rather than the hand we wish we had been dealt. We can learn to use our skills, products, and services in a way that we haven't before. We can find a different shelter that will protect us from hungry birds in a soot-stained world.

Life is a dance, but it can't be choreographed. It requires leaning into curiosity about what will come next instead of demanding that the dance conform to our carefully scripted steps. When we attempt to force outcomes and next steps—when we try to predict what can't be predicted and when we try to control what can't be controlled—we get tangled up and can't tango on.

A thriller wouldn't be as much fun to watch if you knew exactly how it ends. A football game would be boring if you knew who's going to win. Travel would lose its luster if you walked around with your nose stuck in a guidebook, meticulously checking off each "important" sight while missing the magic unfolding around you.

Yet, when it comes to life, we demand a detailed guidebook, a line-by-line script of how things will pan out. But life is more like a jungle gym and less like a ladder. It defies predictions, logic, and order. Nothing in nature is linear. There are no straight branches on a tree. A volcano explodes into life in a spectacularly nonlinear fashion, spewing lava that destroys everything it touches—until it cools, solidifies, and over time creates rich, fertile soil.

The wisdom isn't in your five-year plan or your script. The wisdom is within. The light isn't at the end of the tunnel. The light is within. If you can act like an improv actor—if you can accept each offer from life with a mindset of "Yes and . . . "—life becomes a lot more fluid. You can step into new roles, delight in the twists and turns, and arrive at unexpected destinations.

The future favors the open-eyed and the open-minded. If you don't stick to your script—if you let go of what you expected to see and open your eyes to what's actually there—you'll notice what you'd otherwise miss.

Uncertainty is a feature, not a bug. It's something to be embraced, not erased. The more we look for a clear and well-lit path, the more we choose paths well traveled by other people and the less we can see and chart our own. There's more than one right way to play a poker hand, more than one right way to market a product, and more than one right way to organize a book.

Far too many people wait to make a move until they know exactly what comes next—which means they never move. Life often lights the path ahead only a few steps at a time. There's no trailer previewing the trails ahead and no flashlight powerful enough to illuminate what's to come. As you take each step, and as you experiment with different paths, you go from not knowing to knowing and from darkness to light.

The only way to know is to start walking—*before* you see a clear path.

Yes, you've never launched this specific product before. You've never attended law school before. You've never had a job like this before. But you've launched other products, attended other schools, and had other jobs in the past.

There was a time when it was the first time that you did anything. You've been here before, and you emerged intact. You endured setbacks, solved unforeseen problems, and developed critical skills that you can apply to your next mission.

Sometimes you'll surf the waves of uncertainty. Other times the waves will surf you. But if you swim only in familiar waters, you'll never discover the unexpected.

There's always a gap between the world as it is and the world as we wish it to be.

We can see the gap as a threat.

Or we can see the gap as our own blank canvas, and be ready to bring out our creative best.

Which will you choose?

# 13

# Metamorphosis

*One must have chaos in oneself to give birth to a dancing star.*

—FRIEDRICH NIETZSCHE,
*THUS SPOKE ZARATHUSTRA*

*I don't know where we are going but I know exactly how to get there.*

—BOYD VARTY,
*THE LION TRACKER'S GUIDE TO LIFE*

## Your next life

To become a butterfly, the caterpillar must accept its own death.[1]

The process begins when an impulse deep within the caterpillar signals that it's time for a radical change. When that signal arrives, the caterpillar hangs itself upside down from a twig or a leaf and forms a chrysalis.

Inside the chrysalis, the caterpillar begins to literally eat itself, emitting enzymes to dissolve and digest all its tissues. Although the transition of the caterpillar into a butterfly is often glamorized in popular culture, there's nothing graceful about it. If you were to open the chrysalis, you'd find a rotting caterpillar.

When the caterpillar digests itself, the only survivors are a group of cells called imaginal discs—whose name comes from the word imagination. These are the Lego blocks of the caterpillar—its first principles. Fed by the nutritious soup inside the chrysalis, these imaginal discs allow the caterpillar to develop eyes, wings, legs, and everything else it will need to become a butterfly. Out of that disgusting mess, a marvelous butterfly emerges.

Even when it sheds its old skin, the snake is still a snake. For us, though, the transition from one life phase to another is sometimes more violent. It can require us to become something else, in a complete metamorphosis—like the transformation of the caterpillar into a butterfly.

My time for metamorphosis arrived back in 2016. Up until then, I had done some shedding of old skin—transitioning from rocket science to law and then to academia—but the foundation of my career had been built on a steady paycheck from a steady employer.

Shortly after I got tenure as a professor, I realized that this life was no longer for me. I didn't want to write academic articles that only a handful of professors would read. What's more, I had been teaching the same classes, answering the same questions, and attending the same committee meetings for years.

My life as a caterpillar had become comfortable—too comfortable. I had stopped learning and growing.

But even after the signal for transformation arrived, I initially ignored it. I considered academia an important safety net. Tenure guaranteed me a paycheck for life. That guarantee allowed me to explore other ventures—like writing books about rocket science and speaking to industry-leading businesses—without risking it all. If my other projects didn't pan out, I'd always have the security of tenure to catch me if I fell.

Then I had an epiphany. I realized that my safety net had become a straitjacket.

As long as I kept one foot in academia, I would remain tethered. I couldn't fully make the leap to other fields because my academic commitments were depleting my limited supply of time and creative energy.

In other words, the same net that once provided me with safety and comfort—the career that I once loved—was now confining me. I couldn't fully step into who I was becoming without completely letting go of who I once was.

A safety net that's there to catch you can also restrain you. It can make you believe that you're safe only above the net. *Play only over here, not over there,* the net says. *Stop taking healthy risks and avoid new leaps the net can't support.*

The safety nets in my life felt practical, but it wasn't security or stability that kept me clinging to them. That was just the story I was telling myself.

Rather, it was fear. Fear of letting go. Fear of missing life as a caterpillar. Fear of not knowing if I could ever make it as a butterfly. *Sure, there are so many butterflies out there, but I'm a caterpillar, damn it! That's all I know.*

Then I remembered: Letting go can be an act of love. There's birth in death. As Joseph Campbell writes, "The earth must be broken to bring forth life. If the seed does not die there is no plant. Bread results from the death of wheat. Life lives on lives."[2]

Yes, life lives on lives. Our old selves become compost for our new selves. Our old truths become seeds for new revelations. Our old paths become lighthouses for new destinations.

So I decided to spin myself into a chrysalis and digest my past as fuel for my future. My former career in rocket science provided me with wings for critical thinking—and formed the subject matter for a book. Academia provided the legs for teaching and captivating audiences. A decade of writing gave me the antennae for storytelling. These imaginal discs—my first principles—helped me to create the new me.

The transformation of the caterpillar into the butterfly isn't immediate. A caterpillar doesn't run away from itself. It becomes itself. It embodies itself. It stays in that chrysalis and tends to that wasteland until it locates its imaginal discs and forms what it will need as a butterfly.

I spent a few years in my own chrysalis while I was still in academia testing out different selves and futures. It was only after I achieved some level of success in writing and speaking—when I had formed the body parts I needed to fly—that I decided to leave.

Make no mistake: Rotting isn't fun. You can't bypass the disorder, the collapse, and the decay of what once was. You'll doubt yourself the most when you're closest to your next transformation. Just when the rotting begins, you'll be tempted to go back to your life as a caterpillar. Society will do its best to convince you to resist that transformation and keep participating in business as usual. *Look what you're about to leave behind*, they'll say. *You're about to turn into waste—and to digest everything you've worked so hard to build.*

But digesting doesn't mean forgetting. Quite the opposite: Letting go requires remembering your past and the clues the caterpillar left you to navigate life as a butterfly. Economists call these sunk costs—the time, money, and effort you expended to major in art history, go to law school, or start a business. But these aren't costs. They are gifts, from your former self to your current self.

Was your job a failure if it gave you the skills you need to thrive? Was your relationship a failure if it taught you the meaning of love? Was your art history major a failure if it gave you the tools to appreciate creativity?

When you're in that chrysalis, don't compare yourself to the butterflies flying around. They've been at this for a while, and you're still forming your wings. A young tree wouldn't look at a full-grown tree and feel ashamed. We wouldn't criticize a seed for not having any roots. We'd give it the time and the water it needs to grow.

Do the same for yourself. Even when you feel like you'll be forever rotting in that chrysalis, you're becoming the person you're meant to be. You're returning to your essence so that you can act from that essence, and not from your programming. You'll find your way out—as long as you don't stunt your own transformation or allow others to keep you confined in the chrysalis.

And remember: You don't owe anyone the caterpillar you used to be. Your metamorphosis might trigger people who've grown accustomed to seeing you as a caterpillar. Your transformation might remind them of their stagnation. Your rebirth might cause them discomfort, but it might also wake them up from their own slumber. And if they don't want to wake up—or if they can't wrap their head around your transformation—it's their problem, not yours.

Steps forward often require steps down. "Our next life," Glennon Doyle writes, "will always cost us this one. If we are truly alive, we are constantly losing who we just were, what we just built, what we just believed, what we just knew to be true."[3] Any real change requires you to die before you are reborn—and know that dying can be the beginning, not the end.

You may not know it yet, but you're walking around with imaginal discs within you ready to sprout a butterfly. Say thank you to the caterpillar and let it go. Let what's dying serve as fertilizer for what's awakening.

As you emerge out of your chrysalis, the possibilities will appear endless. You've got wings, and you can fly in a million different directions.

You can look at that infinite abyss and feel paralyzed. Or you can loosen your grip on your past and see where the universe leads you—wingbeat by curious wingbeat.

The Greek word for butterfly is *psyche*. And *psyche* means soul.[4]

When you undergo a metamorphosis, you won't lose yourself.

You'll discover the depths of your soul.

# A life lived carefully

*You never*
*Face failure*
*Walk off the beaten path*
*Leap into the unknown*
*Change your routines*
*Eat forbidden fruits*
*Sing really loudly*
*Dance really badly*
*Go outside in the rain*
*Show your imperfections*
*Cry wild tears*
*Confess your love*
*Get your heart broken*

*You paint all your walls white*
*Look ahead only to the safe course*
*Stifle your finest impulses*
*Shrink away from your calling*
*Say what others expect you to say*
*Punish your inner child for wanting to play*
*Dismiss your thoughts because they're your own*
*Stay with the danger of no danger*
*Walk the same paths*
*Defer your dreams*
*Squeeze yourself into boxes others have drawn*
*Extinguish the fire that burns in your heart*
*Dim the light that dances in your eyes*
*And slaughter a little piece of your soul every day*

*A life lived carefully is a half-dead life*

*Because the purpose of life isn't to be fine*

*It's to be alive*

Visit ozanvarol.com/genius to find worksheets, challenges, and exercises to help you implement the strategies discussed in this part.

# Epilogue

*Henceforth I ask not good-fortune,*
*I myself am good-fortune.*
—WALT WHITMAN, "SONG OF THE OPEN ROAD"

You were created from pieces of the universe.

The iron flowing in your blood, the calcium in your bones, and the carbon in your brain were made in the chaos of red giants billions of years ago.[1]

If you look only at the last 300 years of your family tree, you'll find that you have over 4,000 direct ancestors.[2] Take out just one of them, and you wouldn't be here today.

So much had to conspire to bring you here. For you to be reading these words is nothing short of a miracle.

So be you—unapologetically and spectacularly you.

Discard what doesn't serve you, so you can discover your core.

Declutter your mind so you can see the wisdom within.

Delight in getting to know yourself because there's only—and ever will be—one of you.

Swim with the big fish playing in the depths of your oceans.

Follow your body to places where your mind hasn't allowed you to go.

Embrace the purple that lights up your soul.

Find the extraordinary in the ordinary.

Stand on the shoulders of giants—and help the next generation stand on yours.

Channel the energy that brought you into existence.

Turn it into the art that only you can create.

Stop looking for gurus and heroes.

You are the one you've been waiting for.

Butterfly, it's time for you to fly.

And if you'll excuse me, I have to go.

My battery is low and it's getting dark.

# What's Next?

Now that you've learned how to awaken your genius, it's time to put these principles into action.

Head over to ozanvarol.com/genius to find the following:

- A summary of key points from each chapter
- Worksheets, challenges, and exercises to help you implement the strategies discussed in the book
- A sign-up form for my weekly newsletter, where I share one big idea that you can read in three minutes or less. Readers call it "the one email I look forward to each week."

I travel the globe frequently to give keynote talks to organizations across numerous industries. If you're interested in inviting me to talk to your group, please visit ozanvarol.com/speaking.

If you enjoyed this book, please tell your friends and post a review online. Even in a world of ads and algorithms, books thrive on word of mouth. Ideas spread because generous people like you choose to share them with others. I'm grateful for your support.

# Acknowledgments

The word *grateful* doesn't do justice to how I feel about making a living by creating art—writing, speaking, and sharing my ideas with the world.

So, first and foremost, thank YOU for reading, reviewing, and sharing my books. What an honor to picture you holding this book in your hands. You've given me an incredible gift that I cherish every day—and I hope you've found something in these pages that brought you alive.

I'm grateful to my rock-star literary agent, Richard Pine, for championing my work and taking a chance on me when I was a budding writer—which launched this rocket that we've been on ever since. Thank you to the rest of the all-stars at InkWell, particularly Alexis Hurley and Eliza Rothstein.

This is my second book with PublicAffairs. Thank you to my editor, Benjamin Adams, for illuminating my blind spots and supporting my unconventional ideas. Thanks also to my production editor Melissa Veronesi, marketing maven Miguel Cervantes, publicity maven Johanna Dickson, and Pete Garceau who designed the beautiful cover for the book.

I'm privileged to work with a wonderful team who support my creative endeavors:

Brendan Seibel is the invisible performer in everything I do. Thank you, Brendan, for helping me research, fact-check, and edit this book (all errors are my own) and for leaving everything you touch significantly better than how you found it.

David Moldawer helped me find the gems in the mess of ideas floating through my mind and shape the proposal for this book.

Allison McLean and Elizabeth Hazelton amplify my message through their publicity and marketing genius.

Brandi Bernoskie and her team at Alchemy+Aim design beautiful web pages for my books and other endeavors.

Chris West, my good friend and creative collaborator, along with his team at Video Narrative, refine my online narrative and produce extraordinary videos that bring my ideas to life.

The exceptional team at the Washington Speakers Bureau champion my speaking platform and connect me to audiences across the globe.

When I was in middle school, I told my parents I wanted to be an astronaut. "You can do it," they said. When I later told them I wanted to be a professor, "You can do it," they said. When I later told them I'd quit academia and become a full-time writer and speaker, "You can do it," they said. I wish everyone would have parents as supportive as mine. *Sizi çok seviyorum.*

Shortly after I first learned to read and write, I'd sit in front of my grandfather's typewriter and write stories. I'm deeply grateful to that little boy for following his heart and putting one word after another with no idea where it'd lead one day. The best of this book came from his creative vision and playful nature.

Our dogs, Einstein and Sputnik, remind me every day of what's truly important in life (food, cuddles, play, and sleep). It's a privilege to share my life with them. ("Why want another universe when this one has dogs?," as Matt Haig put it in the multiverse novel *The Midnight Library*).

Finally, Kathy—my wife, my cosmic constant, my partner-in-everything. I'm so grateful that I get to do this life with you. Thank you for inspiring me, for igniting my soul, and for making me a better person. Your genius never ceases to amaze me.

# Notes

## Introduction

1. Zora Neale Hurston, *Dust Tracks on a Road* (New York: Harper-Collins, 2010).

## Chapter 1: Uneducate

1. Guy Raz, "How Do Schools Kill Creativity?," *TED Radio Hour*, October 3, 2014, www.npr.org/2014/10/03/351552772/how-do-schools-kill-creativity.

2. Gillian Lynne, *A Dancer in Wartime* (London: Vintage, 2012), 14.

3. William Poundstone, *Carl Sagan: A Life in the Cosmos* (New York: Henry Holt and Co., 1999), 12.

4. Neil Postman and Charles Weingartner, *Teaching as a Subversive Activity* (New York: Dell Publishing Co., 1969), 60.

5. Tim T. Morris, Danny Dorling, Neil M. Davies, and George Davey Smith, "Associations Between School Enjoyment at Age 6 and Later Educational Achievement: Evidence from a UK Cohort Study," *npj Science of Learning* 6, no. 1 (June 15, 2021), pubmed.ncbi.nlm.nih.gov/34131153/.

6. Postman and Weingartner, *Teaching as a Subversive Activity*, 62.

7. Richard P. Feynman, as told to Ralph Leighton, *"What Do You Care What Other People Think?" Further Adventures of a Curious Character* (New York: W. W. Norton & Co., 2001).

8. Jacob W. Getzels and Philip W. Jackson, *Creativity and Intelligence: Explorations with Gifted Students* (London: John Wiley & Sons, 1962), 31.

9. Erik L. Westby and V. L. Dawson, "Creativity: Asset or Burden in the Classroom?," *Creativity Research Journal* 8, no. 1 (1995): 1–10, www.gwern.net/docs/psychology/1995-westby.pdf.

10. Postman and Weingartner, *Teaching as a Subversive Activity*, 62.

11. Postman and Weingartner, *Teaching as a Subversive Activity*, 29.

12. Tom Peters, "Say 'No' to Normalcy," *Journal for Quality and Participation* 21, no. 3 (May/June 1998): 64, www.proquest.com/open view/30dc2926802784d40c9b3e9dac54cd13/1?pq-origsite=gscholar &cbl=37083.

13. Quoted in "Modern Living: Ozmosis in Central Park," *Time*, October 4, 1976, content.time.com/time/subscriber/article/0,33009,918412,00 .html.

14. David Bayles and Ted Orland, *Art and Fear: Observations on the Perils (and Rewards) of Artmaking* (Santa Cruz, CA: Image Continuum, 1993), 79.

## Chapter 2: Discard

1. Elle Luna, *The Crossroads of Should and Must: Find and Follow Your Passion* (New York: Workman Publishing Co., 2015).

2. Catrin Sian Rutland, Pia Cigler, and Valentina Kubale, "Reptilian Skin and Its Special Histological Structures," in *Veterinary Anatomy and Physiology*, edited by Catrin Sian Rutland and Valentina Kubale (London: IntechOpen, 2019), 150–152; Stephen Divers and Scott Stahl, *Mader's Reptile and Amphibian Medicine and Surgery*, 3rd ed. (St. Louis: Elsevier, 2019), 732.

3. Maranke I. Koster, "Making an Epidermis," *Annals of the New York Academy of Sciences* 1170, no. 1 (August 4, 2009): 7–10, nyaspubs .onlinelibrary.wiley.com/doi/10.1111/j.1749-6632.2009.04363.x.

4. Philip Galanes, "For Arianna Huffington and Kobe Bryant: First Success. Then Sleep," *New York Times*, September 28, 2014, www.nytimes .com/2014/09/28/fashion/arianna-huffington-kobe-bryant-meditate.html.

5. Rebecca Solnit, *A Field Guide to Getting Lost* (New York: Penguin Books, 2006).

6. E. Bruce Goldstein, *Encyclopedia of Perception* (Thousand Oaks, CA: Sage Publications, 2009), 492.

7. John A. Banas and Stephen A. Rains, "A Meta-Analysis of Research on Inoculation Theory," *Communication Monographs* 77, no. 3 (2010), nca.tandfonline.com/doi/abs/10.1080/03637751003758193#.Ypw V7JDMLlw.

8. Carl R. Rogers, *On Becoming a Person: A Therapist's View of Psychotherapy* (Boston: Houghton Mifflin, 1995), 332.

9. Lowell L. Bennion, *Religion and the Pursuit of Truth* (Salt Lake City, UT: Deseret Book Co., 1959), 52.

10. Emma Goldman, "What I Believe," *New York World*, July 19, 1908.

11. David Kortava, "Lost in Thought: The Psychological Risks of Meditation," *Harper's*, April 2021, harpers.org/archive/2021/04/lost-in -thought-psychological-risks-of-meditation/.

12. M. Farias, E. Maraldi, K. C. Wallenkampf, and G. Lucchetti, "Adverse Events in Meditation Practices and Meditation-Based Therapies: A Systematic Review," *Acta Psychiatrica Scandinavica* 142 (2020): 374– 393, onlinelibrary.wiley.com/doi/full/10.1111/acps.13225.

13. F. Scott Fitzgerald, "The Crack-Up," *Esquire*, February 1, 1936, classic.esquire.com/article/1936/2/1/the-crack-up.

14. Graham M. Vaughan, "Henri Tajfel: Polish-Born British Social Psychologist," *Britannica*, April 29, 2022, www.britannica.com/biography /Henri-Tajfel.

15. Henri Tajfel, "Experiments in Intergroup Discrimination," *Scientific American* 223, no. 5 (November 1970): 96–103, www.jstor.org /stable/24927662.

16. David Foster Wallace, "Tense Present: Democracy, English, and the Wars over Usage," *Harper's*, April 2001.

17. Amy E. Boyle Johnston, "Ray Bradbury: *Fahrenheit 451* Misinterpreted," *LA Weekly*, May 30, 2007, www.laweekly.com/ray-bradbury -fahrenheit-451-misinterpreted/.

18. Elizabeth N. Simas, Scott Clifford, and Justin H. Kirkland, "How Empathic Concern Fuels Political Polarization," *American Political Science Review* 114, no. 1 (February 2020): 258–269, www.cam bridge.org/core/journals/american-political-science-review/article/how -empathic-concern-fuels-political-polarization/8115DB5BDE548FF6AB 04DA661F83785E.

19. David J. Lick, Adam L. Alter, and Jonathan B. Freeman, "Superior Pattern Detectors Efficiently Learn, Activate, Apply, and Update Social Stereotypes," *Journal of Experimental Psychology: General* 147, no. 2 (February 2018): 209–227, pubmed.ncbi.nlm.nih.gov/28726438/.

20. Daniel J. Isenberg, "Group Polarization: A Critical Review and Meta-Analysis," *Journal of Personality and Social Psychology* 50, no. 6 (1986): 1141–1151, psycnet.apa.org/record/1986-24477-001.

21. Susan David, "The Gift and Power of Emotional Courage," TED-Women, November 2017, www.ted.com/talks/susan_david_the_gift_and _power_of_emotional_courage/.

22. Glen Pearson, "African Famine: 'I See You,'" *HuffPost Canada*, August 9, 2011, www.huffpost.com/archive/ca/entry/africa-famine_b_92 2063.

23. Pearson, "African Famine."

24. Scott Neuman, "On Anniversary of Apollo 8, How the 'Earthrise' Photo Was Made," *The Two-Way*, NPR, December 23, 2013, www

.npr.org/sections/thetwo-way/2013/12/23/256605845/on-anniversary-of-apollo-8-how-the-earthrise-photo-was-made.

25. Archibald MacLeish, "Riders on Earth Together, Brothers in Eternal Cold," *New York Times*, December 25, 1968, archive.nytimes.com/www.nytimes.com/library/national/science/nasa/122568sci-nasa-macleish.html.

26. Jim Lovell, "Apollo 8 Astronaut Remembers Looking Down at Earth," Smithsonian National Air and Space Museum, December 21, 2018, airandspace.si.edu/stories/editorial/apollo-8-astronaut-remembers-looking-down-earth.

27. "Edgar Mitchell's Strange Voyage," *People*, April 8, 1974, people.com/archive/edgar-mitchells-strange-voyage-vol-1-no-6/.

28. Pico Iyer, "Why We Travel," *Salon*, March 18, 2000, www.salon.com/2000/03/18/why/.

29. Chip Heath and Dan Heath, *Switch: How to Change Things When Change Is Hard* (New York: Broadway Books, 2010), 208.

30. Daniel M. Stancato and Dacher Keltner, "Awe, Ideological Conviction, and Perceptions of Ideological Opponents," *Emotion* 21, no. 1 (February 2021): 61–72, psycnet.apa.org/buy/2019-46364-001.

31. Jonathon McPhetres, "Oh, the Things You Don't Know: Awe Promotes Awareness of Knowledge Gaps and Science Interest," *Cognition and Emotion* 33, no. 8 (2019): 1599–1615, www.tandfonline.com/doi/full/10.1080/02699931.2019.1585331.

32. T. S. Eliot, "Little Gidding," in *Four Quartets* (New York: Harcourt Brace and Co., 1943).

## Chapter 3: Detox

1. Arthur C. Brooks, "This Holiday Season, We Can All Learn a Lesson from Beethoven," *Washington Post*, December 13, 2019, www.washingtonpost.com/opinions/this-holiday-season-we-can-all-learn-a-lesson-from-beethoven/2019/12/13/71f21aba-1d0e-11ea-b4c1-fd0d91b60d9e_story.html.

2. Maynard Solomon, *Beethoven* (New York: Schirmer, 2012).

3. Craig Wright, *The Hidden Habits of Genius: Beyond Talent, IQ, and Grit—Unlocking the Secrets of Greatness* (New York: Dey Street Books, 2020).

4. Blaise Pascal, *Pensées*, translated by Gertrude Burford Rawlings (Mount Vernon, NY: Peter Pauper Press, 1900), 65.

5. "Free Your Mind," En Vogue, *Funky Divas*, EastWest Records, 1992.

6. Clive Thompson, "End the Tyranny of 24/7 Email," *New York Times*, August 28, 2014, www.nytimes.com/2014/08/29/opinion/end -the-tyranny-of-24-7-email.html.

7. Nicholas Carr, *The Shallows: What the Internet Is Doing to Our Brains* (New York: W. W. Norton & Co., 2010), 120.

8. Herbert A. Simon, "Designing Organizations for an Information-Rich World," *Computers, Communication, and the Public Interest*, edited by Martin Greenberger (Baltimore: Johns Hopkins University Press, 1971), 40.

9. Melina R. Uncapher and Anthony D. Wagner, "Minds and Brains of Media Multitaskers: Current Findings and Future Directions," *Proceedings of the National Academy of Sciences* 115, no. 40 (October 1, 2018): 9889–9896, www.pnas.org/doi/full/10.1073/pnas.1611612115.

10. Kermit Pattison, "Worker, Interrupted: The Cost of Task Switching," *Fast Company*, July 28, 2008, www.fastcompany.com/944128 /worker-interrupted-cost-task-switching.

11. Statista, "Daily Time Spent on Social Networking by Internet Users Worldwide from 2012 to 2022," March 21, 2022, www.statista.com /statistics/433871/daily-social-media-usage-worldwide/.

12. Marc Brysbaert, "How Many Words Do We Read per Minute? A Review and Meta-Analysis of Reading Rate," *Journal of Memory and Language* 109 (December 2019), www.sciencedirect.com/science/article /abs/pii/S0749596X19300786.

13. Robert A. Heinlein, *Stranger in a Strange Land* (New York: Ace Books, 1987), 98.

14. Oliver Burkeman, "Treat Your To-Read Pile Like a River, Not a Bucket," www.oliverburkeman.com/river.

15. Chip Heath and Dan Heath, *Decisive: How to Make Better Choices in Life and Work* (New York: Currency, 2013); Amar Cheema and Dilip Soman, "The Effect of Partitions on Controlling Consumption," *Journal of Marketing Research* 45, no. 6 (December 2008): 665–675, www.jstor .org/stable/20618855.

16. Marcia Reynolds, "Zebras and Lions in the Workplace: An Interview with Dr. Robert Sapolsky," *International Journal of Coaching in Organizations* 4, no. 2 (2006): 7–15, libraryofprofessionalcoaching.com/ concepts/managing-stress-and-challenges/zebras-and-lions-in-the-work place-an-interview-with-dr-robert-sapolsky/.

17. Rosamund Stone Zander and Benjamin Zander, *The Art of Possibility: Transforming Professional and Personal Life* (Boston: Harvard Business School Press, 2000), 177.

18. Tim Ferriss, *The 4-Hour Work Week: Escape the 9–5, Live Anywhere, and Join the New Rich* (New York: Crown, 2009), 70.

19. Jia Tolentino, *Trick Mirror: Reflections on Self-Delusion* (New York: Random House, 2020), 66–67.

20. Pamela Rothon, "A Conversation with Corita Kent," *American Way* 3, no. 11 (November 1970): 7–14.

## Chapter 4: Spectacularly You

1. Brené Brown, *Braving the Wilderness: The Quest for True Belonging and the Courage to Stand Alone* (New York: Random House, 2019), 160.

2. The reality was slightly different from the Hollywood depiction. Cash first auditioned by himself after surprising Sam Phillips at the door of Sun Records and was then invited to return with a backing band. After listening to the group's gospel songs, Phillips rejected the idea of marketing them as a gospel act and asked them to return again with new material. In a later audition, Cash finally sang "Folsom Prison Blues." Colin Escott with Martin Hawkins, *Good Rockin' Tonight: Sun Records and the Birth of Rock 'n' Roll* (New York: Open Road Integrated Media, 2011).

3. *Walk the Line*, screenplay by Gill Dennis and James Mangold, directed by James Mangold (20th Century Fox, 2005).

4. Robert L. Doerschuk, "One Vision Beyond Music: On Simplicity, Context, and the Necessity of Urgency," *Keyboard*, June 1989.

5. Bruce Springsteen, *Born to Run* (New York: Simon & Schuster, 2017), 166.

6. David Rubenstein, "Oprah Winfrey," *The David Rubenstein Show: Peer to Peer Conversations*, March 1, 2017, www.bloomberg .com/news/videos/2017-03-01/the-david-rubenstein-show-oprah -winfrey?srnd=peer-to-peer.

7. Jane L. Levere, "Airline Safety Videos That Passengers Might Watch," *Seattle Times*, January 31, 2014, www.seattletimes.com/life /travel/airline-safety-videos-that-passengers-might-watch/.

8. Paula Caligiuri, "When Unilever Bought Ben & Jerry's: A Story of CEO Adaptability," *Fast Company*, August 14, 2012, www.fastcompany .com/3000398/when-unilever-bought-ben-jerrys-story-ceo-adaptability.

9. Nick Craig, *Leading from Purpose: Clarity and the Confidence to Act When It Matters Most* (New York: Hachette Book Group, 2018).

10. "Nick Craig on Leading from Purpose," *Purpose and Profit with Kathy Varol* (audio podcast), June 9, 2021, purposeandprofit.libsyn

.com/5-nick-craig-on-leading-from-purpose; Nick Craig, "Do You Lead with Purpose?," Knowledge at Wharton, September 26, 2018, knowledge .wharton.upenn.edu/article/do-you-lead-with-purpose/.

11. For additional examples of businesses that have created remarkable products, see Seth Godin, *Purple Cow: Transform Your Business by Being Remarkable* (New York: Portfolio, 2009).

12. Cameron Crowe, "Joni Mitchell Defends Herself," *Rolling Stone*, July 26, 1979, www.rollingstone.com/feature/joni-mitchell-defends -herself-61890/.

13. Laura Shapiro, *Something from the Oven: Reinventing Dinner in 1950s America* (New York: Viking, 2004).

14. Claudia H. Deutsch, "At Kodak, Some Old Things Are New Again," *New York Times*, May 2, 2008, www.nytimes.com/2008/05/02 /technology/02kodak.html.

15. Rupert Neate, "Kodak to Stop Making Cameras," *Guardian*, February 9, 2012, www.theguardian.com/business/2012/feb/09/kodak -to-stop-making-cameras.

16. The story of Fuji is based on the following sources: Christopher Sirk, "Fujifilm Found a Way to Innovate and Survive Digital. Why Didn't Kodak?," CRM.ORG, September 17, 2020, crm.org/articles/fujifilm -found-a-way-to-innovate-and-survive-digital-why-didnt-kodak; Ushijima Bifue, "Fujifilm Finds New Life in Cosmetics," nippon.com, April 25, 2013, www.nippon.com/en/features/c00511/; Aidan McCullen, *Undisruptable: A Mindset of Permanent Reinvention for Individuals, Organisations, and Life* (Chichester, UK: Wiley, 2021).

17. Richard Nieva, "YouTube Started as an Online Dating Site," CNET, March 14, 2016, www.cnet.com/tech/services-and-software /youtube-started-as-an-online-dating-site/.

18. Ankit Ajmera, "Slack Reference Price for Direct Listing Set at $26/ Share," Reuters, June 19, 2019, www.reuters.com/article/us-slack-listing -reference-price/slack-reference-price-for-direct-listing-set-at-26-share -idUSKCN1TK31V?il=0; Haidee Chu, "'Glitch' Died so Slack Could Take over Offices Everywhere, but Traces of the Game Live On," *Mashable*, February 25, 2020, mashable.com/article/slack-glitch.

19. Ciarán Ó Murchadha, *The Great Famine: Ireland's Agony 1845– 1852* (London: Continuum International Publishing, 2011).

20. Ann Gibbons, "The Great Famine: Decoded," *Science*, May 21, 2013, www.science.org/content/article/great-famine-decoded.

21. George Stroumboulopoulos, "Interview with BlackBerry Co-CEO Jim Balsillie," *The Hour*, CBC, April 1, 2008, www.youtube.com /watch?v=wQRcEObmSRM.

22. Adam Grant, *Think Again: The Power of Knowing What You Don't Know* (New York: Viking, 2021), 16.

23. George Parker, "Xerox Was Actually First to Invent the PC, They Just Forgot to Do Anything with It," *Business Insider*, February 29, 2012, www.businessinsider.com/xerox-was-actually-first-to-invent-the-pc-they -just-forgot-to-do-anything-with-it-2012-2.

24. François Jacob, "Evolution and Tinkering," *Science* 196, no. 4295 (June 10, 1977): 1163, DOI: 10.1126/science.860134.

25. Robert Root-Bernstein et al., "Arts Foster Scientific Success: Avocations of Nobel, National Academy, Royal Society, and Sigma Xi Members," *Journal of Psychology of Science and Technology* 1, no. 2 (October 2008): 53.

26. Tom Bilyeu, "Amelia Boone: How to Cultivate Mental Toughness," Impact Theory, March 7, 2017, impacttheory.com/episode/amelia-boone/.

27. Thomas C. Hayes, "Walker Balances Bulk with Ballet," *New York Times*, April 11, 1988, www.nytimes.com/1988/04/11/sports/walker -balances-bulk-with-ballet.html.

## Chapter 5: Discover Your Mission

1. This story is based on the following sources: Judy Klemesrud, "'Rocky Isn't Based on Me,' Says Stallone, 'But We Both Went the Distance,'" *New York Times*, November 28, 1976, www.nytimes.com /1976/11/28/archives/rocky-isnt-based-on-me-says-stallone-but-we -both-went-the-distance.html; Josh Cornfield, "Rocky's Muse: Boxer Who Inspired Stallone Gets His Moment," Associated Press, May 4, 2017, apnews.com/article/c32bbd68efbf4a2987719eb6a32bcff4; "*Rocky*: Video Commentary with Sylvester Stallone," produced by Jennifer Peterson and Mark Rance (MGM Home Video, 2000), www.youtube.com /watch?v=TBjKQi5c_As.

2. Robert Krulwich, "How Do Plants Know Which Way Is Up and Which Way Is Down?," *Krulwich Wonders*, NPR, June 22, 2012, www .npr.org/sections/krulwich/2012/06/21/155508849/how-do-plants -know-which-way-is-up-and-which-way-is-down.

3. Gil Bailie, *Violence Unveiled: Humanity at the Crossroads* (New York: Crossroad Publishing Co., 1997), xv.

4. Lizzo, "Juice," *Cuz I Love You* (2019): "If I'm shinin', everybody gonna shine."

5. Bruce McClure and Deborah Byrd, "Gamma Cephei, aka Errai, a Future North Star," EarthSky, September 22, 2021, earthsky.org /brightest-stars/gamma-cephei-errai-future-north-star/.

6. Jim Carrey, commencement address, Maharishi International University, Fairfield, Iowa, May 24, 2014, www.miu.edu/graduation-2014.

7. Boyd Varty, *The Lion Tracker's Guide to Life* (Boston: Houghton Mifflin Harcourt, 2019).

8. Jocelyn Hoppa, *Isaac Asimov: Science Fiction Trailblazer* (Berkeley Heights, NJ: Enslow Publishers, 2009), 8.

9. Seth Godin, "And Maybe It's Enough," Seth's Blog, April 6, 2022, seths.blog/2022/04/and-maybe-its-enough/.

10. Robert I. Sutton, "Kurt Vonnegut on 'Having Enough': A Reminder from the No Asshole Rule," *Fast Company*, March 10, 2011, www .fastcompany.com/1737273/kurt-vonnnegut-having-enough-reminder -no-asshole-rule.

11. Max Kutner, "How to Game the College Rankings," *Boston*, August 26, 2014, www.bostonmagazine.com/news/2014/08/26/how -northeastern-gamed-the-college-rankings/.

12. Luxi Shen and Christopher K. Hsee, "Numerical Nudging: Using an Accelerating Score to Enhance Performance," *Psychological Science* 28, no. 8 (June 30, 2017): 1077–1086, journals.sagepub.com/doi /abs/10.1177/0956797617700497.

13. Bethany McLean, "How Wells Fargo's Cutthroat Corporate Culture Allegedly Drove Bankers to Fraud," *Vanity Fair*, May 31, 2017, www.vanityfair.com/news/2017/05/wells-fargo-corporate-culture-fraud.

14. Nicholas Iovino, "$480M Wells Fargo Shareholder Settlement Approved," *Courthouse News Service*, December 18, 2018, www.court housenews.com/480m-wells-fargo-shareholder-settlement-approved/.

## Chapter 6: Unlock the Wisdom Within

1. John F. Kennedy, commencement address, Yale University, June 11, 1962, www.jfklibrary.org/about-us/about-the-jfk-library/kennedy -library-fast-facts/rededication-film-quote.

2. Glennon Doyle, *Untamed* (New York: Dial Press, 2020), 55.

3. David Lynch, *Catching the Big Fish: Meditation, Consciousness, and Creativity* (New York: Jeremy P. Tarcher/Perigee, 2007), 1.

4. This is one possible meaning of the word abracadabra derived from the Aramaic phrase *avra kehdabra*. Lawrence Kushner, *The Book of Words: Talking Spiritual Life, Living Spiritual Talk* (Woodstock, VT: Jewish Lights Publishing, 2011), 11.

5. Nana Ariel, "Talking Out Loud to Yourself Is a Technology for Thinking," *Psyche*, December 23, 2020, psyche.co/ideas/talking-out -loud-to-yourself-is-a-technology-for-thinking.

6. Julia Cameron, *The Artist's Way: A Spiritual Path to Higher Creativity* (New York: Jeremy P. Tarcher/Putnam, 1992).

7. For more on strategic procrastination, see Adam Grant, "Why I Taught Myself to Procrastinate," *New York Times*, January 16, 2016.

8. Gerry Leisman et al., "Thinking, Walking, Talking: Integratory Motor and Cognitive Brain Function," *Frontiers in Public Health* 4 (May 25, 2016): 94, www.ncbi.nlm.nih.gov/pmc/articles/PMC4879139/.

9. Marily Oppezzo and Daniel L. Schwartz, "Give Your Ideas Some Legs: The Positive Effect of Walking on Creative Thinking," *Journal of Experimental Psychology: Learning, Memory, and Cognition* 40, no. 4 (2014): 1142–1152.

10. "Quentin Tarantino," *The Joe Rogan Experience*, June 29, 2021, open.spotify.com/episode/5cdu4y60lq6QXyUbhMpVWH.

11. William Poundstone, *Carl Sagan: A Life in the Cosmos* (New York: Henry Holt and Co., 1999), 104.

12. Charles J. Limb and Allen R. Braun, "Neural Substrates of Spontaneous Musical Performance: An fMRI Study of Jazz Improvisation," *PLoS ONE* 3, no. 2 (February 27, 2008): e1679, journals.plos.org/plosone/article?id=10.1371/journal.pone.0001679.

13. Guy Raz, "What Does a Creative Brain Look Like?," *TED Radio Hour*, October 3, 2014, www.npr.org/transcripts/351549673.

14. Ellen M. Calder, "Personal Recollections of Walt Whitman," *Atlantic Monthly*, June 1907, www.theatlantic.com/past/docs/issues/07jun/recollections.htm.

15. Chip Heath and Dan Heath, *Decisive: How to Make Better Choices in Life and Work* (New York: Currency, 2013).

16. David Robson, "A Brief History of the Brain," *New Scientist*, September 21, 2011, www.newscientist.com/article/mg21128311-800-a-brief-history-of-the-brain/.

17. The story about Isaac Newton is based on the following sources: Thomas Levenson, "The Truth About Isaac Newton's Productive Plague," *New Yorker*, April 6, 2020, www.newyorker.com/culture/cultural-comment/the-truth-about-isaac-newtons-productive-plague; Ada Palmer, "Self-Care & Healthy Work Habits for the Pandemic," *Ex Urbe*, July 30, 2020, www.exurbe.com/self-care-healthy-work-habits-for-the-pandemic/.

18. Isaac Newton, letter to Robert Hooke, February 5, 1675, in *The Correspondence of Isaac Newton: 1661–1675*, vol. 1, edited by H. W. Turnbull (London: Cambridge University Press, 1959), 416.

19. The courtroom analogy was inspired by an interview with Olivier Sibony: Bill Huyett and Tim Koller, "How CFOs Can Keep Strategic Decisions on Track," *McKinsey & Company*, February 1, 2011,

www.mckinsey.com/business-functions/strategy-and-corporate-finance/our-insights/how-cfos-can-keep-strategic-decisions-on-track.

20. Reed Hastings, "Reed Hastings on Netflix's Biggest Mistake," *Forbes*, September 11, 2020, www.forbes.com/sites/forbesdigitalcovers/2020/09/11/reed-hastings-no-rules-rules-book-excerpt-netflix-biggest-mistake/?sh=5e0d0b0332d9.

21. Hastings, "Reed Hastings on Netflix's Biggest Mistake."

22. Hastings, "Reed Hastings on Netflix's Biggest Mistake."

23. Reed Hastings, "How Netflix Changed Entertainment—and Where It's Headed," TED Talk, April 2018, www.ted.com/talks/reed_hastings_how_netflix_changed_entertainment_and_where_it_s_headed/.

24. Mark Harris, *Mike Nichols: A Life* (New York: Penguin Books, 2022), 369, 435.

## Chapter 7: Unleash the Power of Play

1. The R.E.M. story is based on the following sources: Kory Grown, "R.E.M. Reflect on 'Radical' *Out of Time* LP," *Rolling Stone*, November 21, 2016, www.rollingstone.com/feature/rem-losing-my-religion-out-of-time-album-124296/; Hrishikesh Hirway, "R.E.M.—Losing My Religion," *Song Exploder: How Music Gets Made* (Netflix, 2020), www.netflix.com/watch/81025976.

2. Hirway, "R.E.M."

3. Brooke N. Macnamara et al., "Deliberate Practice and Performance in Music, Games, Sports, Education, and Professions: A Meta-Analysis," *Psychological Science* 25, no. 8 (August 2014): 1608–1618.

4. Henry Ford and Samuel Crowther, *My Life and Work* (Garden City, NY: Doubleday, Page & Co., 1922), 92.

5. Daniel H. Pink, *A Whole New Mind: Why Right-Brainers Will Rule the Future* (New York: Riverhead Books, 2005), 187.

6. Lawrence Pearsall Jacks, *Education Through Recreation* (New York: Harper & Brothers, 1932).

7. Atul Gawande, *The Checklist Manifesto: How to Get Things Right* (New York: Picador, 2011).

8. René Proyer and Willibald Ruch, "The Virtuousness of Adult Playfulness: The Relation of Playfulness with Strengths of Character," *Psychology of Well-Being Theory Research and Practice* 1, no. 1 (January 2011), DOI:10.1186/2211-1522-1-4.

9. Alice Isen, Mitzi M. S. Johnson, Elizabeth Mertz, Gregory F. Robinson, "The Influence of Positive Affect on the Unusualness of Word

Associations," *Journal of Personality and Social Psychology* 48, no. 6 (June 1985): 1413–1426, DOI:10.1037//0022-3514.48.6.1413.

10. Alice Isen, Kimberly A. Daubman, and Gary P. Nowicki, "Positive Affect Facilitates Creative Problem Solving," *Journal of Personality and Social Psychology* 52, no. 6 (1987): 1122–1131, https://psycnet.apa.org/doiLanding?doi=10.1037%2F0022-3514.52.6.1122.

11. Oliver Burkeman, "How Pixar Conquered the Planet," *Guardian*, November 12, 2004, www.theguardian.com/film/2004/nov/12/3.

12. Megan McArthur, "A NASA Astronaut's Lessons on Fear, Confidence, and Preparing for Spaceflight," TED Talk, November 2020, www.ted.com/talks/megan_mcarthur_a_nasa_astronaut_s_lessons_on_fear_confidence_and_preparing_for_spaceflight/.

13. Kory Grow, "R.E.M. Reflect on 'Radical' *Out of Time* LP," *Rolling Stone*, November 21, 2016, www.rollingstone.com/feature/rem-losing-my-religion-out-of-time-album-124296/.

14. Richard P. Feynman and Ralph Leighton, *"Surely You're Joking, Mr. Feynman!": Adventures of a Curious Character* (New York: W. W. Norton, 1985).

15. Michael T. Ghiselin, "Perspective: Darwin, Progress, and Economic Principles," *Evolution* 49, no. 6 (December 1995): 1029–1037, www.jstor.org/stable/2410428.

16. Amy Stewart, "Talking with Elizabeth Gilbert About Her Novel of Botanical Exploration," *Garden Rant*, October 2, 2013, gardenrant.com/2013/10/elizabeth-gilberts-novel-of-botanical-exploration.html.

17. Aaron Sorkin, "Aaron Sorkin Teaches Screenwriting," MasterClass, www.masterclass.com/classes/aaron-sorkin-teaches-screenwriting.

18. Chip Heath and Dan Heath, *Decisive: How to Make Better Choices in Life and Work* (New York: Currency, 2013); Stuart Brown with Christopher Vaughan, *Play: How It Shapes the Brain, Opens the Imagination, and Invigorates the Soul* (New York: Penguin/Avery, 2009), 131–132.

19. Vanessa Van Edwards, "Priming Psychology: How to Get People to Do What You Want," Science of People, www.scienceofpeople.com/priming-psychology/.

20. Chip Heath and Dan Heath, *Switch: How to Change Things When Change Is Hard* (London: Random House Business Books, 2011), 157.

## Chapter 8: Dare to Create

1. Stephen King, *On Writing: A Memoir of the Craft* (New York: Pocket Books, 2002), 9–16.

NOTES TO CHAPTER 8    253

2. Emma Kelly, "15 Books You Didn't Know Stephen King Wrote," *Newsweek*, April 22, 2021, www.newsweek.com/stephen-king-novels -you-didnt-know-he-wrote-1584233.

3. Arthur Schopenhauer, *Parerga and Paralipomena*, vol. 2, *Short Philosophical Essays*, translated by Adrian Del Caro (Cambridge: Cambridge University Press, 2015).

4. *Rocketman*, screenplay by Lee Hall, directed by Dexter Fletcher (Paramount Pictures/New Republic Pictures, 2019).

5. Clare O'Connor, "How Sara Blakely of Spanx Turned $5,000 into $1 billion," *Forbes*, March 14, 2012, www.forbes.com/global/2012/0326 /billionaires-12-feature-united-states-spanx-sara-blakely-american-booty .html?sh=650816f37ea0.

6. Sara Blakely, "I Never Had a Business Plan" (Instagram post), July 20, 2020, www.instagram.com/p/CC3SpZGASE_/.

7. Kevin Kelly, "68 Bits of Unsolicited Advice," Technium, April 28, 2020, kk.org/thetechnium/68-bits-of-unsolicited-advice/.

8. Philip Glass, *Words Without Music: A Memoir* (New York: Liveright Publishing Co., 2016).

9. William Goldman, *Adventures in the Screen Trade: A Personal View of Hollywood and Screenwriting* (New York: Grand Central Publishing, 2012).

10. Ignaz Philipp Semmelweis, *The Etiology, Concept, and Prophylaxis of Childbed Fever*, translated by K. Codell Carter (Madison: University of Wisconsin Press, 1983).

11. Nahlah Ayed, "The Dirt on Handwashing: The Tragic Death Behind a Life-Saving Act," CBC Radio, May 28, 2020, www.cbc.ca /radio/ideas/the-dirt-on-handwashing-the-tragic-death-behind-a-life-saving -act-1.5587319.

12. Nicholas P. Leveillee, "Copernicus, Galileo, and the Church: Science in a Religious World," *Inquiries* 3, no. 05 (2011), www.inquiries journal.com/articles/1675/copernicus-galileo-and-the-church-science -in-a-religious-world.

13. Christopher Graney, "The Inquisition on Copernicus, February 24, 1616: A Little Story About Punctuation," Vatican Observatory, February 24, 2016, www.vaticanobservatory.org/sacred-space-astronomy /139212-2/.

14. King, *On Writing*, 184.

15. Rufus W. Griswold (unsigned), untitled review of *Leaves of Grass*, *Criterion*, November 10, 1855.

16. "*Leaves of Grass*," *New York Daily Times*, November 13, 1856.

17. Elizabeth Gilbert, *Big Magic: Creative Living Beyond Fear* (New York: Riverhead Books, 2015), 125.

18. Lao-tzu, *Tao Te Ching*, translated by Stephen Mitchell (New York: Harper Perennial Modern Classics, 2006).

19. Bob Ross, "Happy Accident," *The Joy of Painting*, March 25, 1987.

20. Dean Keith Simonton, "Creativity as Heroic: Risk, Success, Failure, and Acclaim," in *Creative Action in Organizations: Ivory Tower Visions and Real World Voices*, edited by Cameron M. Ford and Dennis A. Gioia (Thousand Oaks, CA: Sage Publications, 1995), 88.

21. Gary Kauffman, "Babe Ruth Would Now Be Listed as a Contact Hitter," How They Play, May 27, 2022, howtheyplay.com/team-sports/strikeouts-have-skyrocketed-since-Babe-Ruth.

22. Josh Waitzkin, *The Art of Learning: An Inner Journey to Optimal Performance* (New York: Free Press, 2008), 113.

23. Rudy Francisco, "Most of What I Know," *I'll Fly Away* (Minneapolis: Button Poetry, 2020): "The ground has taught me / more about flight / than the sky ever could."

24. Alysa Landry, "Navajo Weaver Shares Story with Authentic Rugs," *Native Times*, March 16, 2009, www.nativetimes.com/archives/22/1217-navajo-weaver-shares-story-with-authentic-rugs.

25. Jason Fried, "A Mistake Is Just a Moment in Time," Signal V. Noise, September 10, 2016, m.signalvnoise.com/a-mistake-is-just-a-moment-in-time/.

26. The story about Jerry Seinfeld is based on the following sources: Michael Neill and Michael Alexander, "Success Was a Shore Thing Once Jerry Seinfeld Stuck to Being a Stand-Up Kind of Guy," *People*, September 5, 1988; Steven Rea, "Jerry Seinfeld's True Comedy," *Entertainment Weekly*, March 1, 1991.

27. Lionel Messi, "Adidas: Overnight Success," Adidas commercial (2012), vimeo.com/44340483.

28. Steve Martin, *Born Standing Up: A Comic's Life* (New York: Scribner, 2007), 1.

29. Mark Harris, *Mike Nichols: A Life* (New York: Penguin Books, 2022), 531.

30. Tim Ferriss, *Tribe of Mentors: Short Life Advice from the Best in the World* (Harper Business: New York, 2017).

31. Seth Godin, *Permission Marketing: Turning Strangers into Friends and Friends into Customers* (New York: Simon & Schuster, 1999).

## Chapter 9: Detecting Bullshit

1. Jacob Margolis, "How a Tweet About the Mars Rover Dying Blew Up on the Internet and Made People Cry," *LAist*, February 16, 2019, laist.com/news/jpl-mars-rover-opportunity-battery-is-low-and-its-getting-dark.

2. Chuck Palahniuk, *Lullaby* (New York: Anchor Books, 2003), 18–19.

3. Soroush Vosoughi, Deb Roy, and Sinan Aral, "The Spread of True and False News Online," *Science* 359, no. 6380 (March 9, 2018): 1146–1151, www.science.org/doi/10.1126/science.aap9559.

4. Jonathan Swift, "The Art of Political Lying," *Examiner*, November 9, 1710.

5. Alex Mayyasi and Priceonomics, "Why Cereal Has Such Aggressive Marketing," *Atlantic*, June 16, 2016, www.theatlantic.com/business /archive/2016/06/how-marketers-invented-the-modern-version-of-breakfast /487130/.

6. John Harvey Kellogg, *Plain Facts for Old and Young* (Battle Creek, MI: J. H. Kellogg, MD, 1881).

7. Loren K. Ammerman, Christine L. Hice, and David J. Schmidly, *Bats of Texas* (College Station: Texas A&M University Press, 2011), 18.

8. Robynne Boyd, "Do People Only Use 10 Percent of Their Brains?," *Scientific American*, February 7, 2008, www.scientificamerican.com /article/do-people-only-use-10-percent-of-their-brains/.

9. Shuang Rong et al., "Association of Skipping Breakfast with Cardiovascular and All-Cause Mortality," *Journal of the American College of Cardiology* 73, no. 16 (April 30, 2019): 2025–2032, pubmed.ncbi.nlm .nih.gov/31023424/.

10. Elizabeth Pratt, "Eating Breakfast Every Morning May Be Better for Your Heart," *Healthline*, April 23, 2019, www.healthline.com/health -news/skipping-breakfasts-raises-your-risk-of-cardiovascular-disease.

11. Ryan W. Miller, "Eating Breakfast? Skipping a Morning Meal Has Higher Risk of Heart-Related Death, Study Says," *USA Today*, April 23, 2019, www.usatoday.com/story/news/health/2019/04/23/skipping -breakfast-tied-higher-risk-heart-disease-death-study/3547295002/.

12. Shelly Insheiwat, "Study: Skipping Breakfast Increases Risk of Heart Disease Mortality by 87 Percent," FOX 11 Los Angeles, April 23, 2019, www.foxla.com/news/study-skipping-breakfast-increases-risk-of -heart-disease-mortality-by-87-percent.

13. E. J. Mundell, "Skipping Breakfast a Bad Move for Your Heart?," WebMD, April 23, 2019, www.webmd.com/heart/news/20190423 /skipping-breakfast-a-bad-move-for-your-heart.

14. Tyler Vigen, "Spurious Correlations," https://tylervigen.com /spurious-correlations.

15. Peter Attia, "The Bad Science Behind 'Skipping Breakfast,'" Peter Attia, MD, May 12, 2019, peterattiamd.com/skipping-breakfast/.

16. George Plimpton, "Ernest Hemingway, The Art of Fiction No. 21," *Paris Review* 18 (Spring 1958), www.theparisreview.org/interviews/4825 /the-art-of-fiction-no-21-ernest-hemingway.

17. Richard P. Feynman, "What Is and What Should Be the Role of Scientific Culture in Modern Society," in *The Pleasure of Finding Things Out: The Best Short Works of Richard P. Feynman* (New York: Basic Books, 1999), 111.

18. Matt Preuss, "Investor Letter: Enron—Ask Why," Visible, April 27, 2016, visible.vc/blog/investor-letter-enron-ask-why/.

19. "Why We Praise Meaningless Jargon and Fail to Realize the Emperor Has No Clothes," Farnam Street, fs.blog/the-emperor-has-no-clothes/.

20. Peter Whoriskey, "As Drug Industry's Influence over Research Grows, so Does the Potential for Bias," *Washington Post*, November 24, 2012, www.washingtonpost.com/business/economy/as-drug-industrys -influence-over-research-grows-so-does-the-potential-for-bias/2012/11/24 /bb64d596-1264-11e2-be82-c3411b7680a9_story.html.

21. Stephan Guyenet, "Conflict of Interest," *Whole Health Source*, August 28, 2008, wholehealthsource.blogspot.com/2008/08/conflict-of -interest.html.

22. Upton Sinclair, *I, Candidate for Governor: And How I Got Licked* (Berkeley: University of California Press, 1994), 109.

23. For more on absolute versus relative risk, see Peter Attia, "Studying Studies: Part I—Relative Risk vs. Absolute Risk," Peter Attia, MD, January 8, 2018, peterattiamd.com/ns001/.

24. Mark Twain, *Chapters from My Autobiography*, serialized in *North American Review* (September 1906–December 1907). Twain attributes the comment to British prime minister Benjamin Disraeli.

25. "Blowing Smoke: Vintage Ads of Doctors Endorsing Tobacco," *CBS News*, March 7, 2012, www.cbsnews.com/pictures/blowing-smoke -vintage-ads-of-doctors-endorsing-tobacco/.

26. Ayelet Waldman, *A Really Good Day: How Microdosing Made a Mega Difference in My Mood, My Marriage, and My Life* (New York: Alfred A. Knopf, 2017).

27. Richard Conniff, "When Continental Drift Was Considered Pseudoscience," *Smithsonian*, June 2012, www.smithsonianmag.com /science-nature/when-continental-drift-was-considered-pseudoscience -90353214/.

28. Rollin T. Chamberlin, "Some of the Objections to Wegener's Theory," *Theory of Continental Drift; a Symposium on the Origin and Movement of Land Masses, Both Inter-continental and Intra-continental, as Proposed by Alfred Wegener* (Tulsa: American Association of Petroleum Geologists, 1928), 87.

29. Lisa Florman, *Concerning the Spiritual—and the Concrete—in Kandinsky's Art* (Stanford, CA: Stanford University Press, 2014), 33.

30. Carl Sagan, *Broca's Brain: Reflections on the Romance of Science* (New York: Random House, 1979), 15.

31. Joseph McClain, "Feynman's Advice to W&M Student Resonates 45 Years Later," *W&M News*, September 9, 2020, www.wm.edu/news /stories/2020/feynmans-advice-to-wm-student-resonates-45-years-later.php.

32. Richard Feynman. "What Is Science?," presented at the 15th annual meeting of the National Science Teachers Association, New York, 1966, www.feynman.com/science/what-is-science/.

33. Julia A. Minson, Nicole E. Ruedy, and Maurice E. Schweitzer, "There Is Such a Thing as a Stupid Question: Question Disclosure in Strategic Communication," *Advances in Consumer Research* 40 (2012): 271–275, www.acrwebsite.org/volumes/1012889/volumes/v40/NA-40.

34. Werner Heisenberg, *Physics and Philosophy: The Revolution in Modern Science* (London: Penguin Books, 2000), 25.

35. Neil Postman and Charles Weingartner, *Teaching as a Subversive Activity* (New York: Dell Publishing, 1969).

36. Tim Ferriss, *Tools of Titans: The Tactics, Routines, and Habits of Billionaires, Icons, and World-Class Performers* (Boston: Mariner Books, 2016).

37. Isaac Asimov, *It's Been a Good Life*, edited by Janet Jeppson Asimov (Amherst, NY: Prometheus Books, 2002), 259.

## Chapter 10: Look Where Others Don't Look

1. The story about Clifton Pollard is based on the following sources: *Breslin and Hamill: Deadline Artists*, HBO documentary, 2018; Jimmy Breslin, "Digging JFK Grave Was His Honor," *New York Herald Tribune*, November 26, 1963, www.newsday.com/opinion/digging-jfk-grave-was -his-honor-jimmy-breslin-1.6481560; Kat Eschner, "The Man Who Dug JFK's Grave, Twice," *Smithsonian*, March 14, 2017, www.smithsonian mag.com/smart-news/man-who-dug-jfks-grave-twice-180962457/.

2. Arthur Schopenhauer, *The World as Will and Representation*, vol. 2, translated by E. F. J. Payne (New York: Dover Publications, 1966), 391.

3. Marnie Hunter, "Happy Anniversary, Wheeled Luggage!," CNN, October 4, 2010, www.cnn.com/2010/TRAVEL/10/04/wheeled.luggage .anniversary/index.html.

4. Reed Hastings, as told to Amy Zipkin, "Out of Africa, onto the Web," *New York Times*, December 17, 2006, www.nytimes.com/2006/12/17 /jobs/17boss.html.

5. Salvador Dalí, "Photography, Pure Creation of the Mind," *L'Amic de les Arts* 18 (September 30, 1927): 90–91.

6. Alexandra Alter, "Best Sellers Sell the Best Because They're Best Sellers," *New York Times*, September 19, 2020, www.nytimes .com/2020/09/19/books/penguin-random-house-madeline-mcintosh.html.

7. Russell Smith, "How Algorithms Are Changing What We Read Online," *The Walrus*, September 8, 2020, thewalrus.ca/how-algorithms -are-changing-what-we-read-online/.

8. John Herrman, "What if Instagram Got Rid of Likes?," *New York Times*, May 31, 2019, www.nytimes.com/2019/05/31/style/are-likes-and -followers-the-problem-with-social-media.html.

9. Rebekah Scanlan, "Crying Influencer Slammed After Instagram Meltdown," *NZ Herald*, July 23, 2019, www.nzherald.co.nz /lifestyle/crying-influencer-slammed-after-instagram-meltdown/IFCLY 7BFDD4NBHOC3GF447PUW4/.

10. Kurt Schlosser, "Instagram Surpasses 500 Million Users—95 Million Photos and Videos Shared Daily," *GeekWire*, July 21, 2016, www.geekwire.com/2016/instagram-500-million-users/; Raffi Krikorian, "New Tweets per Second Record, and How!," Twitter engineering blog, August 16, 2013, blog.twitter.com/engineering/en_us/a/2013 /new-tweets-per-second-record-and-how.

11. Jeff Haden, "20 Years Ago, Jeff Bezos Said This 1 Thing Separates People Who Achieve Lasting Success from Those Who Don't," *Inc.*, November 6, 2017, www.inc.com/jeff-haden/20-years-ago-jeff-bezos -said-this-1-thing-separates-people-who-achieve-lasting-success-from -those-who-dont.html.

12. Kimberly Adams, "US Users Are Leaving Facebook by the Millions, Edison Research Says," *Marketplace*, March 6, 2019, www .marketplace.org/2019/03/06/tech/exclusive-look-numbers-showing -users-leaving-facebook-by-the-millions/.

13. Jim Jarmusch, "Things I've Learned," *MovieMaker*, June 5, 2013, www.moviemaker.com/jim-jarmusch-5-golden-rules-of-moviemaking/.

14. Ernest Hemingway, *A Moveable Feast: The Restored Edition* (New York: Scribner, 2010).

15. William Deresiewicz, "Solitude and Leadership," *American Scholar*, March 1, 2010, theamericanscholar.org/solitude-and-leadership/.

16. Robert Frost, "The Road Not Taken," *Atlantic Monthly* (August 1915).

17. "Study: 70% of Facebook Users Only Read the Headline of Science Stories Before Commenting," *Science Post*, March 5, 2018, thescience post.com/study-70-of-facebook-commenters-only-read-the-headline/.

18. Sarah Zhang, "The One-Paragraph Letter from 1980 That Fueled the Opioid Crisis," *Atlantic*, June 2, 2017, www.theatlantic.com/health /archive/2017/06/nejm-letter-opioids/528840/.

19. Ronald Melzack, "The Tragedy of Needless Pain," *Scientific American*, February 1, 1990, www.scientificamerican.com/article/the -tragedy-of-needless-pain/.

20. Art Van Zee, "The Promotion and Marketing of OxyContin: Commercial Triumph, Public Health Tragedy," *American Journal of Public Health* 99, no. 2 (February 2009): 221–227, www.ncbi.nlm.nih.gov/pmc /articles/PMC2622774/.

21. Pamela T. M. Leung, Erin M. Macdonald, Irfan A. Dhalla, and David N. Juurlink, letter to *New England Journal of Medicine*, June 1, 2017, www.nejm.org/doi/full/10.1056/NEJMc1700150.

22. Marilynn Marchione, "Painful Words: How a 1980 Letter Fueled the Opioid Epidemic," Associated Press, May 31, 2017, apnews.com /article/health-ma-state-wire-us-news-business-epidemics-9307eb6e8b3c 4970bb2a6344a09b0170.

## Chapter 11: I Am Not Your Guru

1. Jordan Ellenberg, *How Not to Be Wrong: The Power of Mathematical Thinking* (New York: Penguin Books, 2015).

2. Henry David Thoreau, *Walden; or, Life in the Woods* (Boston: Ticknor and Fields, 1854).

3. Amanda Palmer, *The Art of Asking, or, How I Learned to Stop Worrying and Let People Help* (New York: Grand Central Publishing, 2014).

4. Richard Zacks, *An Underground Education: The Unauthorized and Outrageous Supplement to Everything You Thought You Knew About Art, Sex, Business, Crime, Science, Medicine, and Other Fields of Human Knowledge* (New York: Anchor Books, 1999), 19.

5. Maya Angelou, Distinguished Annie Clark Tanner Lecture, 16th annual Families Alive Conference, May 8, 1997, Weber State University, Ogden, Utah, awpc.cattcenter.iastate.edu/2017/03/21/the-distinguished -annie-clark-tanner-lecture-may-8-1997/.

6. Michael H. Keller, "The Flourishing Business of Fake YouTube Views," *New York Times*, August 11, 2018, www.nytimes.com/interactive /2018/08/11/technology/youtube-fake-view-sellers.html.

7. Max Read, "How Much of the Internet Is Fake? Turns Out, a Lot of It, Actually," *New York*, December 26, 2018, nymag.com/intelligencer /2018/12/how-much-of-the-internet-is-fake.html.

8. Taylor Lorenz, "Rising Instagram Stars Are Posting Fake Sponsored Content," *Atlantic*, December 18, 2018, www.theatlantic .com/technology/archive/2018/12/influencers-are-faking-brand-deals /578401/.

9. *Miss Americana*, directed by Lana Wilson (Tremolo Productions, 2020).

10. Andre Agassi, *Open: An Autobiography* (New York: Alfred A. Knopf, 2009).

11. Laura Belgray newsletter, talkingshrimp.activehosted.com/index.php ?action=social&chash=b6edc1cd1f36e45daf6d7824d7bb2283.983&s =1b1ffcfd9ceaa89d13a6921ec91e51ef.

12. Marc Andreessen, "Pmarca Guide to Personal Productivity," *Pmarchive*, June 4, 2007, pmarchive.com/guide_to_personal_productivity .html.

## Chapter 12: Let Go of Your Future

1. Tom D. Crouch, *Wings: A History of Aviation from Kites to the Space Age* (New York: W. W. Norton & Co., 2004), 8.

2. Erin Blakemore, "The First Nonstop Flight Across the Atlantic Lasted 16 Harrowing Hours," History, June 13, 2019, www.history.com /news/first-transatlantic-flight-nonstop-alcock-brown.

3. Paul Krugman, "Why Most Economists' Predictions Are Wrong," *Red Herring*, June 10, 1998, web.archive.org/web/19980610100009 /http://www.redherring.com/mag/issue55/economics.html.

4. David Emery, "Did Paul Krugman Say the Internet's Effect on the World Economy Would Be 'No Greater Than the Fax Machine's'?," Snopes, June 7, 2018, www.snopes.com/fact-check/paul-krugman-inter nets-effect-economy/.

5. Philip E. Tetlock, *Expert Political Judgment: How Good Is It? How Can We Know?* (Princeton, NJ: Princeton University Press, 2017).

6. Tetlock, *Expert Political Judgment*, xx.

7. Colin F. Camerer and Eric J. Johnson, "The Process-Performance Paradox in Expert Judgment: How Can Experts Know So Much and Predict So Badly?," in *Toward a General Theory of Expertise: Prospects and Limits*, edited by K. Anders Ericsson and Jacqui Smith (Cambridge: Cambridge University Press, 1991), 195–217.

8. Stephen Fleischfresser, "Ultra-Violet Confirms 'Darwin's Moths,'" *Cosmos*, August 20, 2018, cosmosmagazine.com/nature/evolution /ultra-violet-experiment-confirms-darwins-moths/.

## Chapter 13: Metamorphosis

1. Ferris Jabr, "How Does a Caterpillar Turn into a Butterfly?," *Scientific American*, August 10, 2012, www.scientificamerican.com /article/caterpillar-butterfly-metamorphosis-explainer/.

2. Joseph Campbell, *A Joseph Campbell Companion: Reflections on the Art of Living* (Mill Valley, CA: Joseph Campbell Foundation, 2011).

3. Glennon Doyle, *Untamed* (New York: Dial Press, 2020), 74.

4. Elena I. Antonakou and Lazaros C. Triarhou, "Soul, Butterfly, Mythological Nymph: Psyche in Philosophy and Neuroscience," *Arquivos de Neuro-Psiquiatria* 75, no. 3 (March 2017): 176-179, www.researchgate.net/publication/315598495_Soul_butterfly_mythological_nymph_Psyche_in_philosophy_and_neuroscience.

## Epilogue

1. Carl Sagan, *Demon Haunted World: Science as a Candle in the Dark* (New York: Ballantine Books, 1997).

2. Tim Urban, "Your Family: Past, Present, and Future," Wait But Why, January 28, 2014, waitbutwhy.com/2014/01/your-family-past-present-and-future.html.

**Ozan Varol** has been a rocket scientist and an award-winning professor, and is now a bestselling author. A native of Istanbul, Varol grew up in a family of no English speakers and moved to the United States by himself at age 17 to attend Cornell University. While there, he served on the operations team for the 2003 Mars Exploration Rovers mission.

An acclaimed expert in creativity, innovation, and critical thinking, Varol has been called a "true original" by Adam Grant and dubbed a "superhero" by Daniel Pink. His work has been described as "must read" by Susan Cain and featured in the *Wall Street Journal*, *Time*, BBC, CNN, *Fast Company*, *Washington Post*, and more. His first book, *Think Like a Rocket Scientist*, was translated into nearly 25 languages and named a top book of 2020 by Inc.com. You can follow him at ozanvarol.com.

PublicAffairs is a publishing house founded in 1997. It is a tribute to the standards, values, and flair of three persons who have served as mentors to countless reporters, writers, editors, and book people of all kinds, including me.

I. F. STONE, proprietor of *I. F. Stone's Weekly*, combined a commitment to the First Amendment with entrepreneurial zeal and reporting skill and became one of the great independent journalists in American history. At the age of eighty, Izzy published *The Trial of Socrates*, which was a national bestseller. He wrote the book after he taught himself ancient Greek.

BENJAMIN C. BRADLEE was for nearly thirty years the charismatic editorial leader of *The Washington Post*. It was Ben who gave the *Post* the range and courage to pursue such historic issues as Watergate. He supported his reporters with a tenacity that made them fearless and it is no accident that so many became authors of influential, best-selling books.

ROBERT L. BERNSTEIN, the chief executive of Random House for more than a quarter century, guided one of the nation's premier publishing houses. Bob was personally responsible for many books of political dissent and argument that challenged tyranny around the globe. He is also the founder and longtime chair of Human Rights Watch, one of the most respected human rights organizations in the world.

·　　·　　·

For fifty years, the banner of Public Affairs Press was carried by its owner Morris B. Schnapper, who published Gandhi, Nasser, Toynbee, Truman, and about 1,500 other authors. In 1983, Schnapper was described by *The Washington Post* as "a redoubtable gadfly." His legacy will endure in the books to come.

Peter Osnos, *Founder*